FREEHAND
GRAPHICS STUDIO SKILLS

· · · · · · · · · · · · · · ·

Don Parsons

William W. Hurley II

Sebastian Hassinger

Contributing Editors:
David Bergsland
Robin McAllister
Russ Taber

Hayden
Books

Acquisitions Editor

Robin Graham

Development Editor

Beth Millett

Copy/Production Editor

Peter Kuhns

Technical Editor

Carla Rose

Publishing Coordinator

Rosemary Lewis

Cover and Book Designer

Anne Jones

Manufacturing Coordinator

Brook Farling

Production Team Supervisor

Laurie Casey

Production Team

Heather Butler

Dan Caparo

Kim Cofer

Terrie Deemer

Tricia Flodder

David Garratt

Beth Rago

Pamela Volk

Christy Wagner

Indexer

Cheryl Dietsch

FreeHand Graphics Studio Skills

©1996 Hayden Books

Library of Congress Catalog Number: 96-77062
ISBN: 1-56830-302-5

Printed in the United States of America 1 2 3 4 5 6 7 8 9 0

Warning and Disclaimer

Publisher	Lyn Blake
Publishing Manager	Melanie Rigney
Managing Editor	Lisa Wilson
Marketing Manager	Nancy Price

About the Authors

Don Parsons is currently president and co-founder of Infinite Media, Inc., an Internet-based multimedia company. Over the past two years, he has been conducting all levels of Internet training and has been a guest speaker at conferences addressing various Internet related topics. Prior to starting Infinite Media, Mr. Parsons worked 10 years at Apple Computer, Inc. in various technical support, writing, and training positions. At Apple, he was part of a three person team that designed and developed an intranet self-paced training solution. His areas of expertise include Internet technologies, intranet solutions, and media integration. Mr. Parsons received his degree from the University of Texas at Austin.

William W. Hurley II is a multimedia producer with experience in development, training, and project management for multimedia. Mr. Hurley attended Texas State Technical College Audio/Video Production program. He also has produced and recorded original soundtracks and sound effects and has created original graphics for multimedia productions. Mr. Hurley provides training on audio engineering and MIDI, and multimedia production services. He is a member of the Macromedia Development and Netscape Development Partners organizations.

Sebastian Hassinger has written numerous books on Internet development topics, including the *60-Minute Guide to Shockwave for Director*. He is a principle in OuterNet Connection Strategies, Inc. and DigitalDownload, Inc. two Austin-based high-tech companies. Previously, Mr. Hassinger dabbled furiously with typography, layout, and design, creating identities for his companies in print and online.

Trademark Acknowledgments

All terms mentioned in this book that are known to be trademarks or services marks have been appropriately capitalized. Hayden Books cannot attest to the accuracy of this information. Use of a term in this book should not be regarded as affecting the validity of any trademark or service mark. FreeHand, Extreme 3D, and Macromedia xRes are trademarks of Macromedia, Inc. Fontographer is a registered trademark of Macromedia, Inc.

Acknowledgments

Don Parsons

I owe a great deal of appreciation to family and friends who do not realize how much they helped me on this project. To my parents, thanks for supporting me in getting that first computer back in 1983. Who would have thought it would help me launch an entire career? Also, thanks for going to such great lengths to help take care of some of the things that a book project does not allow. To my friends Corky Matney, Dawn Matney, Sue Loughary, Kelly Ebersole, and Clint Novosad: Thanks for not giving up on me when I was always off working on "the book." Thanks to the staff of the Austin DBM office for the guidance. And last, but not least, thanks to William and Sebastian for sticking it out with me through the entire project. I could not have done it without them.

William W. Hurley II

Thank you Mom, Dad, and Charlie. You have always shown support for everything I have done. Also, thank you to everyone who helped to make this project a reality: Robin Graham, Beth Millett, Sebastian Hassinger, Don Parsons, and everyone at Hayden Books. This book was a team effort.

I would like to thank the Macromedia part of our team, John C. "Bud" Colligan, Rachel Schindler, Carrie Myers, and everyone else at Macromedia who helped our efforts. Above all, I would like to thank God, and my loving wife. Both are constants in my life, and neither could I live without. Trish, your love and support during this project were unparalleled, and I can't begin to tell you how much you mean to me.

Sebastian Hassinger

Thanks to everyone at Hayden for sticking it out and seeing the project through sometimes harrowing times. Thanks also to my co-authors, for their expertise, professionalism, and cooperation. Ted Ollier proved to be an invaluable resource when it came to the Fontographer section, and I'd like to offer him hearty thanks for his assistance and for the use of his fonts. Finally, to simply acknowledge the sacrifice, love, and support I receive from Nina, Eyre, and Haefen on a daily basis is not enough. I stand in awe of them, the most important people in my life.

Hayden Books and Macmillan Computer Publishing would like to extend appreciation and thanks to Russ Taber, Robin McAllister, and David Bergsland for their significant contributions to this project.

Hayden Books

The staff of Hayden Books is committed to bringing you the best computer books. What our readers think of Hayden is important to our ability to serve our customers. If you have any comments, no matter how great or how small, we'd appreciate your taking the time to send us a note.

You can reach Hayden Books at the following:

Hayden Books
201 West 103rd Street
Indianapolis, IN 46290
317-581-3833

Email addresses:

America Online: Hayden Bks
Internet: hayden@hayden.com

Visit the Hayden Books Web site at `http://www.hayden.com`

Contents at a Glance

Table of Contents

IX

Part II: Fontographer

Part IV: Macromedia xRes

Introduction

In the not-too-distant past, the art of illustration did not involve computers at all. Given the fast pace of technological advances in our world, some of us might have forgotten when graphic design was an entirely analog art. Former tools of the trade included the pen, ink, straight edge, compass, bendable spline, and many equally low-tech devices. All of those tools proved to be effective, but the process was extremely labor-intensive and required finely honed, specialized skills.

Just as word processing software made it easier to write by simplifying the mechanical process, illustration software has made the illustration process much easier. It is rare now to find artists and craftsmen who use purely traditional methods to create graphics. To meet the needs of the legions of users and artists with their individual preferences and tastes, a vast array of software tools has sprung up courtesy of the software industry.

The earliest offerings, looked at today, appear quite crude. Simple drawing and painting programs came first, but they were soon followed by applications that blazed trails into new territories with their capabilities and feature sets. Superpaint, CorelDRAW!, and others explored what exactly it was that artists wanted to do with computers, and how exactly software tools could help them achieve their goals. As these software packages evolved, they defined the categories of computer graphics as we know them today. Graphic design, desktop layout, desktop video, and many other types of applications came into being, and the categories they belong to continued to mature and grow more sophisticated.

Functional Categories of Graphics Applications

Graphics applications can be categorized in any number of ways. The best way to group this type of software may be according to how they are programmed to work. From this viewpoint, graphics applications fall into four primary categories: drawing, painting, three-dimensional rendering, and charting. Software in each of these categories is designed to help us generate graphics. The differences are in the types of graphics they help you create, and the procedures you follow in creating them.

Drawing Programs: Object-Oriented Graphic Design

Drawing programs create, maintain, and manipulate graphics in the form of objects. Each graphic object has associated with it information that defines what type of object it is; for example, line, rectangle, ellipse, arc, or polygon. More complex images are made up of combinations of multiple graphic objects.

FreeHand is a textbook example of a "drawing" program. Drawing programs resemble most the tools of the old-fashioned graphic designer, such as the ruler and compass. The emphasis is on line drawing and creating images out of colored shapes that are bounded by drawn lines. Commercial graphic design, product packaging design, logo design, and any other type of work that relies on clean, precise illustration (see Figure 1.1) are created now with drawing programs. Fonts and typefaces are also manipulated, thanks to Adobe's PostScript page-description language, as drawn objects (see Figure 1.2).

Figure 1.1

Object-oriented art. Note the small black "handles" that indicate control points on objects.

Figure 1.2

The same image, magnified. The "smoothness" of the image remains the same regardless of its scale.

In fact, PostScript is the reason for another name for drawing programs: outline graphics. The emphasis is on the lines that define the image. The reason lines are so important is that they represent the portion of the image that the program "describes" mathematically in the document being created. This means that every time the graphic is displayed on a monitor or printed, its appearance is calculated and created on the fly. The main advantages to this system are that the graphic can be created at the best resolution the target device supports. A 72dpi monitor receives a 72dpi object, and a 1200lpi imagesetter receives an image for its resolution. Secondly, changes to the entire graphic document are limitless, because all the steps that went into the file are, in effect, "recorded" in the objects' descriptions. Therefore, a single element can be modified or removed without disturbing any of its neighboring elements.

Painting Programs: Virtual Canvas and Oil

Painting programs are good tools for creating a different type of graphic, closer to the traditional art of painting with oils. The artist creates the image by applying colors in various shapes, blending them, and layering them to create the final image. In terms of how the program achieves this technically, a good analogy is a page of graph paper. You could create an image by coloring individual cells on the graph to create a pattern. The image that you create would depend on how you organized the colors on the graph paper.

If you want to draw a vertical red line, you can color some portion of one column of cells red. If you want to change it to a horizontal line, you have to redraw the line. This time you color cells along a row. It becomes more difficult to achieve results if you want to create a diagonal line because there is no way to organize square cells aligned on a grid in a diagonal.

When you change a graphic such as a line in a painting program, you have to change all the points along the line. In a drawing program, you only have to change the location of the end points, and the software recalculates everything in between. Figures 1.3 and 1.4 show a paint program image and a close-up showing its pixels (similar to graph paper).

Painting programs store graphic information in a large matrix, similar to graph paper. Each cell in the matrix contains a value that represents the color for one picture element. In fact, the other term for painting programs, "bitmap" graphic programs, comes from this method for representing images.

These programs are useful when you want to edit digitized images created by devices such as digital cameras and scanners. These devices create images by looking at the world as if they were viewing it through a transparency with graph lines like an image created on graph paper. The camera measures the color it sees in each cell. The numerical value recorded for each picture element is then saved. To display the image on-screen, the computer set dots on the screen to fill in the colors recorded for the matrix of picture elements. You see the information as a reproduction of the original scene. Paint programs let you change picture element values to modify the overall image.

Figure 1.3

A detail from "Herstory," by
Judi Moncrieff, created in
Macromedia xRes.

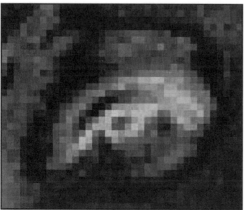

Figure 1.4

The detail from "Herstory,"
magnified. Note the grid of
pixels.

3D Rendering: Repeating Reality

The third, and, for the purposes of this book, final category of graphics application is the 3D illustration and rendering application. This is the most recently developed class of desktop computer application, in part because of the incredible processing demands rendering puts on a processor. Only recently have CPUs in desktop computers had the necessary power to work with this software, and therefore, only relatively recently these types of applications have become available. 3D programs are a little like sculpture, a little like animation, a little like illustration, puppetry, mathematics, physics, and many more crafts and trades.

3D programs enable you to create the illusion of reality, or of a computer-generated reality. Mathematical representations of lines form the basis for models of real objects. These lines resemble closely the lines that form objects in drawing programs, with one significant difference: 3D programs add information about the line's third dimension; drawing programs record information about a given line in only two dimensions. Given this amount of detailed data about an object, achieving some illusion of reality should be simple, yes? Actually, no. The amount of information, as incredibly voluminous as it can be, can create nothing more than a highly accurate "wireframe model." That is, an object that looks as though someone decided to create a sculpture out of coat hangers or pipe cleaners (see Figure 1.5).

Figure 1.5

A 3D model in Extreme 3D.

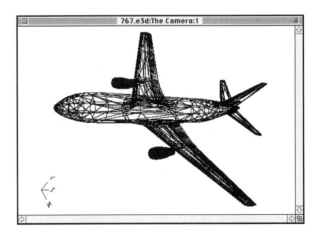

To elevate these "wicker men" to something resembling reality, applications had to be given two key features: light simulation and textures. These are achieved through more geometrical magic, and combined they are referred to as "rendering" techniques. In the case of textures, a 2D image is "wrapped" to a wireframe model by translating it to three dimensions. Lighting effects are created through complex algorithms with names such as "Phong shading" and "ray tracing."

With all these components working in tandem, 3D graphics programs are the perfect tool for jobs that require an illusory quality, or when reality itself is not good enough. A perfect, well-known example of this type of application is the movie *Jurassic Park*. Probably the best-known computer-generated graphics in the world, the dinosaurs in the movie were created using high-power 3D graphics applications.

The capabilities of drawing, painting, and 3D programs are continually increasing. Although each type of software has inherent differences, you can combine many of their advantages in your work to create more sophisticated imagery. For example, you can use FreeHand to generate artwork that will be printed on product packaging. The graphic can be opened in Extreme 3D, in which you can map onto the surface of the packaging a 3D-rendered sample. xRes can then be used to prepare a version of the final image for Web pages. Fontographer can then be used to modify an existing typeface to create a unique corporate logo.

The Genesis of Software Suites

The combination of similar programs occurred a few years ago with business applications. While graphics applications were still differentiating themselves from each other, business applications had long before become sophisticated word processors, spreadsheets, and presentation software, that were then combined into business "suites."

In the last two years, software marketing departments have begun to bundle together powerful applications that represent the best in word processing, spreadsheet, communication, and presentation software and sell them as a single product. These bundles are called "suites." Companies were buying all the separate applications to meet their various needs anyway, and the no-hassle, deep-discount appeal of the single bundled product was irresistible. Today, this consolidation of feature sets and marketing hype is being duplicated in the graphic design categories.

Macromedia's Vision: "Studios"

One company that has been aggressive in combining the best of drawing, painting, and 3D software into powerful, friendly software is Macromedia, Inc. Macromedia has been active in the computer graphics world from the early days because of its popular and powerful multimedia development tool Director®. As it grew, the company has sought to duplicate the success of the larger, more mature business software companies by developing or acquiring applications that cover the entire gamut of graphic tool categories.

In 1995, Macromedia made a number of company and software acquisitions that crystallized into FreeHand™ Graphics Studio, the product featured in this book.

Macromedia recently acquired Altsys, the Richardson, Texas, company that developed FreeHand and Fontographer®. FreeHand has been at the forefront of computer illustration for many years, and represents the cutting edge of specialized, line-based graphics applications.

Macromedia's accumulation of graphic applications continued with the development of Extreme 3D™ in August of 1995. A 3D authoring application, it combines the capabilities of Macromedia's 3D products, including MacroModel, into a single, integrated package. It is now part of the Director Multimedia Studio bundle, replacing MacroModel™.

Macromedia also recently purchased xRes from Fauve Software. The only part of the graphics puzzle that Macromedia was missing was a bitmap graphics application, which is why Macromedia xRes™ was created.

With these acquisitions in the Macromedia® lineup, the company unveiled a suite of tools called FreeHand Graphics Studio in January, 1996. The bundle shipped in February, when version 2.0 of xRes and version 1.0 of Extreme 3D were completed.

Macromedia's FreeHand Graphics Studio is a tool belt full of all the software that every graphic designer needs. From illustration to typography, from manipulating bitmaps to creating rendered objects, Studio is all things to all people. What makes this studio so important is that each software application is considered "top of class" in its respective category.

Surprisingly, these powerful applications have been neglected in the publishing world; there simply aren't many books available that discuss professional techniques with these applications, and, at the time of this writing, none that addresses the FreeHand Graphics Studio.

About This Book

This book has been split into sections—one for each application. Every section includes hands-on, practical examples that reveal some of the obvious and not-so-obvious strengths possessed by Studio's applications. Abstract overviews and background materials also are provided for newcomers to a particular graphics category. Seasoned veterans can find detailed exercises and projects that incorporate advanced features of Macromedia's latest Studio offering.

A unique addition that is designed for all audiences is the project that follows Chapter 11. The project is a comprehensive exercise that is designed to show how Studio's parts can be used with each other as a near-seamless whole. Macromedia has successfully integrated Studio's four applications with each other, and areas where the programs overlap (such as color and textures) can occasionally be exploited to create some of the most interesting results.

When you work through the tutorials and the project, make sure you use the sample files and demo applications included on the CD that accompanies this book. Macromedia has included save-disabled versions of the Studio applications, and the authors provide sample files for the exercises.

Each application included with FreeHand Graphics Studio is explored individually. You are encouraged to choose the application you are most interested in, or least familiar with, as a starting point for reading. Of course, if you would rather take a tour of the complete Studio program, the book can be read from start to finish.

You are now invited to begin exploring FreeHand Graphics Studio; we hope the information you find in this book helps you make the most of this powerful set of graphic tools. Thank you!

Part I

FreeHand

FreeHand is the flagship application in the FreeHand Graphic Studio suite, and is one of the most widely-used computer illustration programs. FreeHand's powerful illustration tools let you create graphic objects that can be imported into other Studio programs to make more sophisticated images.

You can create shapes in FreeHand, then import them into Extreme 3D and render the shapes as three-dimensional objects. FreeHand graphics also can be imported directly into xRes and combined with bitmap graphics to create professional art. Graphics can also be imported into Fontographer to use as characters in a custom font.

Chapter 1

FreeHand Basics

One of the biggest differences between FreeHand and other graphics applications is the way FreeHand creates and manipulates graphic elements. This program defines graphics like a connect-the-dots puzzle: it records the locations of key points that define the shape of a graphic object and maintains a description of the lines that connect those points. These lines are referred to as paths, which can be straight or curved. You can construct point and path combinations manually a point at a time, or with tools to create standard objects.

For example, imagine you want to create an illustration of the United States flag. If you create each of the 50 stars manually by drawing the 10 individual lines that make up each of the five point stars, electronic illustration offers almost no added value. If, on the other hand, you use FreeHand's polygon tool and specify that the polygon you want is a five point star, perfect stars would be a simple click away. After you draw the first star, you can duplicate it and finish the job in less than 60 seconds. Figure 1.1 demonstrates how points and paths can be combined to create the United States flag.

Figure 1.1

Each star is made up of 10 points and 10 paths. Each rectangle is made up of 4 points and 4 paths.

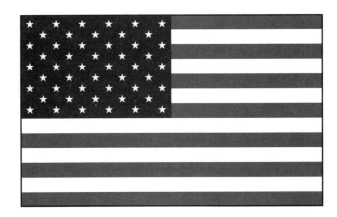

What makes creating this flag so simple in FreeHand? Two factors:

- Tool functionality: FreeHand is capable of drawing perfect five point stars.
- Technique: The FreeHand user knows how to make FreeHand duplicate and place the graphic objects automatically.

Figure 1.2 shows a different variety of basic point, path, and handle combinations.

Figure 1.2

Example points, paths, and handles.

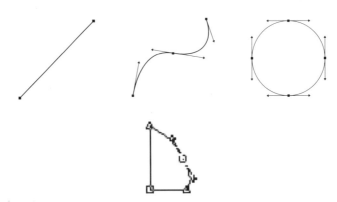

Each point has a different appearance and action:

- Corner points (square) connect straight segments and act as end points.

- Curve points (round) provide a smooth (rounded) transition between any two line segments.

- Connector points (triangles) connect straight path segments and curved segments, or create an obtuse angle between curve segments.

Most editing tasks consist of moving points and adjusting the paths that connect them. Every point has two handles that are used to define the shape of paths—these handles appear in Figure 1.2. You can also combine points and paths to create complex graphics. No matter how complex an image, it is still comprised of individual objects. In contrast, bitmap graphic applications like xRes manipulate the individual pixels that "paint" the image.

FreeHand has tools and commands to create and modify common graphic elements. Circles are drawn with the circle tool, eliminating the need to draw a circle by placing points individually and manually adjusting their paths. Should you need to rotate an object, you can avoid the drudgery of rearranging an object's points individually by using the Rotate command.

Many comparisons can be made between drawing with conventional drawing tools and drawing with FreeHand. With conventional tools, you use a straight edge to make straight lines and a compass for drawing circles. These tools and the images they create are very simple, but they are used together to make more complex graphics.

When drawing any graphic, you are constantly considering what shape or partial shape is needed to create the next part of the graphic, and which of the available tools is best suited for helping you accomplish the task. Drawing with FreeHand involves the same process—thinking about a complex drawing as being composed of smaller parts—but there are many more options.

The biggest advantage FreeHand has over conventional drawing tools is the number of tools that aid the drawing process. The challenge is to learn to use these tools effectively and efficiently. Learning to draw with pencil and paper takes time because of the need to develop the dexterity and skill to create the effect you want. You may find yourself consciously considering which tool can minimize the number of steps, help simplify the job, or increase quality.

Floating Palettes

FreeHand uses floating palettes that contain many of the most often used graphic tools and functions . Some examples are pictured in Figure 1.3. Floating palettes "float" above the windows that contain the graphics. Any palette can be dragged around the screen and placed wherever you desire. When you click in a document window, all palettes remain in front of that window.

Figure 1.3

A new document with the default palettes: the Toolbox, Inspector, Color Mixer, and Color List.

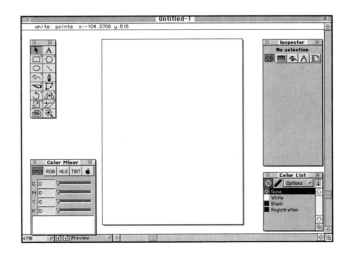

To access palettes not already open, pull down the Window menu. You will see a list of available palettes. Select the palette name in this menu to open it. Figure 1.4 shows the palettes listed in the Window menu.

Figure 1.4

FreeHand Window menu (Palette list).

Window	
New Window	⌘ ⌥N
✓ Toolbox...	⌘7
✓ Inspector...	⌘I
Color Mixer...	⌘⇧C
Color List...	⌘9
Type...	⌘T
Align...	⌘⇧A
Halftone...	⌘H
Layers...	⌘6
Styles...	⌘3
✓ Transform...	⌘M
Other	▶
✓ Untitled-1	

To close the palette, simply click on the "close" box in the left corner of the menu bar.

Tip

If a number of palettes are open in your workspace you'll have little room to work. You can shrink the palette to the identifying menu bar by clicking on the minimize box in the right corner of the palette's menu bar. To see the full palette, just click on the button again. (The Type menu is the only palette with no minimize/maximize button.)

FreeHand's palettes can be broken into two categories: object tools and object attributes. Object tool palettes include Toolbox, Layers, Operations, Xtra Tools, Transform, and Align. These palettes create and control the basic graphic elements and also the actions you can perform on those elements. Object Attributes palettes are used to apply and edit characteristics such as color or text point size. The Inspector, Color Mixer, Color List, Halftone, Styles, and Type palettes are in this category.

Although all the palettes serve some purpose, the Toolbox, Inspector, and Layers palettes are the most important for understanding the basics of how you can work with graphics in FreeHand.

Toolbox

The Toolbox contains the basic tools that you use to create graphics. The Toolbox comprises several functional groups, as shown in Figure 1.5.

One group shown in Figure 1.5 are the tools you use to draw shapes. Others are used to perform some task on the objects you have created.

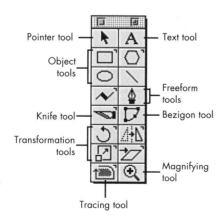

Pointer tool — Text tool
Object tools
Freeform tools
Knife tool — Bezigon tool
Transformation tools
Magnifying tool
Tracing tool

Figure 1.5

The Toolbox broken into functional groups.

17

Note that some of the tools have a small carat mark in the upper right corner of the tool icon. This indicates that the respective tool has options you can adjust to control how the tool actually functions. Double-clicking the tool brings up a dialog box that presents all the options that pertain to that particular tool.

Pointer Tool

The Pointer tool selects, moves, and adjusts points, paths, and objects after they have been created. You will probably use this tool more than any other because it is used to select objects before using other tools, and also must be used to adjust and move objects. Because the Pointer tool is not capable of creating graphics, you will learn more about using the Pointer tool as you become more familiar with the other tools.

Tip

When you have any tool selected and need quick access to the Pointer tool, hold down the Command key (Macintosh) or the Control key (Windows). The icon will change to the Pointer. Release the key and the tool you have been using reappears.

Text Tool

The Text tool is used to add text (called text objects) to your graphics. Text is a special type of object in FreeHand. On a simple level, each letter within a segment of text is nothing more than a graphic object; many tools and attributes are available to control text appearance. Chapter 3 is devoted specifically to text objects in FreeHand.

USING THE TEXT TOOL

1. Create a new document by selecting New from the File menu.

2. Make sure that the toolbox is open by selecting Toolbox from the Window menu.

3. Select the Text tool in the Toolbox.

4. Click somewhere near the center of the new document.

5. Type your name.

6. Select the Pointer tool in the Toolbox and click somewhere in the new document, but not on your name, to end text insert mode for that text object.

7. Click on your name to select it. Note that you have selected the text object as a whole and no insertion point is set.

8. The Type menu has numerous menu items for making changes to text. Change the font and size of your name.

Object Tools

The third group includes the graphic object tools: lines, rectangles, ellipses, and polygons. The Rectangle and Polygon tools have additional options. As shown in Figure 1.6, the Rectangle tool lets you set the corner radius to specify how rounded the corners will be. The corner radius is equal to the radius of a circle drawn from the corner point in the measurement style you have selected.

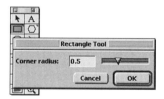

Figure 1.6

Option for Rectangle tool: Rectangles can have rounded corners.

EXPERIMENTING WITH THE CORNER RADIUS

1. In the document you have just created, enable the rulers by selecting Ruler from the View menu.

2. Reset the zero point by dragging the crosshairs in the upper left hand corner of the page to the point where you want to begin to draw your round-cornered rectangle.

3. Drag a guide from each ruler (top and side) to the zero point.

4. Double-click on the Rectangle tool in the Toolbox.

5. Enter .5 in the dialog box.

6. Draw the rectangle, starting at the zero point.

7. Drag another guide from the side ruler to the point where the curve stops and the straight line begins. (This will be at the half-inch mark.)

8. Repeat the exercise using a different value for the corner radius.

The Polygon tool also has several options (see Figure 1.7). If the Shape radio button is set for Polygon, the only option is the number of sides. If the shape is set for Star, another setting appears that determines how much of an angle there is between each star point. The angle is controlled by a slider that ranges from acute to obtuse.

Figure 1.7

Options for Polygon tool: Polygons can either be simple polygons or stars. Polygons and stars always have equal angles and equal sides.

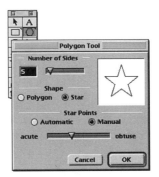

 **Tip**

To make a perfect square or a perfect circle, hold down the Shift key when using the Rectangle or Ellipse tool. Use this same trick to constrain a line to 45° increments.

Free Form Drawing Tools

The free form drawing tools are the Freehand, Pen, and Bezigon tools. These tools are versatile, but involve more work on your part. The advantage is that you can use these tools to create shapes that cannot be created by the Rectangle, Polygon, Ellipse, or Line tools.

The icon you see in your Toolbox for the Freehand tool will be one of three pictured in Figure 1.8. The Freehand Tool has distinct personalities: Freehand, Variable Stroke, and Calligraphic Pen.

Figure 1.8

The three Freehand tool icons: Freehand, Variable stroke, and Calligraphic pen.

The icon that appears in the Toolbox depends on the radio button chosen in the Freehand tool option window. Each of these three tools has different options (see Figure 1.9).

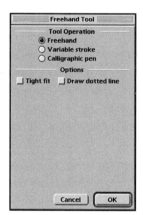 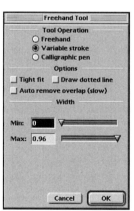 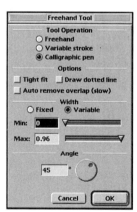

Figure 1.9

Options for the Freehand tools.

To use this tool, click in the document window and, while holding down the mouse button, start dragging the cursor around. As the cursor moves, a path appears. The path will end when you release the mouse button. After you draw a path, you will see points along it. You can select the Pointer, click on any one of those points, and move it. This will change the shape of the path. If you click the path between points and then drag, you will move the entire path.

Tip

To draw a straight line with the Freehand tool, hold down the Option key (on the Macintosh) when you click to create the second point. To constrain the line to 45° increments, add the shift key to the combination.

Figure 1.10 shows the three different types of strokes the Freehand tool can create. A graphic tablet will help you make smoother strokes with this tool.

Figure 1.10

Freehand stroke examples.

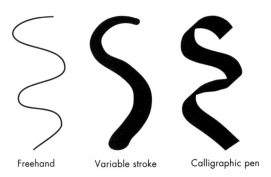

Freehand   Variable stroke   Calligraphic pen

The Freehand tool creates a stroke that is as wide as the current Stroke Width. Each stroke may be defined to end or "cap" in a specified manner. (This will be discussed more in Chapter 2.)

The Variable stroke tool creates an object composed of bordering lines and a fill. The lines are as wide as the current Stroke Width; the fill is the color or texture defined in the Inspector palette. The overall stroke (filled area plus outside bordering lines) centers on the stroke's point of origin and the bordering lines center on the nominal width of the stroke. The minimum width of the Variable stroke is twice the width of the current Stroke Width. The variable stroke always has rounded ends.

Figure 1.11 shows a path created with a Variable stroke with a minimum and maximum of 16 points in width and a line weight of four points. Notice that the stroke centers at the zero point; the nominal width is at eight points on either side; and the bordering line extends two points inside and outside the stroke's given width.

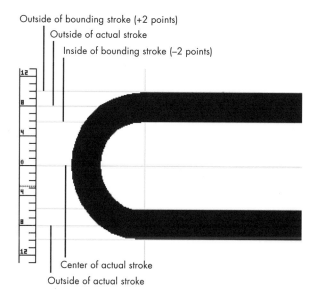

Outside of bounding stroke (+2 points)
Outside of actual stroke
Inside of bounding stroke (–2 points)

Center of actual stroke
Outside of actual stroke

F i g u r e 1 . 1 1

A path created with the Variable stroke tool.

Variable stroke enables you to set a width range in the Freehand Tool dialog box. This tool is best used with a pressure sensitive graphic tablet because it is capable of creating a narrower path with lighter stylus pressure and a wider path with harder stylus pressure. The minimum and maximum values in the Freehand tool options dialog box set limits on how narrow and how wide the path can be.

If you do not have such a tablet, you can make adjustments to the width of the stroke by pressing the Right or Left Arrow key while dragging. Every time you press the Left Arrow key the stroke will become narrower, down to the minimum you have allowed in the Tool Options dialog box. Each time you press the Right Arrow key, the stroke becomes wider.

T i p

The Variable stroke tool remembers the last width it drew and will begin the next stroke at the same width if you are using the arrow keys to control it. To create a different starting width, you may need to "scribble" on the pasteboard.

The Calligraphic pen has a similar width range setting. The path created by the Calligraphic pen varies in width depending on the direction of the path at any given point; this direction is determined by the angle assigned the pen's "nib." An angle of 0° will result in all strokes ending horizontal to the page; a 90° angle will produce strokes that end vertical to the page.

23

When you draw an outlined figure, you run into problems when lines overlap one another. The Auto Remove Overlap button solves them quickly and easily.

THE FREEHAND, VARIABLE STROKE, AND CALLIGRAPHIC PEN TOOLS

1. Double-click on the Freehand tool icon in the Toolbox.

2. Select the Freehand radio button and click OK. Experiment with it by drawing different free-form paths. Be sure to include one or more straight line segments.

3. Select the Pointer tool and make changes to the path by moving points and adjusting handles.

4. Using the Variable stroke tool, draw a line that smoothly becomes wider and narrower, with a width ranging from .028 inches to .25 inches (be sure the Stroke Width in the Inspector palette allows you to create a stroke this narrow).

5. Use the same width settings and a variable setting to draw an "S" with the Calligraphic pen tool. Set the angle at 0°, 45°, and 90° respectively (remember to alter the width of your stroke with the arrow keys). Redraw the shape with a fixed setting of .25 inches.

6. Using each of the tools, sign your first name.

The Pen and Bezigon tools allow you to place a sequence of points defining a path. A point is placed at the coordinates of each mouse click. However, two essential differences exist between the Pen and Bezigon tools. The first concerns what happens if you drag the mouse after setting a point's location. With the Pen tool, a handle will appear and you will drag the end of a handle, altering the shape of the path between the point you have just plotted and the previous point. With the Bezigon tool, you will drag the entire point, repositioning it on the page.

These tools also differ in the type of point that is placed. The Pen tool places curve points; the Bezigon tool places corner points. Shapes drawn with the Pen tool tend to be smooth; those drawn with the Bezigon tool tend to be angular.

With the Pen tool, you control path as well as points on the first pass. With the Bezigon tool you position the points to create the basic shape, and you can adjust the path later. Beginners tend to prefer the Bezigon tool because it is more natural. Advanced users prefer the Pen tool because it allows you to work much faster.

THE PEN AND BEZIGON TOOLS

1. Open file FreeHand/Ch1/FREEFRM.FH5 on the disc included with this book. Note that there are two paths grayed out in the document.

Pen Tool

2. Select the Pen tool from the Toolbox.

3. Click on Point A.

4. Click on Point B on the same path and drag the handle until you create a path between points A and B.

5. Click on Point C and drag the handle until it follows the path between points B and C.

Bezigon Tool

6. Select the Bezigon tool from the Toolbox.

7. Click on Point 1.

8. Click on Point 2. Notice that the path you just created is straight, but in step 11 you will come back and add the curve.

9. Continue clicking on points 3, 4, and 5.

10. Now that all the points are placed, you can have FreeHand close the shape by double clicking on Point 1.

11. Hold down the Option key (in Windows use the Alt key) and click on the center of the path between points 1 and 2. Drag the mouse in the direction of the curve until your curve matches the template.

Knife Tool

The icon for the Knife tool resembles an X-acto knife blade. It is used to cut paths just as you would use such a knife in the real world. After a cut has been made through a path, you can remove a segment of a path or replace it with a custom segment. Figure 1.12 shows options for the Knife tool.

Figure 1.12

Knife tool options: set for straight cut, with a cut width of 0.

The first two options are usually the ones you'll use most. FreeHand lets you drag the cursor around—cutting every path on the selected object that you cross. Straight sets a starting point wherever you press down the mouse button. With the mouse button depressed, drag to a destination point and then release. Any path on the selected object that is exactly between the two points is cut.

The width of the cut can also be changed. The numbers that you see in the window depend on the unit of measure set for the entire document. If the unit of measure is set to Points, the number can range from 0 to 72. At 0, the Knife tool will cut a path in two—just like an infinitely thin X-acto knife blade. Values from 1 to 72 actually make a cut as wide as the number specifies. For example, a setting of 72 will remove 72 points of the path.

The remaining options let you control how the cuts are made. Before you can use the check box to set Close cut paths, you will need some background information. If the path that defines the outer perimeter of an object reconnects with itself, the object is said to be "closed." The path of a closed object has no visible start or stop point. The path of an open object has two ends.

If the Close cut paths check box is checked and you cut a closed object, the object will remain closed around the cut. For example, if you cut completely across the entire object, you will create two closed objects on either side of the cut. On the other hand, if you cut part of the way into a closed object, FreeHand will construct a path around the cut. Figure 1.13 illustrates both of these examples.

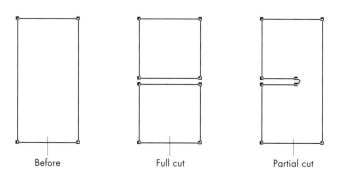

Before   Full cut   Partial cut

Figure 1.13

A closed rectangle and the effects of the Knife tool. A full cut creates two closed objects, while a partial cut creates a new path shape.

If the Close cut paths option is not checked, FreeHand makes no attempt to keep a closed path closed after the cut.

The Tight fit check box is used with the Knife tool in Freehand mode. When this option is turned on, FreeHand makes a cut that more closely follows the path you cut through the object.

USING THE KNIFE TOOL

1. Open file FreeHand/Ch1/KNIFE.FH5 on the disc.

CD ROM

2. Click on Object 1 with the Pointer tool.

3. Double-click on the Knife tool. The window shown in Figure 1.12 will appear. Select the same settings shown in Figure 1.12 and click on OK.

4. Object 1 and Object 2 show you where to click to set the cut start point, and where to drag the mouse. The straight line between the start and end points is the path that the Knife tool cuts through object paths. Click at the start point and drag to the end point for both objects.

5. An object must be selected before it can be cut with the Knife tool. Therefore, a new point appeared on Object 1 along the cut path, but not on Object 2. Perform the necessary steps to cut Object 2 along the proposed cut path.

Transformation Tools

The next four tools in the Toolbox do not create graphic objects, but transform previously drawn shapes by rotating, reflecting, scaling, and skewing. You can transform an object in two ways; both require that the object be selected before it can be transformed.

The first method uses direct manipulation.

1. Select the object and the desired tool in the Toolbox.

2. Click on the screen. The location of your initial click determines the point around which all transformations take place.

3. Drag the cursor. You will see the object change according to the tool being used.

For example, if you are rotating the object, it will rotate around that initial point.

 Tip

If you click on the object and pause until you see the 4-headed Pointer tool, ✛ you will be able to observe the transformation in keyline mode. The initial mode is only the outline of the shape, or the rectangle bounding the group.

The second method involves the Transform palette in the Window menu. This method lets you perform the same transformations, but with numerical input. For example, if you want to rotate an object by 45 degrees, enter 45 in the Rotation angle field as illustrated in Figure 1.14. There are also fields that allow you to enter the center point, the point around which the transform takes place. The default values are the center of the object within the document's coordinates system. The Transform palette also lets you to alter the shape of the object without affecting its contents, or to alter the contents.

Figure 1.14

Transform palette with the Rotation tool selected, and a 45 degree rotation angle set.

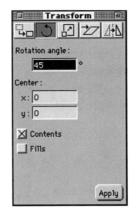

 **Tip**

Double-clicking on any of the Transformation tools will bring up the Transform palette with the appropriate tool selected.

Rotate Tool

The Rotate tool rotates the selected object by an angle on a 360-degree scale around a specified center point.

ROTATING OBJECTS

1. Open file FreeHand/Ch1/ROTATE.FH5 on the disc.

 **CD ROM**

Rotation Tool

2. Select Object 1 with the Pointer tool, and select the Rotate tool from the Toolbox.

3. Click on the cursor on Start Point, and drag the cursor to Stop Point. You just rotated Object 1 by 30 degrees around Start Point.

Rotation with Transform Palette

4. Select Object 2 with the Pointer tool, and open the Transform palette from the Window menu.

5. Click on the Rotation tool icon in the Transform palette.

6. Enter the following numbers:
Rotation angle: 30
x: 100
y: 265
Press Enter.
You just rotated Object 2 by 30 degrees around the point 100,265.

The rotation point is defined in points (1/72 inch) relative to the 0/0 position on the page. 0/0 is the lower left position; positions to the right and above the zero point are described as positive numbers; positions to the left and below the zero point are described as negative numbers.

Reflection Tool

Many graphic programs include a command that allows you to flip an object, producing a mirror opposite of the original graphic. The options that you normally have are flip horizontal and flip vertical. If you are creating a face, you can create one eye, then duplicate and flip it horizontally to save time.

REFLECTING OBJECTS

 **CD ROM**

1. Open file FreeHand/Ch1/REFLCT.FH5 on the disc.

Reflection Tool

2. Select Eye 1 with the Pointer tool, and choose the Reflection tool from the Toolbox.

3. To flip a copy of the eye and not the original, select Clone from the Edit menu. This creates one copy of the object in the exact location of the original.

4. Click the cursor on Start Point, and drag the cursor to Stop Point. You just flipped the copy horizontally around Start Point.

Reflection with Transform Palette

5. Select Eye 2 with the Pointer tool, and open the Transform palette from the Window menu.

6. Click on the Reflection tool icon in the Transform palette.

7. Clone Eye 2.

8. Enter the following numbers:
Rotation angle: 90
x: 0
y: 0
Press Enter.
You just flipped the copy horizontally around point 0,0.

When reflecting objects using the Transform palette, you usually will use 90 degrees to flip horizontally and 180 degrees to flip vertically.

Scale Tool

At some point you will need to change the size of an object after you have created it to make it smaller or larger. Although you can resize some objects with the Pointer tool, occasionally you will want to resize the object by a specific percentage or unit of measure. The Scale tool is the answer.

Scaling using the Transform palette includes an additional feature: the ability to scale, or not scale, lines in the object. Occasionally when you print a graphic that has been reduced, thin lines can cause printing problems or not print at all.

SCALING OBJECTS

1. Open file FreeHand/Ch1/SCALE.FH5 on the disc.

CD ROM

Scale Tool

2. Select Object 1 with the Pointer tool, and select the Scale tool from the Toolbox.

3. Click the cursor on Start Point, and drag the cursor around within the SCALE.FH5 document window. Before you release the mouse button, press the Shift key while dragging the cursor. Notice that the Shift key causes height and width to scale evenly.

Scaling with Transform Palette

4. Select Object 2 with the Pointer tool, and open the Transform palette from the Window menu.

5. Click on the Scale tool icon in the Transform palette.

6. Enter the following numbers:
   Scale factor % : 150
   Notice that the "Uniform" button has been selected. If you deselect the button, you can scale x and y coordinates by different percentages.

When you resize objects with the Pointer tool, you are resizing them arbitrarily (by eye) with little control over their final size. You can, however, resize the object uniformly or arbitrarily, and can resize from the center or from any of the four corners. Objects that can be resized with the Pointer tool include rectangles, ellipses, and grouped objects.

SCALING FROM DIFFERENT POINTS

1. Create a new document from the File menu.

2. Draw a regular shape (a rectangle or ellipse) using a tool from the Tool palette.

Scaling from a Corner Point

3. Select the object with the Pointer tool, then position the pointer on one of the corner points.

4. Drag the cursor around within the document window. Notice that the opposite corner point acts as an anchor for the object. Before you release the mouse button, press the Shift key while dragging the cursor. Notice that the Shift key causes height and width to scale evenly.

Scaling from a Center Point

5. Select the object with the Pointer tool, press and hold down the option key, then position the pointer on one of the corner points.

6. Drag the cursor around within the document window. Notice that the object resizes around its center point. Pressing the Shift key while dragging the cursor causes height and width to scale evenly.

Skew Tool

It is easier to draw objects in 2D than it is to include perspective. The addition of perspective makes graphics look more interesting, but getting the angles correct is difficult. The Skew tool adds skewing on horizontal and vertical axes to an object that has been drawn without perspective. This allows you to draw two-dimensional objects and add perspective after all proportions have been set correctly.

SKEWING OBJECTS

 CD ROM

1. Open file FreeHand/Ch1/SKEW.FH5 on the disc.

Skew Tool

2. Select Object 1 with the Pointer tool, and select the Skew tool from the Toolbox.

3. Click the cursor on Start Point, and drag the cursor around within the SKEW.FH5 document window. Before you let go of the mouse button, press and hold down the Shift key while dragging the cursor. Notice that the Shift key causes the object to skew only on the horizontal axis or the vertical axis, but not both at the same time.

Skewing with Transform Palette

4. Select Object 2 with the Pointer tool, and open the Transform palette from the Window menu.

5. Click on the Skew tool icon in the Transform palette.

6. Enter the following numbers:
Skew angle h: 10
Skew angle v: 20

Trace Tool

Using the Trace tool to draw a scanned image helps you create a convincing representation of real objects and people. This tool lets you select a region of a graphic, and FreeHand automatically traces the edges of anything within the region. The use of this tool sounds simple and straightforward, but it can be involving. Figure 1.15 shows a traced image. You can see that the general shapes are drawn but that a lot of clean up and smoothing will be needed. Tracing is discussed in detail in Chapter 4.

Figure 1.15

A scanned image and the traced artwork.

Magnifying Glass

The Magnifying Glass lets you zoom in or out on your graphic. After you select this tool, click on the area of the graphic where you want to take a closer look. To zoom out press and hold down the Option key (Macintosh), or the Alt key (Windows), and click the mouse.

 Tip

To look at one section of the page close up, marquee (draw a box around) the area with the Magnifying Glass tool. The area will then fill the entire window, or enlarge to 6400 percent, whichever is greater.

Inspector Palette

An important palette you will use often is the Inspector palette. This special palette lets you view and change information about points, paths, objects, text blocks, pages, and documents. One thing that all these have in common is each has a specific set of attributes. The content of the Inspector can vary greatly, depending on the icon selected in the icon row at the top of the Inspector palette. Figure 1.16 shows just a couple of possible examples.

Figure 1.16

Sample variations of the Inspector palette.

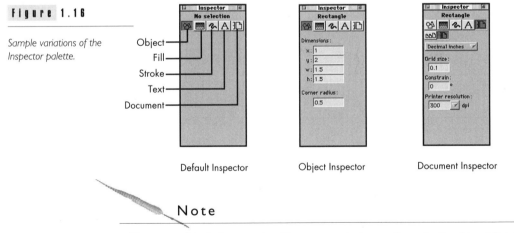

Default Inspector   Object Inspector   Document Inspector

Note

To see an all inclusive sample of Inspector variations, refer to the FreeHand Quick Reference Card that comes with FreeHand.

Object Inspector

The Objects icon in the Inspector palette displays most of the attributes for paths, rectangles, polygons, ellipses, and lines. The exact contents are determined by the object you have selected at the time. Figure 1.17 shows the three most common possibilities.

Object selected

Path selected

Point selected

Figure 1.17

Three variations of the Object Inspector.

Rectangles, ellipses, and grouped objects show object dimensions in X and Y coordinates; these values represent the lower-left corner of the object on the page. The W and H values represent the width and height of the object. You can manually change these values to move the object or resize it. Rectangles have one more option: the radius of the corners for rounded corner rectangles.

Paths create one of two Inspector variations. The first is when the entire path is selected. You will see a count of the total number of points in the path and a check box for Even/Odd fill. If this option is selected, the entire closed object will be filled with the selected fill color and pattern except areas that overlap the object. Overlap regions will be white (see Figure 1.18).

Figure 1.18

A path with Even/Odd fill turned on.

The next option is a Closed checkbox. A closed object has a path line extending between the start and end point. If this item is unchecked, that part of the path will not be present, and the object cannot be filled with any color or pattern.

The final decision you have to make in the Path Inspector is to assign a Flatness to the object. Flatness is a value that affects the printing speed of documents. Higher flatness values create longer line segments in curves, which "flatten" them. Usually a flatness value (relative to how that value will affect the printing process) of three is appropriate.

Another variation of the Path Inspector references individual points on the path. This can be particularly useful when aligning objects. This Path Inspector window also gives information about the way a point behaves: it reveals whether a point is a corner, curve, or connector point. You can change its nature by selecting another point type. The "Curve Handles" section of the Inspector enables you to collapse the handles on a point, allowing it to be a simple pivot.

Document Inspector

Attributes for FreeHand documents include units of measure settings that are used throughout the document. Figure 1.19 shows the Inspector with the Document icon selected.

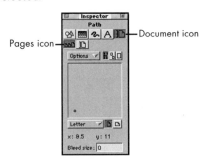

Figure 1.19

The Document Inspector permits changes to document attributes.

Each document has a unit of measure system that applies to all pages in the document. The pop-up menu in Figure 1.16 shows the selected unit of measure is decimal inches. Other options include points, picas, inches, and millimeters.

FreeHand has a few different mechanisms designed to help you place points and objects on the page. If you select Grid from the View menu the grid system will show you dotted lines that represent the grid. When Snap to Grid is checked in the View menu, the grid determines where you can place graphic components. The number you enter in the Grid size field in the Document Inspector determines possible placement. For example, if the document is set to use inches and the grid size you entered is 1, you can place objects on the 1-inch boundaries, but not in between.

Although it seems that you gain greater control with smaller and smaller grid sizes, you can actually make some types of illustration easier if you make the grid size larger. A large grid size reduces the amount of time to precisely place things. Also, you can always change grid size to different values throughout the illustration process to meet your exact needs at any given time.

Constrain degrees also applies when Snap to Grid is turned on. It defines the angle at which rectangles and ellipses will be drawn, and establishes a new starting axis for objects drawn with the Polygon, Pen, Line and Bezigon tools. The default is 0°.

The final document attribute in the Document Inspector is printer resolution. This setting indicates the resolution of the printer you will ultimately print to (not the proofing printer). If the final printer is, say, an imagesetter, the resolution should probably be 2400. FreeHand uses this information to calculate the number of default steps in blends and the resolution of gradients and radial fills. This information is also used to resize bitmap images to best match the resolution of the output device.

Page Inspector

A document can have 292 pages. The document represented in Figure 1.20 has three pages. Each rectangle in the page thumbnail region represents a page, and each is numbered. The Options pop-up menu allows you to add, duplicate, or remove pages. The icons to the right of the Options menu enable you to set the magnification used in the thumbnail region. In Figure 1.20, page 1 is selected. Clicking on page 2 will activate it, double-clicking it will take you to the page in the document window.

Figure 1.20

The Page Inspector permits making changes to page attributes.

Each page can have an independent page size and orientation. The pop-up menu below the thumbnail region offers eight options of standard page sizes. If the size you want is not in the list, you can select Custom and enter the page dimensions in the X and Y fields that appear below the pop-up menu. If a standard page size is selected, X and Y will report each page dimension, but will not allow you to change them directly. Next to the pop-up menu are two page orientation icons. Select the left icon to put the page in portrait mode; select the right to put the page in landscape mode. Figure 1.20 shows page 1 in portrait, and page 2 in landscape.

The field for setting Bleed size allows you to specify how far over the edge of the page objects will continue to print before the printer is instructed to cut off the graphics. By letting objects "bleed" over the edge of the page, the print version of the page can be physically cropped with the graphics on the page going right to the edge instead of being cut off before the edge, which leaves a border.

Measurement and Placement Tools

A FreeHand document can be used as if it were a blank canvas. You may want to consider this when creating graphics that take more of a free-form style, such as drawings of people or birds, logos, and other illustrations that are not dependent upon exact scale. Numeric accuracy is not as important, and may not even be desirable. For other types of work, however, structure and accuracy may be critical, such as with scale drawings or illustrations that must match one another in size and relative line weights. They would certainly include a series of icons that would be used in conjunction with one another.

Rulers

If you need rulers for reference, select Rulers in the View menu. The rulers will appear along the top and left edges of the document window. If multiple documents are open, only the topmost document will be affected. Figure 1.21 shows the ruler measuring inches.

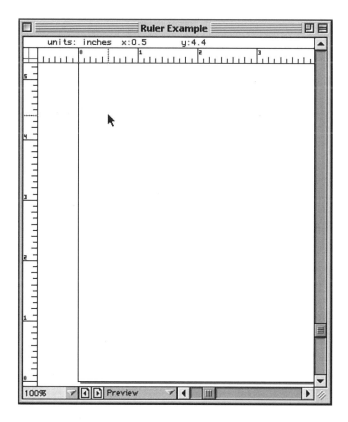

F i g u r e 1 . 2 1

The Ruler in inches.

The units of measure used with the ruler depend on the Inspector palette's document settings. As the cursor moves over the document, gray lines appear in the ruler indicating cursor position. The 0,0 point on both rulers is called the Origin. The default location for the Origin in a new document is at the lower left corner of the page. You can place the Origin anywhere else on the page by clicking in the square where the horizontal and vertical rulers meet, and dragging to the location on the page where you want to place the Origin. You can replace the Origin as often as you like. It affects only the ability to position items on the electronic page.

 Tip

You can simplify many tasks by strategically placing the Origin point. All the transformation tools work from a point relative to the Origin point. If you place the Origin at the desired center point on your object, you can enter 0 for X and Y in the Transform palette.

Information Bar

Another option in the View menu is Info Bar, which adds the bar pictured in Figure 1.22 at the top of the document window below the title bar. If rulers are also turned on, the Info Bar will appear between the title bar and the ruler. In Figure 1.22 the units of measure are points and the coordinates of the cursor are x: 1.861112 and y: -0.458334.

Figure 1.22

Information Bar example.

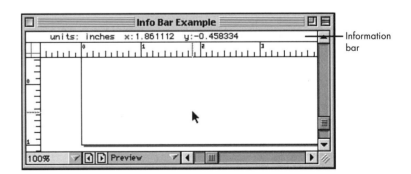

The information that appears will depend on which tool is selected and what you are doing. Nevertheless, the information bar only displays coordinates for the current location of the cursor, and gives the width and height of elements on the page. To accurately position an object, and to size it precisely, use the Object Inspector.

Guides

Some forms of illustration need a high degree of accuracy. Objects may need to be placed in exact locations on the page, or specific points within an object need exact placement. In either case, this type of work could take hours. Fortunately, FreeHand has a feature called Guides that provides accuracy and is also fast.

You can think of guides as placement magnets. When you are placing an object and it moves close to a guide, the object will gravitate to the guide. Individual points are also attracted to guides in this way. For example, if you want the lower-left corner of a rectangle to be 5 inches from the bottom of the page and 2 inches from the left edge, place a horizontal guide at 5 inches, and a vertical guide at 2 inches. (Remember, if you need *exact* placement, use the numbers in the information bar when you drag your guides into position. Don't eyeball it!) Now you can drag the rectangle so that its lower-left corner is close to the horizontal and vertical guides; when it gets close to guide let go of the mouse. Boing! Even if you did not drag the rectangle to the exact position, the guides will pull it into place.

The Guide layer in the Layers palette lets you show or hide all guides at one time, as does selecting or deselecting Guides in the View menu. Selecting Snap To Guides in the View menu turns guide "magnets" on or off.

 Tip

Guides default to a Cyan color, which you may already be using for objects or fills in your illustration. To change Guide color, select Preferences in the File menu. Select Colors, click on Guides and select a color that is not used in your illustration.

Ruler Guides

FreeHand provides two types of guides. The first, ruler guides, are either perfectly horizontal or vertical. An example of each is shown in Figure 1.23.

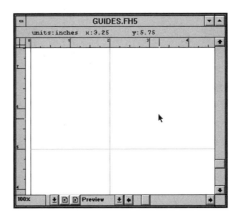

Figure 1.23

Ruler Guides are horizontal and vertical.

Horizontal guides are created by clicking within the horizontal ruler at the top of the document and dragging down into the content area of the document window to the desired location. Vertical guides are created by dragging from the vertical ruler.

Path Guides

Another form of guides are path guides. They serve the same purpose as ruler guides, but they can be any angle, size, or shape. This is an extremely useful and flexible feature, but most FreeHand users do not realize that it exists.

Any graphic object that you create can be turned into a path guide by selecting the object and then selecting the Guides layer in the Layers palette. The paths of the object will instantly turn to the guide color.

Guide Editor

Most of the time you will create or move guides simply by clicking and dragging. Occasionally this may not be the best way to create or change guides. Suppose, for example, you need to place a guide precisely and also need to place several evenly spaced guides simultaneously. Under these circumstances the Guide editor (View menu, Edit Guides) becomes important. The Guide editor pictured in Figure 1.24 shows a horizontal guide at 396, and a vertical guide at

306. The numbers represent the number of points (the unit of measurement for this document) from the Origin point. The third guide in Figure 1.25 is a path guide. The Guide editor gives no location information for path guides.

Figure 1.24

The Guide editor helps manage guides.

When you click on Release in this dialog box, you can move a guide from the Guides layer to the Foreground layer if the guide is selected in the list. Any path that is not in the Guides layer no longer functions as a guide. The Delete button eliminates a guide. To create a guide from scratch in the Guide editor, click on Add..., and use the dialog box pictured in Figure 1.25.

Figure 1.25

Add Guides dialog box can be used to create new guides.

The Add Guides dialog box can only be used to create horizontal and vertical guides, but it does provide more flexibility when creating these guides. For example, this dialog box simplifies the process of creating numerous guides at once. The first option specifies how some number guides will be created. The dialog box labeled Add by Count in Figure 1.25 shows how you can create five guides. The first guide will be located on row 0, and the last on 500. FreeHand automatically calculates the even separation, which is 125 points. The dialog box labeled Add by Increment in Figure 1.25 shows how you can create guides with 20 points in between, with the same first (0) and last (500) positions as before. FreeHand automatically calculates that this will require 26 guides.

The first option, Add by Count, allows you to specify how many guides will be created. Based on the position of the first and last guides, FreeHand will space the guides evenly on the page. The second option, Add by Increment, allows you to specify how far apart the guides will be. Based on the position of the first and last guides, FreeHand will add guides in between in the increment you have defined.

WORKING WITH GUIDES

 CD ROM

1. Open the file FreeHand/Ch1/GUIDES.FH5 on the disc.

Ruler Guides

2. Drag a ruler guide from the vertical ruler on the left to the center of the document. Use the Info Bar to help you find the center. Your target is X = 306.

3. Drag a ruler guide from the horizontal ruler at the top to the center of the document. Your Info Bar target is Y = 396.

Path Guides

4. Select the Ellipse tool in the Toolbox.

5. Position the cursor where the two new guides intersect.

6. Macintosh users: press and hold down the Shift and Option keys. Windows users: press and hold down the Shift and Alt keys. Now click and drag until you have created a circle of about 1 inch in diameter.

7. If the Layers palette is not open, open it now. While the circle is still selected, click on the Guides layer. This converts the circle to a guide.

Guide Editor

8. Select Edit Guides…from the View menu.

9. Select and delete the three guides you just created. Click on OK to get the actual guides in the document to disappear.

10. Re-open the Guides editor, and click on the Add…button.

11. Select the Horizontal and Increment radio buttons.

12. Fill in the blanks with the following values:
    Increment: 20
    First: 0
    Last: 780
    Press the Add button.

13. Notice that FreeHand creates a lengthy list of horizontal guides. Press OK.

14. Perform steps 11 through 13 and create vertical guides with a 20 point separation, starting at column 0.

Paths, Points, and Handles

The shape of all FreeHand graphics is defined by some sequence of points. Paths are lines that run from one point to another. Every one of these path segments has exactly two points—one at each end. These segments are connected end to end to form more complex objects. Handles that extend out from points define the shape of a path, and the direction and length of a handle defines the course of a path segment. Some point, path, and handle segments are shown in Figure 1.26.

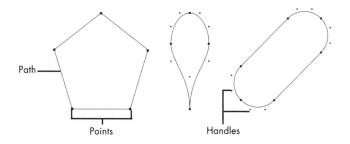

Figure 1.26

A closer look at points, paths and handles.

Path Direction

Although you can see that each path has shape, it is not as apparent that paths also have direction. In other words, you may not know that one end of a path is considered the start point and the other is the end point. Closed objects appear to have no ends at all. Surprisingly, FreeHand maintains information that indicates which point is the official start point, and which is the official end point. Even closed objects have start and end points. The term used to refer to these attributes is "path direction."

In most cases, you do not have to worry about path direction. One good example of when path direction makes a difference is when you need to extend retracted point handles (discussed in the next section).

Point Types and Handles

FreeHand has three different types of points—corners, curves, and connectors. The differences among these three are based on the way their handles work.

Each point has exactly two handles. Some points may appear to have no handles, and others may appear to have only one. Handles that appear to be missing are fully retracted. When a handle is not fully retracted, it is extended by some amount. The longer the handle, the more that segment of the path wants to continue in the path's current direction. As the path moves farther away from the point and its handle, the more it is affected by the control of the next point and its handle. Figure 1.27 shows examples of the same points with variations in handles.

Figure 1.27

Changing the handles affects the shape of the path between points.

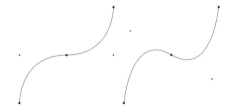

To extend a handle, press and hold down the Option key (Macintosh) or Alt key (Windows). Click once on the point, and then click and drag away from the point. The first handle to extend from the point will control the path segment following the point. Repeat the procedure and a second handle extends from the point; this controls the path segment preceding the point. Figure 1.28 illustrates the extension order regarding path direction.

Note

The order in which handles may be dragged from a point depends on the path direction. The first handle you can drag out will be in the direction of the path segment created after the point. The second handle you drag out will be in the direction of the path segment created before the point.

Figure 1.28

A point with retracted handles is a corner point. The first handle drawn for a point controls the direction of the path segment that follows the point. The second handle controls the segment that preceeds the point.

Curve Points and Handles

Curve points are designed to make paths that follow a smooth curved transition from one side of the point to the other. Figure 1.29 shows several examples of curve point path segments.

Figure 1.29

Curve point and handle examples.

Two handles extend from opposite sides of a curve point. Both handles combined always form a straight line and run parallel to the path as it passes through the point. Changing the angle of one side always affects the angle of the other side. Each can have different lengths, so the curve does not have to be symmetrical on both sides of the point.

Corner Points and Handles

Corner points make paths that change direction abruptly as the path passes through the point. Figure 1.30 shows a few corner point examples.

Figure 1.30

Corner point and handle examples.

Two handles extend from a corner point. Both handles are independent of the opposite handle. The default corner point has both handles fully retracted.

47

Connector Points and Handles

Connector points smoothly alter straight lines into curved lines. Figure 1.31 shows a connector point path segment. Actually, they don't alter straight lines into curved lines. They provide a transition point where a straight line ends and a curved line begins.

Figure 1.31

Connector points help make smooth transitions between straight and curved path segments.

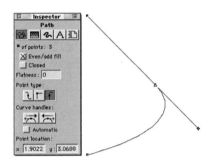

Although you can extend both handles from a connector point, typically you will only need to extend the handle on the side of the point that is to be curved.

Changing Point Type

One of the first important details to keep in mind when constructing graphic objects is that you choose the most appropriate point type for the desired path. If you create a corner point, then later need to make a smooth curve, you can easily change it. Simply select the point and choose the desired point type in the Object Inspector (see Figure 1.32).

Figure 1.32

Changing point type in the Object Inspector.

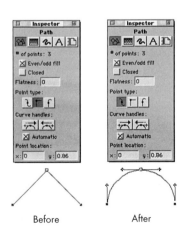

Before   After

WORKING WITH POINTS AND HANDLES

Often, you will want to change a corner point to a curve point. This exercise shows you how to do so.

1. Create a new document.

2. From the Tools palette, select the Rectangle tool; be sure that its corner radius is set to 0°.

3. Draw a two-inch square (144 points).

4. Open the Inspector palette and select the Object Inspector.

5. From the Arrange menu, select Ungroup. Notice that this changes the object you created from a "rectangle" to a closed path.

6. With the Pointer tool, select the bottom left point on the object.

7. Press and hold down the Option key (Macintosh), or Alt key (Windows), then extend both handles. (Notice in the Inspector that this is a Corner point.) Move them around to change the shape of the object.

8. Use the Curve Handles buttons at the bottom of the palette to retract both handles (click both buttons).

9. Select the Connector point from the Inspector and extend the handle that will extend. (This indicates the direction of the path. The connector point toward the end of the path.)

10. Notice that the connector handle can only affect the object in a limited way.

11. Retract the handle.

12. Select the Curve point from the Inspector and extend the handles. Notice how the handles work in conjunction with one another and how they affect adjacent points and handles.

Working with Graphic Objects

Up to this point in the book, you have learned about FreeHand object shapes. Beginning with this chapter, you will learn how to interpret and manipulate many other object attributes. This chapter also begins to explain how you combine different objects to build more complex illustrations.

Objects and Attributes

Chapter 1 introduced you to FreeHand's basic objects library. FreeHand also provides tools for creating custom objects. With the Inspector, you even have tools for changing objects' attributes. Some attributes apply to all graphic objects; other special attributes apply only to a specific object type. For example, rectangles can have a corner radius. FreeHand uses the corner radius number to determine how big the quarter circle will be to make each corner of the rectangle.

Stroke

One of the most basic of all the object attributes is the stroke, the line that is drawn along the perimeter of the object. An object's stroke can be turned off so that no line is drawn. To turn stroke off, select the object, select the Path icon in the Inspector, and choose None in the pop-up menu just below the Path icon (see Figure 2.1).

Figure 2.1

Turning stroke off for an object.

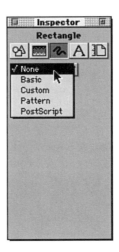

Even this simple attribute provides you with a number of different characteristics, such as cap and join settings, miter limits, dash qualities, and arrowheads. Regarding width, the thinnest standard stroke width is 0.25 of a point; this width is called "Hairline." The widest standard stroke is 12 points. Narrower and wider widths are possible. Figure 2.2 shows the contents of the Stroke Widths sub-menu. By selecting one of these items you can set the object's stroke width.

Thinner	⌘ ⌥ <
Thicker	⌘ ⌥ >
✓ Hairline	
0.5 pt	
1 pt	
1.5 pt	
2 pt	
4 pt	
6 pt	
8 pt	
12 pt	

Figure 2.2

Standard stroke widths in Arrange, Stroke Widths.

Cap

Cap specifies how FreeHand actually "caps off" the end of a path.

■ Butt cap is flush with the end of the path (it butts up against it).

■ Round cap extends a curved edge one-half the stroke width beyond the end of the path.

■ Square cap extends a flat edge one-half the stroke width beyond the end of the path.

Figure 2.3 shows each cap option and illustrates how each cap is drawn.

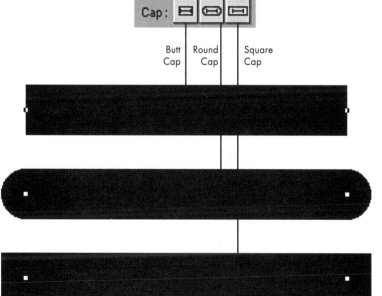

Figure 2.3

Cap icons and the type of cap each represents.

53

Join

Join specifies how FreeHand bevels the outside edge of a path as two path segments join. The three types of join are Miter, Round, and Bevel. Each path can have only one type of join defined. If FreeHand alters a Miter join to become a Bevel join because the join has exceeded the Miter Limit, *(see below)* the other Miter joins are not affected.

Figure 2.4 shows each join option and illustrates how each join is drawn.

Figure 2.4

Join icons and the type of transition each represents.

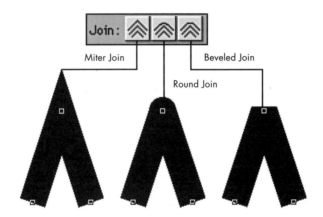

Miter limit

The Miter limit restricts the length of a mitered joint (see Figure 2.5). As an angle becomes more acute, the thickness at the apex (Miter Join) increases. Miter limit calculates using the allowable thickness of the miter using the ratio of the thickness of the Miter Join to the thickness of the line. When the ratio is exceeded, the join changes from Miter to Beveled. If the line is 3 points wide and the miter limit is 1.5, the join will change when the Miter Join exceeds 4.5.

Figure 2.5

The Miter Limit controls the thickness of the Miter Join.

Dashes

You can create a dashed line manually, but it would be ridiculously time-consuming. Fortunately, FreeHand includes a variety of dashed lines (see Figure

2.6) that are particularly useful when creating graphics such as maps or coupons.

Figure 2.6

FreeHand's dashes menu from the Dashed Stroke drop-down list.

Sometimes the selection of dashes FreeHand provides isn't acceptable for your needs; to remedy this, FreeHand lets you create custom dashes (see Figure 2.7). From the stroke inspector, be sure Basic is selected as the stroke type and click on the dash drop-down list. Press and hold down the Option key (Macintosh) or Alt key (Windows) and select a dash to use as the basis of your new style.

Figure 2.7

Custom dashes are added to the bottom of the Dashed Stroke drop-down list.

To create your new style, enter up to four different lengths for the dashes in the "On" boxes and up to four lengths for the spaces in the "Off" boxes. When you click on "OK" the new dashed stroke appears at the bottom of the list.

Arrowheads

Putting an arrowhead at the end of a path is a helpful feature when developing illustrations, such as maps, that need to have portions labeled as shown in Figure 2.8.

Figure 2.8

Paths with FreeHand's arrowheads.

To put arrowheads on either end of a path, you must first select the target path. Next, open the Path Inspector. At the bottom of the Inspector are two pop-up menus as pictured in Figure 2.8. This is one place that path direction is important and obvious. The left pop-up menu defines the arrowhead that will be put on the *start* of the path; the right pop-up controls the *end* of the path. Either one can specify a particular arrowhead, or either can be set to None, which is the default. The actual size of the arrowhead depends on the path width.

 Tip

If your arrow is pointing the wrong way, you can either change the arrowhead in the Inspector or reverse the direction of the path from the Arrange, Path Operations menu.

One overlooked feature of this tool is the capability to create custom arrowheads. For example, you may want a proportionally larger pointer, or perhaps a star. To create these unique arrowheads, go to Arrowheads, New and use FreeHand's drawing tools to create the arrowhead of your choice. The new arrowhead will now appear in the selection menu. Notice that you can select an open or filled version of the new arrowhead.

You can also create a custom arrowhead, such as the star in Figure 2.9, by using any of the tools in your FreeHand document. Cut the object from the document and paste it into the Arrowhead window, where you can resize it.

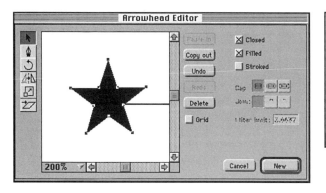

Figure 2.9

Your new custom arrowhead will appear in the selection menu.

Tip

Custom arrowheads apply only to the document in which they were created. To export any arrowhead, hold down Command-Option (Macintosh) with the arrowhead selected. Click the Copy Out button to export the arrowhead to the clipboard, then copy it into your new file.

To create a "palette" of arrowheads, keep the arrowhead art in an arrowhead palette document. Whenever you need an arrowhead, simply copy the art to the clipboard, then paste it into the arrowhead palette of the new document.

Fills

Another basic object attribute in the Inspector arsenal specifies the area within the perimeter of an object. The area of an object can either be empty, or it can be filled with a solid color or a pattern. Figure 2.10 shows a graphic object and various Inspector settings, such as the Fill icon. Initially, the Inspector contains nothing under the icon bar but a pop-up menu. The fill types that make up the pop-up menu are pictured in Figure 2.10.

Figure 2.10

The Fill Inspector can be used to set an object's fill characteristics.

57

None and Basic

The exact contents of the Fill Inspector below the first pop-up menu are determined by what type of fill is selected. If None is selected, the remainder of the Inspector is empty. This specifies that there is no fill specified for the object; this makes the content area of the object transparent. The Basic option lets you fill the object with a solid color.

The Overprint button controls whether the object will overprint or knock out the background color. Usually you will want black to overprint. Other applications where you would want to overprint are when two colors abut one another and you need them to blend together. The stroke around the shape that was created last (this color is on top of the other color) will create a *trap*, an area where the two colors blend, which avoids the possibility of the paper showing through. (There is also an Overprint button in the Path Inspector.) The remaining options in the Fill Inspector will be covered more in the Patterns section of this chapter.

Trapping

To avoid the possibility of the paper showing through in areas where two colors abut, printers use a printing process called trapping. The elements of a trap are chokes, spreads, overprints, and knockouts. Each of these describes how the topmost element will interact with elements below it.

When an element is choked, it becomes smaller with respect to the element below it. For example, if a top object was cyan and the element below was yellow, the stroke around the uppermost object would be yellow (the lighter color), making the object appear smaller. If the objects were reversed, the stroke of the upper object would still be yellow, but it would be spread into the background, becoming larger in relation to the background.

In either case, the actual object (less the surrounding stroke) knocks out the color below, retaining its pure color. If the objects were allowed to overprint, the result would be a mix of the inks, producing a green object.

Custom

The Custom option in the Fill Inspector displays a pop-up menu for filling objects with custom fills. One important point to be aware of with all of the Custom options is that none of them actually displays the selected pattern on screen. Instead the object will be filled with a pattern that looks like it only contains the letter "C". Your drawing will print with the appropriate fill pattern when printed on a PostScript capable printer. The "Bricks" Custom option, for example, creates a fill that resembles a wall of bricks (see Figure 2.11). The options include the color used to represent the bricks, and a color for the mortar. The remaining settings define how the brick pattern is drawn.

Figure 2.11

You can customize the Brick color; Mortar color; and Brick width, height, and orientation for the Bricks pattern.

Graduated

When a graduated fill is used, one side of the graphic is one color and the opposite side is either another color or a different shade of the same color. This fill option creates a smooth color transition between the two. This color transition is frequently called a color ramp.

Figure 2.12 shows graduated fill options. This graduated fill is set to start at black, and transition to white. Because the taper is set to Linear, the progression from black to white will be at a consistent rate across the ramp. The angle is set to 270 degrees, which will place black at the top of the object and white at the bottom.

Figure 2.12

The Fill Inspector set for a Graduated fill.

You can specify what colors will be on both ends of the color ramp by assigning colors with the From and To options. You can control the progression from one color to the other with Linear and Logarithmic (see Figure 2.13). Linear produces a slow and gradual ramp, and Logarithmic creates a faster color progression.

Figure 2.13

Linear and logarithmic progressions of the graduated fill.

The angle of the progression is affected by the degree you specify:

■ 0 degrees—From the left to the right

■ 90 degrees—From the bottom to the top

■ 180 degrees—From the right to the left

■ 270 degrees—From the top to the bottom

As you can imagine, acceptable angle values are within the range 0 to 359 degrees.

Tip

Only colors using the same color model (more on this later) may be blended together. CMYK colors may be blended and any spot color may be blended within its tonal range (from 100 to 0 percent) or a spot color may be blended with white. If the program preferences are set to CMYK, any RGB colors selected will default to their CMYK equivalent. Two spot colors or a spot color and a CMYK color cannot be blended.

CREATING CUSTOM GRADUATED FILLS

Linear Fill

1. Open a new document and create a rectangle 72 points wide by 144 points deep.

2. In the Fill Inspector, select Graduated; be sure the taper is Linear and adjust the angle to 270°.

3. Open the Color List and Color Mixer palettes.

4. Using the sliders in the Color Mixer palette, create a color comprised of 100 percent cyan and 75 percent yellow. Drag the resulting color sample onto the Color List palette.

5. Create a second color that is 100 percent yellow and 50 percent magenta. Drag this color onto the Color List palette.

6. Drag the green color swatch onto the From box in the Fill Inspector and the orange swatch onto the To box.

7. Clone this box and move it 84 points to the right. To do this, select Clone from the Edit menu. From the Windows menu, be sure the Transform box is visible, select the Move icon, and type 84 in the x-axis box; type 0 in the y-axis box. Be sure that Contents and Fills are both checked.

Logarithmic Fill

8. Select the new box and in the Fill Inspector change the Fill taper to Logarithmic.

9. Experiment with different angles and color combinations.

Pattern

The Pattern option offers pre-made patterns with which you can fill objects. The pattern is shown within the object using the color in the color box right below the options pop-up menu. You can change the color by dragging a color from either the Color Mixer or the Color List and dropping it on the color box. The slider at the bottom of the Inspector lets you view all the available patterns. When you select one, it appears in the pattern edit box (on the left) shown in Figure 2.14. There are two boxes, the one on the left is the editable pattern. The one on the right shows the pattern at actual size. The box on the right of Figure 2.14 shows you a sample of the pattern at normal size. You can turn the spots black or turn them off by clicking on each square within the edit box.

Figure 2.14

The Fill Inspector set for Pattern lets you use pre-made or custom patterns.

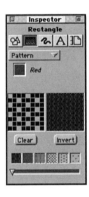

One advantage to the Fill Inspector is that it allows you to create your own patterns. One disadvantage is that you are creating the pattern with a bitmapped image. The quality of most patterns when printed will not be optimized for the resolution capabilities of most PostScript printers. When the patterns are included in a process color document, they may produce unforeseeable and unacceptable results. For these reasons, patterns should only be used for lower resolution black and white images.

CREATING A CUSTOM PATTERN

1. In the Fill Inspector, select Pattern, then reset the color to black.

2. Click on the Clear and Invert buttons so that you can see the squares.

3. Create a diamond pattern with flat tops and sides as you see in the figure.

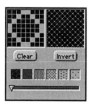

4. Draw a new shape; your pattern will fill it.

5. Invert the pattern if you'd like, or assign it a different color, or both.

PostScript

PostScript is a page description language developed by Adobe Systems. You can think of PostScript as a computer programming language that tells imaging devices such as printers how to draw an image on the page. Normally you would let FreeHand create PostScript code from your drawings. In case you need to include precise PostScript instructions in your drawing, the edit box labeled PostScript code in the Fill Inspector is included (see Figure 2.15).

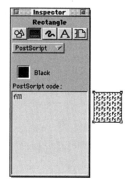

Figure 2.15

The PostScript option of the Fill Inspector.

This box allows you to enter up to 255 characters of PostScript code to use as the fill pattern for an object. The actual pattern will only be used at print time when printing to a PostScript printer. On the screen and when printing to a non-PostScript printer, the fill contains the letters PS in a pattern throughout the object.

An almost limitless number of patterns can be specified in code because every shape that can be described to a printer is described in PostScript. The PostScript language is so flexible that Adobe has published a series of four books for learning the PostScript language. If you're interested, learning to write PostScript can be extremely rewarding.

63

Figure 2.16 shows one example of PostScript code. The phrase "1 srand" sets the random pattern, with any number greater than 0 creating a different pattern. The number of splotches in the pattern is set by the "100." The maximum and minimum radius of the splotches is set by the numbers "5" and "1."

Figure 2.16

These few lines of PostScript code produce a random "spatter" pattern.

What is PostScript?

A simple explanation of PostScript is a language that allows computers and the programs running on them to communicate with imaging devices. The printing and publishing industries (among others) have made PostScript the standard for communicating graphics, type, and entire page descriptions.

All machines talk to one another in code. People put images and pages together using computers and monitors (workstations); the pages are imaged at printers. Each device has its own language. For that reason, we must prepare the pages in the proper manner for each output device.

PostScript is an elegant interpreter that is fluent in many languages. At the workstation, it translates the screen image into PostScript code. At the printer, it translates the same information into the language of the printing device. This "interpreter" is used on printing devices from inexpensive desktop laser printers to very high resolution imagesetters and film recorders.

Because of PostScript you can buy one typeface and print it to many devices. PostScript also lets you describe shapes simply, either by using primitives (rectangles, ellipses, and lines) or by using the points and handles of Bézier curves.

In addition to translating vector-based data, PostScript understands raster-based images, and can correctly interpret TIFF and EPS images, then send these types of files to an imaging device for rendering the original in the best way.

Radial

The Radial option also creates color ramps in an object. The difference is that the ramp proceeds from the outside to the inside in circles. The only other options for controlling how this works include the color used on both ends of the color ramp and where the inside color will be located within the object. Figure 2.17 show possible options and an object with a radial fill.

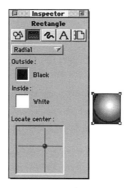

Figure 2.17

Locate center lets you determine where the Inside color will be centered in the object.

CREATING A RADIAL COLOR RAMP

1. Be sure that the Path (stroke) is set to none. In the Fill Inspector, select Radial.

2. Set the colors to black for the outside color and white for the inside color.

3. From the Toolbox, select the ellipse tool and draw a perfect circle three inches (216 points) in diameter. It will appear with the radial fill.

4. Move the center point around to achieve different effects.

5. Change colors from the color mixer or the color list. Notice the variety of effects you can create.

Textured

A nice addition to the texture fill option is that it lets you choose the color to be used. A pop-up menu lets you select the texture (see Figure 2.18).

Figure 2.18

The Texture option of the Fill Inspector.

When you use Texture fill, you cannot actually see the texture on-screen. The object instead contains a pattern that looks like the letter "C." The texture only appears when printing to a PostScript printer.

Tiled

Of all the options in the Inspector palette, this is probably the most powerful and flexible (and the most fun!). Tiling enables you to create a small graphic object (or group of objects), copy it to the clipboard, and then press the Paste In button in the Tiled Fill Inspector to create a repetitive fill pattern. The pattern you create displays on-screen and prints on the printer. Figure 2.19 shows a tile pattern that uses a five point star.

A few controls are available for tiling the graphic, including the angle option. An angle of 0 degrees orients the object exactly as it was when you pasted it. An angle of 20 degrees rotates the object 20 degrees counterclockwise. The orientation can range from 0 to 359 degrees.

The scale option lets you make the object bigger or smaller in the pattern. A value of 100 percent draws the object at the size it was created; you can also use smaller and larger values.

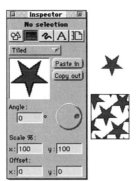

Figure 2.19

Fill Inspector lets you copy the object you want tiled and paste it into a tile.

Offset is used to move the pattern around within the object. If you are not happy with the placement of objects within the fill, you can adjust the pattern horizontally and vertically. You can also use negative numbers.

CREATING AND ADJUSTING TILED PATTERNS

1. Make sure the Path (stroke) is set to none in the Path Inspector. In the Fill Inspector, select Basic.

2. From the Toolbox, select the Rectangle tool and draw a perfect square two inches (144 points) across.

3. From the Color Mixer or the Color List, color the square 100 percent magenta.

4. Using the Polygon tool, create five stars of varying sizes. Color the largest one cyan, two of the small ones yellow, and two of the small ones white.

5. Using the Pointer tool, drag the stars into pleasing positions on top of the magenta square.

6. Use the pointer tool to draw a marquee around the entire group (the square and the stars) and copy them.

7. Press the Tab key to deselect the objects.

8. In the Fill Inspector, select Tiled. Click on the Paste In button. Your patterned fill is now ready to use.

9. Select a shape from the Toolbox (Ellipse, Rectangle, or Polygon) and draw an object approximately three inches by two inches. Watch it fill with your custom pattern.

10. With the shape still selected, adjust the angle, scale, and offset.

You don't need to create a background square for the Pattern Fill for it to work. But working with one allows you to add a solid color background to your pattern. To make this work use a background square that is at least 96 points wide. Otherwise there will be unsightly gaps between the tiles.

 Tip

After you start making Pattern Fills you won't want to stop. Keep a FreeHand Document (or several, if you prefer) of your patterns. Then they will always be available for cutting and pasting into new documents.

Although they are almost addictive, tiling patterns should be used with care. It is easy to create complex graphics that would make great background patterns. The problem is the computer has to image each instance of the graphic within the pattern. If the tile image is complex, you may see a significant slowdown in screen updates, and even slower print times. The worst cases may actually cause the printer to run out of memory during printing.

Object Styles

Object styles are user-definable attribute groups. When you create objects on-screen, you probably will need some of the objects to have common attributes. For example, you may want a number of objects to have the same combination of stroke width, fill color, and fill pattern. Rather than set each one of those attributes one by one, you can define them all in one style. (You can even create a style for that neat pattern you just created, or for a number of them.) You can also name the style to help you remember why it was created. When you want to apply the style, it is as simple as applying a single attribute.

FreeHand provides a floating palette for Styles (under the Windows menu). Figure 2.20 shows the Styles palette and the contents of the Options pop-up menu.

Figure 2.20

The Styles palette and Options pop-up menu.

Most of the settings in the Edit Style window should be familiar. Clicking on the Style pop-up menu will open a menu that contains the names of all the defined styles within the document. When you select one of the styles it switches the Edit Style window to that style.

The Parent pop-up menu allows you to define one style based on another style. The illustration in Figure 2.21 shows how this relationship works. The style named Base calls for a red color fill and a Basic fill pattern, with None set for stroke. Style-1 does not define any values for fill, but defines a stroke that is black, Basic, and has a width of 1 point. Style-2 also does not define values for fill, but defines a stroke that is black, Basic, and has a width of 2 points. To change the fill color for all objects that use Style-1 or Style-2, you only need to change them once in Base.

The third new item in the Edit Style window is the Style Affects pop-up menu. This sub-menu lets you limit the scope of a style definition. In Figure 2.21, Base has this set to "Both Fill and Stroke." Style-1 and Style-2 are set to "Stroke Attributes." These two styles are set this way so that they affect only the stroke and do not override the fill attributes set in Base.

Setting up the styles can be tricky, and it takes a little planning, if you want to do it efficiently. The next exercise will help you see how to set up styles properly.

Figure 2.21

The Edit Style Window for style-1 and style-2.

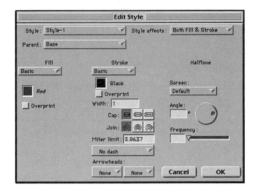

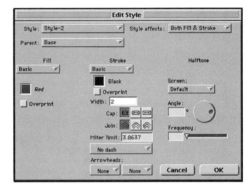

CREATING STYLES

1. Begin by setting up the base style. In the Inspector, set the stroke as None and the fill as basic red.

2. Draw a rectangle: it will automatically become an unstroked box filled with red.

3. Be sure the rectangle is still selected. Go to the Options pop-up in the Style Palette and click on New. The name Style-1 will appear in the palette. Double-click on it and type its new name, Base.

4. Click on the Style Options button and go to Edit Style. You will see that the Edit menu appears, and that the Base style has been defined.

5. Press the Tab key to deselect all.

6. Select New from the Options pop-up. Name this style Base + Stroke 1. (It will add a one-point stroke to the base definition.)

7. Select Edit Style, Parent, Base. Notice that the Fill color is still None.

8. Click on the Fill button and select basic. The Fill color changes to the color in the Base style, which is red.

9. Click on the Stroke button and select basic. Change the color to black, and the width to 1.

10. Under Style Affects, select Both Fill and Stroke.

11. Draw two rectangles and assign them a fill of cyan.

12. With the first rectangle selected, click on the Base style. Notice that the fill changes to red, and it has no stroke.

13. Select the second rectangle and assign it the Base + Stroke 1 style. Notice that its fill is red and it has a 1-point stroke.

14. Deselect the rectangles by pressing Tab.

15. Edit the Base style by changing its color to cyan. Click on OK. Note that the fills on both rectangles changed color.

Combining Simple Graphic Objects

Almost any graphic you will need to develop will be constructed from some combination of simpler graphic objects. The actual complexity of the finished product depends on many factors.

Although all the features discussed here are used to combine graphic objects in some way, not all of them are found in the same locations within FreeHand. Group is a menu item in the Arrange menu; other graphic combining tools are sub-menu items within the Path Operations menu (see Figure 2.22). With the exception of Group (which can be accessed with Command-G [Macintosh] or Ctrl-G [Windows]), all these options also are represented by icons in the Operations palette (Window, Other menu).

Figure 2.22

Tools to help you create complex drawings from primitives supplied by FreeHand may be selected from the menu or the Operations palette.

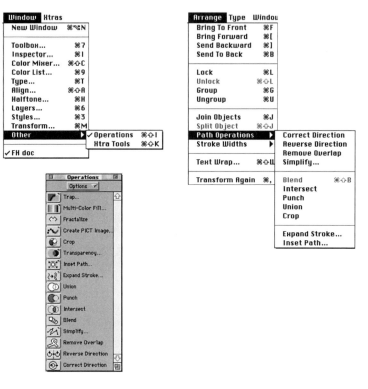

Suppose you want to create a simple icon of everyone's favorite mouse. (Just the head will do.) You could do a lot of drawing or assemble it completely from ellipses (and a few tricks).

BUILDING A MOUSE

1. Create a new document.

2. From the Color List, set a fill of black and a stroke of none.

3. Open the Object Inspector.

4. Draw three circles, measuring 216 points, 120 points, and 24 points. Next, draw an ellipse with a width of 42 points and a height of 54 points.

5. From the Color List, make the stroke of the ellipse black and the fill white.

6. Position the objects so they match the figure shown below.

7. Select the 120 point circle and the ellipse with the pointer tool, then clone the objects.

8. Select the Reflecting Tool. Place it in the center of the large circle and mirror the objects 180 degrees.

9. Open the Operations Palette from the Window, Other menu, and extend it to see all the items.

10. With the pointer tool, select the "face" and "ears," then click on Union in the Operations Palette. The face and ears are now one path, as shown below.

73

11. The Union command brought the element to the front, covering the "eyes." From the Arrange menu, send the object to the back.

12. Select the left eye and the background shape, then click on Punch in the Operations menu. Repeat with the right eye.

13. Place the remaining element inside one eye, clone it, then reflect it into the other one. Make whatever adjustments you need to make with the pointer tool.

14. Select the "eyeballs" and the object, then select Union from the Operations Palette again.

15. If you want to give your mouse a mouth, create a 3-sided polygon and rotate it so that the apex is at the bottom.

16. Position the mouth below the eyes. Adjust the points so that the edges of the mouth are at the outside edge of the eyes and about 1/4 inch from the bottom of the face.

17. Press and hold down the Option key (Macintosh) or Alt key (Windows), then extend the handles on the bottom point to give the mouse a wide grin (see the following figure).

Group

Although well done graphics may appear to be seamless, FreeHand considers all of them combinations of individual components. This is not much of a problem until you want to do something like move them or resize them as one unit. To remedy this potential concern, the Group command (Arrange, Group) enables you combine graphic objects. To break this artificial bond, you can select the grouped object and select Ungroup from the Arrange menu. Figure 2.23 shows a number of separate selected objects and one selected grouped object. Ungrouped objects each have their own set of selection points, while grouped objects have only four points, one defining each corner of the bounding box they fill.

 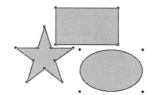

Figure 2.23

Multiple selected objects and one single grouped object.

GROUPING OBJECTS

1. Use the Polygon tool to create seven randomly-sized stars. Be sure Fill is set to black and stroke is set to none.

2. Select three of these stars. Notice how each star is individually defined.

3. Group the stars (select Arrange, Group). Notice that the area of the entire group is now bounded by just the four corner points. By clicking on any star within the group, you can select and move the entire group.

   Occasionally you may need to alter one item in the group. Ungrouping and regrouping is a painstaking, tedious process that creates opportunities for mistakes when regrouping.

4. Press and hold down the Option key (Macintosh) or Alt key (Windows), then click on one of the stars in your group. From the Color List, change the star's Fill to white and its Stroke to black.

Changing Attributes and Grouped Objects

Be careful when making object attribute changes when a grouped object is selected. Combined objects often have different attribute settings. Some components have a stroke, and others will have it turned off. Each component may also have different colors for the fill. If you change an attribute, you possibly could create problems throughout the grouped objects. If you realize that you made this mistake, immediately select Undo from the Edit menu.

You can test this yourself. Select the group of stars from the preceding exercise, go to the Color List, and change the stroke to red (if there's no red in your list, mix one in the Color Mixer [100 percent yellow, 100 percent magenta will work]). Notice that the black stars acquired a red stroke.

Resizing a Grouped Object

When resizing a grouped object, you should consider these questions:

■ Do you also want the stroke width to increase or decrease in proportion to the components you've just resized?

■ If you're using a textured fill, do you want it to be resized too, or should it remain the same?

■ If you combine two elements, do you want them to resize as a unit, or for the inside element to retain its current size?

The best way to resize a grouped object is to use the Transform palette. Note the check boxes for Content, Fills, and Lines at the bottom of the Transform palette. Here, you can indicate which objects and parts of objects are to be resized.

RESIZING GROUPED OBJECTS

1. Create three hexagons with the Polygon tool and assign them a three-point stroke. Fill them with the "stars" pattern you created in an earlier exercise. A polygon is not a "primitive," (only lines, ellipses, and rectangles are) and so, it must be grouped if it is to be resized using the Pointer tool, just like any object you draw in FreeHand.

Resizing all elements within the graphic

2. Group one of the hexagons and resize it to approximately double its size by dragging one of the corners of the group. Notice the fill and the stroke increased proportionally.

Resizing the graphic's size, but leaving fill and line untouched

3. Select a different hexagon. From the Transform palette, scale by 200 percent; be sure the Fills and Lines buttons are unchecked. Next, click on Apply. Compare the size of the lines and fills on this object with the untouched one.

The Contents button relates to the more advanced Paste Inside feature, but works in the same way as fills.

Join

Like the Group command, Join combines separate objects, but in a different manner. Objects that are grouped have some force holding the objects together. When separate objects are joined, the result differs, depending on what type of objects are being joined. If two open paths are joined, they actually become one path. In other words, the end of one path merges with the end of the other path that is nearest it, without taking into account the start point and end point of either path.

Separate closed objects that are joined behave like grouped objects. There are some exceptions to this though. For one thing, these objects can be split apart by selecting Split Object from the Arrange menu. Figure 2.24 shows three closed objects that have been joined. Even/Odd fill has been turned on for the object, and you can see that the area in which they overlap is not colored with the fill color.

Figure 2.24

Closed, joined objects with Even/Odd fill turned on. If these objects were grouped, Even/Odd would not be an option.

Note

Another situation in which Group and Join become important is with text. As you will see in Chapter 3, joining text to a path causes the segment of text to follow the course of the path.

Joining any two objects is as simple as selecting the two objects and choosing Join Objects from the Arrange menu. When joining two un-closed paths, they will be joined at the two ends that are closest to each other (see Figure 2.25).

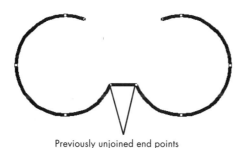

Figure 2.25

Two open paths that were joined where the two points are closest. Start and end points do not take priority.

Previously unjoined end points

JOINING CLOSED OBJECTS OR PATHS

1. Draw a red rectangle with a black border and a yellow ellipse with a black border. Drag the ellipse over the rectangle and center it.

2. Select both objects, then choose Join from the Arrange menu. Notice that two things happen: The ellipse turns the same color as the rectangle (the object on the bottom determines the fill for both objects); and the part of the ellipse that overlapped the rectangle turns white.

3. Open the Object Inspector. Notice that Even/Odd Fill is selected. Deselect it and watch the white area where the shapes overlap fill with red.

Joining Open Paths

1. Use the Freehand tool to draw two semicircles with their open sides facing one another. (Be sure stroke is set to a number.)

2. Select both paths, then choose Join from the Arrange menu. Notice that the nearest two points are linked, so the two become one path.

3. Open the Object Inspector and click on Closed. The other ends of the semicircles are joined and the object is filled with whatever attribute is selected in the Inspector.

Union

Union turns multiple overlapping objects into one object. The objects are merged at the points where they overlap. Overlapping pieces of each object are discarded. Figure 2.26 might make the Union command's purpose clearer.

Figure 2.26

Before and after examples of objects that have been combined with the Union command.

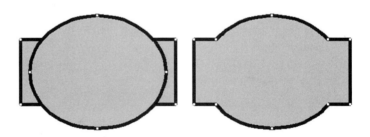

Combining two objects with this command is as simple as selecting the objects and choosing Union. If the objects do not overlap, this command will have the same effect as joining the two objects; you can split them apart by selecting Split

Objects from the Arrange menu. If either object overlaps the other, the two will become one object, and any path and points that are within the common area are discarded.

Tip

Union can be very helpful when you need to create complex shapes. Sometimes it is much easier to use FreeHand's standard shapes and combine them with Union than it is to create the shape by placing points and adjusting handles. Figure 2.27 shows an example of an object that was created with Union-ed shapes.

Figure 2.27

This shape was created with a rectangle and an ellipse that were combined with Union.

Punch

The Punch command in Arrange, Path Operations enables you to cut away portions of one object with the shape of another. Punch can create a hole of any shape in another object or can be used to cut away parts of a shape.

The Punch command is simple to use: you just place one object over another. The path of the upper object becomes the cut-out path. The lower object is modified. If the path of the upper object doesn't cross over any paths in the lower object, you will cut a hole in the lower object. If a portion of the upper object crosses over the path of the lower object, the Punch command will alter the path of the lower object (see Figure 2.28). Should the upper object not be over any part of the lower object when the Punch command is used, the upper object will be discarded, and the lower object will be left unchanged.

upper object
lower object

Figure 2.28

A portion of the upper object's path replaces part of the path on the lower object.

Keep in mind when using this command that you cannot unseparate some Punch operations. There is one difference between using Punch to cut a hole in an object and using Punch to actually change the shape of an object. After you punch a hole in an object, you can separate the objects by selecting Split Objects from the Arrange menu. However, after changing the shape of an object with the Punch command, the two cannot be split apart.

 Tip

Cutting away parts of objects may not seem like a useful method for creating custom objects, but it actually can be a time saver. Sometimes it is quicker to use standard FreeHand shapes and subtract parts you don't need with other basic shapes than it is to draw shapes by hand.

USING UNION AND PUNCH

In this exercise, you'll create a lock with a keyhole. You'll work with some elements from previous lessons so that you can build on your knowledge.

1. Be sure the Fill Inspector is open, with Graduated fill selected.

2. Open the Color Mixer and create two new colors: Mix 0C, 25M, 100Y, and 30K and drag it to the From box in the Fill Inspector; create and drag 0C, 25M, 100Y, and 0K to the To box in the Fill Inspector. Set the angle to 270°.

2. Create a rectangle 186 points wide and 306 points tall. The fill will automatically apply.

3. Clone the rectangle. Use the same center point (press and hold down the Option key [Macintosh] or Alt key [Windows]) to reduce the rectangle to 168 points wide and 280 points tall. Change the angle of the graduated fill to 90°, then group the rectangles.

4. Create a circle 106 points in diameter, a rectangle 54 points wide by 72 points high, and a 66 point square. Position them on top of each other with some overlap. Compare your screen with the figure shown.

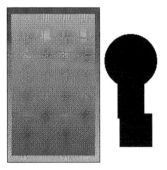

5. From the Window Menu select Align, Horizontal, Align Center. Leave the Vertical alignment unchanged. Now click on Apply.

6. Create a Union of these elements.

7. Place the new object on top of the grouped rectangles, select both objects and center-align them horizontally and vertically. (Select Align Center from both the Horizontal and the Vertical drop-down menus in the Align palette.)

8. With both objects still selected, Punch the keyhole into the lock.

Intersect

Intersect is the inverse of the Union command. Union discards common portions of different objects; Intersect keeps only common parts. Like the Union command, Intersect turns multiple overlapping objects into one object. Any area that is not common to the selected objects is discarded. Figure 2.29 should help illustrate this Intersect command.

F i g u r e   2 . 2 9

Before and after examples of objects that have been combined with the Intersect command.

Combining two objects with this command is as simple as selecting the two objects and choosing Intersect. If the objects do not overlap, this command will delete the two objects. If either of the objects overlaps the other, the two will become one object. Any path and points that are outside the common area are discarded.

 Tip

To create a perfect semicircle in seconds, draw a rectangle. Place a circle on it, position to taste, and choose Intersect.

Layers

FreeHand enables you to distribute individual graphic objects over separate layers. Imagine a picture comprised of multiple layers of transparent film on top of each other. Different components of the overall graphic are printed on each layer of film. Splitting the image into separate layers provides a number of creative possibilities. Changing the background, for example, is as simple as swapping the background layer for another image. In addition, any layer can be subtracted or substituted with another layer. This type of organization also lets you edit a layer separately without any distractions by temporarily removing the other layers and pieces of the drawing.

FreeHand provides a palette for creating and controlling layers. In Figure 2.30 you can see that the Layers palette currently has three layers: Guides, Foreground, and Background. All three are created automatically when you create a new document in FreeHand.

Figure 2.30

Standard Layers palette.

Any object placed in the Background layer will appear grayed out on-screen and will not print. FreeHand places Background below the dividing line seen in Figure 2.30. You can drag any layer below this line, which will gray out the layer on-screen and prevent it from printing when the document is printed.

Any path placed on the Guides layer becomes a guide. The Guide layer in the Layers palette allows you to show or hide all guides at one time. Selecting Snap To Guides in the View menu turns guide "magnets" on or off.

Another layer FreeHand creates with the birth of every new drawing is the Foreground layer. Objects you create are initially placed in that layer by default.

To the left of each name in the Layer palette are three small icons. The rightmost check mark icon makes the graphic objects that reside on that layer disappear. This feature can be used to simplify the document while you are working on specific areas, or to print variations of the images. Just before printing, you can hide any layer you want to exclude on the printed page.

The middle icon either contains a dark fill or no fill with a small "x" in the center. If the circle is darkened, "Preview mode" is active; no fill indicates "Keyline mode." Click on this circle icon to toggle between these two modes. When the layer is in Preview mode, all objects on that layer are displayed with the characteristics set for those objects. For example, if you create objects in a particular layer with various fill colors and patterns, the fills and patterns will appear in Preview mode.

In Keyline mode, only an outline of each object displays. The advantage to Keyline is that it takes less time for FreeHand to redraw graphics in a drawing when you scroll around, but you can still use the object's outline for placement and composition.

The last icon, padlock, enables you to lock and unlock a layer's contents. Locking a layer prevents you from changing it—no moving, deleting, or altering objects. When you finish a layer, locking it will protect the layer from accidental changes.

You can create new layers by clicking on the pop-up menu at the top of the Layers palette and choosing "New." A new, empty layer will appear in the document. You can rename a layer by double-clicking on its default name and typing the new name. Figure 2.31 shows the Layers palette with two custom layers: Circles and Squares.

Figure 2.31

All circle objects are on the Circles layer, and squares are on the Squares layer.

To choose which layer you'd like the next new object to be created in, click on the desired layer in the palette. To move an existing object to a different layer, click on the object and then click on the new destination layer in the Layers palette.

CREATING AND WORKING WITH LAYERS

1. Open the file FreeHand/Ch2/LAYERS.FH5 that was included with this book.

2. Be nice to your eyes by turning off the Foreground and Circles layers (uncheck them).

3. Lock the Foreground and Circles layers.

4. Shift-select every other square (in a checkerboard fashion). Assign a red fill and yellow stroke to these squares.

5. Create a new layer and rename it Squares 2. Press Tab to deselect everything.

6. Lock the two Squares layers, and turn them off.

7. Turn on and unlock the Circles layer. Select every other circle and assign a black fill with a red stroke.

8. Create a new layer. Rename it Circles 2 and drag it between the Circles layer and the Squares layer. Press Tab again to deselect everything.

9. Lock the two Circles layers, and turn them off.

10. Turn on and unlock the Foreground layer. Select all, then press and hold down the shift key and click on the background rectangle (this deselects it).

11. Create a new layer and rename it Dots All. Press Tab to deselect everything.

12. Lock and then turn on all the layers.

Color

Color is an important part of all FreeHand graphic objects. Even in situations when the graphic will only be printed on a black and white printer, you still must consider color issues, such as setting certain parts black, and others white, transparent, or various shades of gray. Understandably, most would consider such a graphic to not contain color. However, color plays an important part in every graphic, from CMYK four-color process drawings to the simplest monochromatic sketches. Fortunately, with FreeHand you do not have to worry as much about the theories behind mixing colors and the interaction between colors.

Color Mixer Palette

One of FreeHand's color-related palettes you are already familiar with, the Color Mixer palette, enables you to define your own colors to be used for strokes and fills. This palette lets you create colors using several different color models —good news for you because it gives you some choice about the best one for your project's needs. In Figure 2.32, you can see the first four color models: CYMK, RGB, HLS, and Tint.

Figure 2.32

Color Mixer Palette for the Macintosh version of FreeHand.

A color model is simply a system for defining specific colors. The difference between each model is in the component colors that are used to make up all the other colors. The fifth model included with FreeHand depends on the computer system; if you are using a Macintosh, you will have access to the standard MacOS color picker. If you are using Windows, the Windows color picker is included.

Note

Before you use the Color Mixer, you should know that the colors you see on-screen are not the colors that will actually print. When mixing colors, be sure to consult a printed color chart.

Selecting a color model in the Color Mixer is as simple as clicking on the button that names the desired color model. When a model is selected, the appropriate color controls appear in the rest of the palette. The first two options are CYMK and RGB (see Figure 2.33).

Figure 2.33

Color Mixer Palette for CYMK and RGB.

Both color models shown in Figure 2.33 work the same, and include a slider for each color component within the model. The sliders are scaled from 0 to 100 percent. When one of these sliders is set to 0 percent, its component color makes up 0 percent of the final color. When a slider is set to 100 percent, that component's color contributes all of its color to the final color.

To determine which of these two primary color models to work in, you need to consider the destination of the artwork. Will the work you produce be printed? If so, use the CMYK palette. Will it be viewed on-screen, such as on a CD or on a computer-generated presentation, as slides, or on the World Wide Web? For these destination media, use the RGB color model. The color model you use should correspond to the Color Preferences you set up in the File menu.

The rectangle in the bottom quarter of the palette actually has two halves. The left half represents the current or previous color. The right half represents the new color being mixed.

The Color Models

CYMK: The four color components for CYMK are cyan, yellow, magenta, and black. In the CYMK model, 0 percent of all four components creates white, and 100 percent creates black. CYMK is unique in that it has a component specifically for black. Theoretically, black can be created with C=100%, Y=100%, and M=100%, which should eliminate the need for a black channel. In reality, however, neither color printers nor the traditional printing process can print an acceptable black by mixing colors in this way. The black channel has been added to address this limitation. 100 percent of black is the best way to create a simple true black.

The best method for creating shades of gray with CYMK is to vary the black color component between 0 percent and 100 percent. Typically, CYMK is the most appropriate model for full-color printing. The CMYK model is known as *subtractive* color because as all the colors are blended they subtract from the light being reflected into your eyes, yielding black. CMYK is designed for use with pigments (ink).

RGB: The three color components for RGB are red, green, and blue. RGB is the opposite of CYMK, in that 0 percent of all three components creates black, and 100 percent creates white. With RGB, you create shades of gray by adjusting all three color components by the same percentage. For example, R=25%, G=25%, B=25% creates a dark gray, and R=75%, G=75%, B=75% creates a light gray.

RGB is best when used for display purposes. If you are working on art that is to be transferred to xRes or Extreme 3D for multimedia or World Wide Web purposes, you will want to use RGB. The RGB model is known as additive color because as all the colors are blended they add to the light being reflected into your eyes, yielding white. RGB color is designed to be projected as light.

HLS: The three components for HLS are hue, luminosity, and saturation. This model is often referred to as HSB—hue, saturation, and brightness. The components for this model work differently from CYMK and RGB. Hue is the color component. The values range from 0 to 360 degrees. Imagine a color circle, and every direction within the 360 degrees represents a different color. The number for hue selects the direction, and hence, the color that will be used. Luminosity or brightness ranges from 0 to 100. This determines how much black (closer to 0) or how much white (closer to 100) will contribute to the final color. Saturation specifies how prominent that color is in the final color. The range for saturation is also 0 to 100 percent, where 0 is non-existent, and 100 is as strong as possible. Saturation of a color is relative to the action upon it by its opposing color on the color wheel. Hence, when cyan is added to red, the red becomes less brilliant; green and magenta, blue and yellow interact in the same manner. Saturation can also be thought of as the color's intensity.

Tint: Strictly speaking, Tint is not a separate color model. A more accurate definition of tint is a mechanism that creates lighter variations of a given color. Thinking back to the CYMK or RGB models, adjustments in tint change all the components that make up the overall color, preserving the relative proportions of the color components. If you're trying to achieve a specific color match, do not use tint with CMYK values. Refer to a color chart and input the desired values in the CMYK mode. Tint works well when combined with other color models available from the Color List and with black.

MacOS/Windows: Neither of these proprietary color sets is a color model. Both are mechanisms provided in the operating system for selecting from a spectrum (finite palette) of colors.

For some, HLS may be easier to work with because it does not require mixing component colors. Instead you use a color wheel to choose the desired color and its intensity. To adjust the extent to which that color is light or dark, just adjust the slider to the right. Moving the slider toward the bottom makes darker colors, and moving the slider higher makes lighter colors. Figure 2.34 shows the Color Mixer in HLS mode; the lack of color in this figure prevents you from appreciating the value of the color table in the palette.

Figure 2.34

Color Mixer palette for HLS.

After you generate a color from one of the color models, your next option is to use Tint. You can switch to Tint to create a lighter variation of the same color. Notice in Figure 2.35 that the full color is at the far right of the tint range for that color. On the left, the color has progressed to white. By adjusting the slider you can select the new color tint along the tint continuum. When you generate the desired tint, you can drag the tint sample to the object you want to color.

Figure 2.35

Color Mixer palette for Tint.

WORKING WITH COLOR MODELS AND TINT

1. Create a new document.

CYMK

2. Open the Color Mixer from the Window menu if it is not already open.

3. Click on the CYMK button. Make sure all four CYMK components are set to 0 percent.

4. In case you aren't familiar with the colors cyan and magenta, set the value for C to 100 percent. If you have a color monitor, you should be looking at a sample of the color cyan. Return C to 0 percent, and set M to 100 percent to see a sample of the color magenta.

5. With the M value still set to 100 percent, set the value for Y to 100 percent. The color you get by mixing those two components is red. Theoretically, this is the same red you would get if you set the values R=100%, G=0%, B=0% within the RGB model.

6. Continuing with the same values set in step 5, set the K channel to 50 percent. This maintains the same color of red, but darkens it substantially.

RGB

7. Click on the RGB button. If none of the settings for CYMK were changed from Step 6, the values should be R=50%, G=0%, B=0%.

8. Change the values to R=100%, G=100%, B=0%. The color is yellow.

9. Slowly drag the B slider from 0% toward 100%. Note that the color below and to the right turns white as you approach 100%.

10. Before switching to HLS, set the color values back to R=100%, G=100%, B=0%.

HLS

11. Click on the HLS button. The values you should see are H=60, L=50, S=100.

12. Change the value for L to 25. This causes the yellow shade to darken. The value for hue was not changed so it should still be the same yellow within the HLS model.

13. Switch momentarily to RGB. Note that the values changed to R=50%, G=50%, B=0%.

Tint

14. Click on the TINT button. The color that you created in Step 12 should be the color displayed in the TINT Color Mixer.

15. Drag the slider slightly below the center of the Mixer to the right until the number at the left equals 35. The small color block to the left of the 35 gives you a sample of the color that is generated. Drag that color sample to the large rectangle at the bottom of the palette. You have just created a lighter version of the same color, and have set it as the current color being edited in the Color Mixer.

As you can see from the exercise steps, when you set colors in one model and then switch models, the color stays the same but the values change. The benefit to this setup is that you can make adjustments in one model, where things may be easier, and then switch models at will. For those who have stringent color matching needs, this little bonus is not acceptable because the gamuts (areas of usable color) between the RGB/HLS model and CMYK vary radically.

Color List Palette

You can think of the Color List palette as a bin in which you can store colors that you often use in your work. The default colors in the Color List in a new document include None, White, Black, and Registration, as illustrated in Figure 2.36. Access the Color List palette through the Windows menu.

Color List palette with the default colors.

In the upper-left corner of the palette are two icons. The left-most rectangle icon is filled with the same color as the selected object. The color of the icon to the right (a 45 degree line) represents the color of the selected object's stroke.

The list of colors below these icons include FreeHand's default colors and any additional colors added by the user. Applying any of these colors to an object is as simple as dragging the color from the list and dropping it on either the fill or the stroke icons. Because FreeHand needs to know which object you are changing, the target object must first be selected. If an object is not selected when you drag color samples into the fill or stroke, the changes will apply to the next object you draw.

Another way to change object colors is to drag the desired color sample from the Color List palette onto the object. This is usually the easiest when you want to change the fill color, but can be tricky for setting the stroke width if it's narrow.

Colors created in the Color Mixer can be dragged and dropped into the Color List, where it will be automatically added to the list. The default name given to the color reflects the color components that make up the color. For example, if you mix the color red using RGB and drop it into the list, the default name will be "100r 0g 0b" ("0c 100m 100y 0k" in CMYK mode). You can change the name by double-clicking on the name and typing the new name.

Another method for adding colors to the list is found in the Options menu at the top of the palette. The options you are likely to see in the list are shown in Figure 2.37.

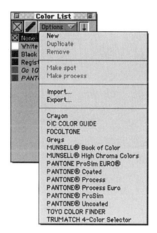

Figure 2.37

Color List Options. This list differs according to the way you installed FreeHand.

The first option, New, takes whatever color is sitting in the right side of the box at the bottom of the Color Mixer and turns it into a new color in the Color List. This is the same as dragging the color directly from the Color Mixer to the Color List.

The Duplicate option makes a copy of whatever color is currently selected in the Color List. The name of the new color will be the same as the original color, with the addition of "Copy of" at the beginning of the name. Remove deletes the color that is currently selected.

Make Spot and Make Process change a characteristic of the selected color. These options are mutually exclusive—selecting one unselects the other. Both represent different methods of printing color.

The biggest difference between Process and Spot is that Process uses four colors to generate almost any color; Spot color uses only one color of ink, toner, or dye for every color that it prints. For example, the Apple Computer,

Inc. logo is made up of six rainbow colors. With a Spot method, six colors are necessary to complete the job. Process color always requires only four colors (CMYK), regardless of how many colors you see on the page. Process color is used when the color printing method involves each of the four color components (cyan, magenta, yellow, and black). Selecting one of these two menu items allows you to designate how the color should be handled in the event you have to perform color separations for the final print. FreeHand comes with a book titled "Commercial Printing Guide" that covers both methods in greater detail.

Import and Export enable you to save color lists and reload them for other products. For example, any time you want to create a graphic that uses your company's trademark colors, you can load the color list file that has those colors already in use.

The remaining options to be found in the Options menu differ among FreeHand setups. All of the remaining optional entries in the Options menu represent pre-configured color lists. Some of those options are a part of various color matching systems. For example, the Pantone system is based on a Spot color system and has a specific and universal standard catalog of colors.

Text Objects

*E*arly versions of FreeHand had limited capabilities for handling text. Now, however, many advanced features previously found only in word processors and page layout programs are part of FreeHand.

The most important new capabilities let you:

- Create separate blocks within the document and flow text through these blocks.
- Access an integrated spell checker.
- Add various fonts, sizes, and styles within text blocks.
- Flow text around or within a graphic object.

Although these new features seem to make FreeHand as much a page-layout program as the PageMaker and Quark programs, the intention is not for FreeHand to consolidate all of the page layout features in the program. Although FreeHand's text capabilities have improved greatly, if you have large quantities of text to format or place, you're better off using a word processor and page-layout program.

Text Basics

Everything that you create in FreeHand is an object of one type or another. This includes text, which has its own object, the text block, that is specifically designed to contain text. The first step toward creating a text block is selecting the Text tool in the Toolbox palette. When you click anywhere within a document it creates a text insertion point. The default distance in height (from the top to the bottom) of the block depends on factors such as the currently selected font and size. You can control initial block size by following the initial click with a drag. For example, you can click where the upper-left corner of the block should be, and drag to where the lower-right corner should be (see Figure 3.1).

Figure 3.1

Manually defining the size of a text block.

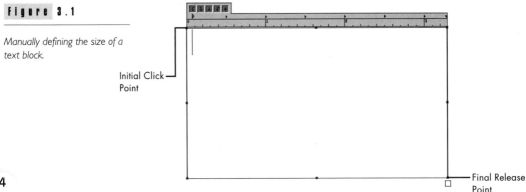

Initial Click Point

Final Release Point

Regardless of which method you use to create the text block, you can always change the block's size. Figure 3.2 shows an example of a text block with some text.

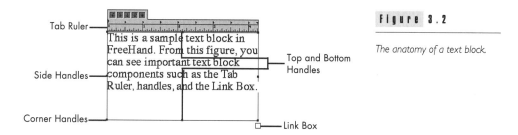

Tab Ruler

Side Handles

Corner Handles

Top and Bottom Handles

Link Box

Figure 3.2

The anatomy of a text block.

ENTERING TEXT

1. Click anywhere on the page.

2. Type your name and address in one continuous line. The text flows off the page.

3. Starting about a half inch from the left side of the page, draw a box about 4 inches long and 3 inches high.

4. Type your name and address as before. Notice that the text wraps from line to line. Now go back and press Enter between your name and address and your address and city.

After a text block is created, it can be resized as needed. Resizing a text block involves dragging the handles that appear along the perimeter of a selected text block. The three types of handles each have a different affect on the text block.

Corner Handles

The least significant type of handle appears on the four corners of a text block. The only function these handles perform is resizing. When you size a text block with the corner handles they change the width, height, or both of the text block.

Side Handles

Adjusting text block size with side handles not only affects the dimensions of the text block, but also changes the space between the characters across the entire width of the text block. This spacing characteristic is called range kerning. By adjusting range kerning as you resize the text block, the location of word wrapping does not change within a segment of text. Kerning is discussed in the section "Using the Text Inspector" later in the chapter. Figure 3.3 shows a before and after example of a text block that has been resized with the side handles.

Figure 3.3

Resizing a text block with the side handles adjusts the width of the block and the range kerning.

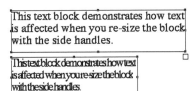

Top and Bottom Handles

Adjustment of the text block size using the top and bottom handles affects more than the dimensions of the text block. Instead of changing width, you change height. In doing so, the space between the lines of text—the leading—also changes. Figure 3.4 shows before and after a text block has been resized with the top and bottom handles. Leading is discussed later in the section on the Text Inspector.

Figure 3.4

Resizing a text block with the top or bottom handles adjusts the height of the block and the leading.

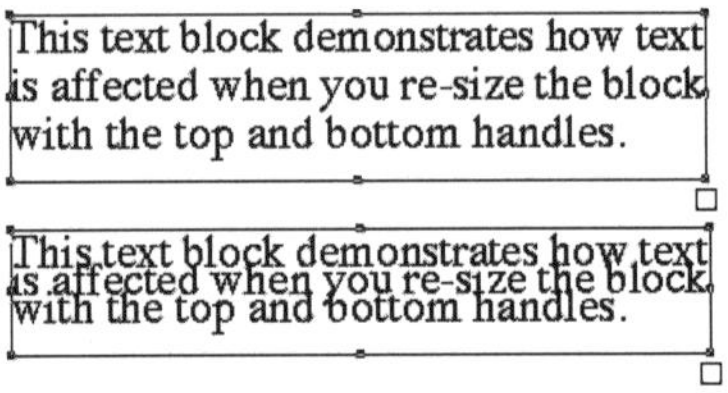

Resizing a Text Box

1. Use the text box you created in the preceding exercise to test the text box features. First, select the Pointer tool.
2. Select a corner handle and alter the size of the text box. Notice that nothing happens to the type unless you make the box smaller than the space for your name and address.
3. Now use a side handle. Notice how it spaces out the letters. From the Edit menu, select Undo Move.
4. Select either the top or bottom handle, then drag out the text box. Note how the leading increases. Select Undo Move.

Tab Ruler

The tab ruler, which magically appears when you create a text box, has several parts, shown in Figure 3.5. The first is a selection of five different tab types. The available tab types listed in order are left, right, center, decimal, and wrapping. With one exception, all of these are standard tabs and they work the same way in FreeHand as they do in most word processors and page-layout programs. The tab style that may be new is the wrapping tab.

Figure 3.5

The Edit Tab dialog box and the Alignment and Leader pop-up menus.

Tabs are placed in the tab ruler in one of two ways: You can click and drag one of the tab types to the desired location on the tab ruler, or double-click on the tab ruler in the desired location. For the latter, the Edit Tab dialog box will appear.

You can select the tab type through the Alignment pop-up menu, and you can select a leader, if desired, to precede the tab. A leader character, such as a period, repeats itself from the location where you press the tab character to the location where the tab is set. Tab leaders are frequently used in tables of contents so that your eye can easily find the page number associated with the topic.

The wrapping tab functions like a left tab, with an extra feature that can be helpful when constructing tables composed of text data. When you put data in table form, a nice but often overlooked feature is to wrap the text in between tabs. Most word processors and page-layout programs enable wrapping only for each line of text, and what appears to be wrapping between tabs is done manually. Wrapping tabs function like mini-columns. When the tab key is depressed, it goes back to the start of the column and moves to the next tab position. Figure 3.6 shows text formatted with wrapping tabs.

Figure 3.6

Wrapping tabs align text in tables.

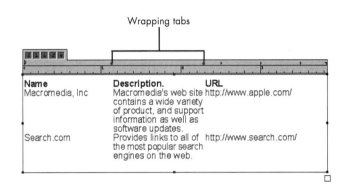

When you use wrapping tabs, keep in mind that as a segment of text proceeds toward a wrapping tab stop, you need to include a tab character to signal the end of the segment so that the text will resume at the wrapping tab. If the same wrapping tab is used for stopping one segment and starting the next, the two segments may be too close to each other, as in Figure 3.6. To address this issue, you can use one wrapping tab to set where one segment should end, and another for where the next segment should start, as shown in Figure 3.7. In addition, you need to add one tab character in the text to stop one segment, and another to proceed to the next tab stop.

Figure 3.7

For more separation between two segments of text, use two wrapping tabs and two embedded tab characters.

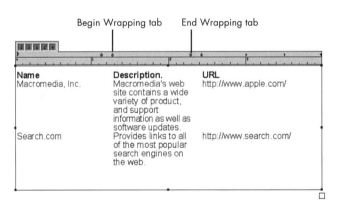

How the wrapping tab works is pretty simple. A vertical start position is defined. When you press the tab key, three things happen. First, a vertical end position is defined, then the program returns you to the vertical start position and advances to the next horizontal tab position. It continues through the entire wrap tab sequence. When you press Enter, the tab recalls the deepest vertical position and adds the appropriate leading, plus additional space to advance to the beginning of the next line.

USING WRAPPING TABS IN TABLES

1. Create a text block approximately six inches wide.

2. The first column will include your name and address (you don't have to start with a tab).

3. Put an end wrapping tab at 1.75 inches, a left tab at 2 inches, and another wrapping tab at 3 inches.

4. From the Font menu, select any 10 point typeface.

5. Type your name, a Shift+Return (that is, soft return), your address, Shift+Return, your city, state, and zip. Press Tab twice. Type your phone number, then press Tab again. Type "The quick brown fox jumps over the lazy old dog" then press Enter (Return). Type your best friend's name. FreeHand jumped to the next line after the longest line.

Linking Text Blocks

One of FreeHand's more important new features is the capability to create multiple text blocks, and link them in such a way that if text overflowed from one, the text would flow into the text block it was linked to. At the bottom-right corner of a selected text block you will see a small square that represents the Link box. The Link box can be in one of three forms as illustrated in Figure 3.8. The empty box indicates no links and no overflowing text. A solid circle indicates overflowing text, but no links. The double arrow indicates that the text box is linked with another text box.

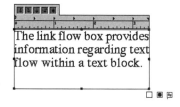

Figure 3.8

The Link box indicates the status of the link flow.

FreeHand provides a few different ways to use the Link box. When you double-click on an empty Link box, (it is not linked and does not have overflowing text), the Link box will resize the text box so that it can contain all the text in it.

99

To link one text block to another text box, click on the Link box and drag it to the text block to which you want to link. When the link is established, every time the "up-stream" text block is selected, you see the Link box display double arrows. A curved line also extends from the Link box to the destination text block. Keep in mind that only one text box may be linked to another text box, and text flows into the beginning of the second ("downstream") box.

To unlink a text box, simply drag from the Link box to an open area in the document. The text and all text linked to that box flow back into the box and the solid circle reappears in the Link box.

LINKING AND UNLINKING TEXT BOXES

In this exercise, you will import text, create text boxes, and link and unlink them.

1. From the File menu, select Place.

 CD ROM

2. Choose the file FreeHand/Ch3/LOREM.RTF from the disc included with this book.

3. The cursor will change to an inverted "L." In the FreeHand document, drag the cursor to form a window approximately 3 inches wide by 1 inch deep. When you release the mouse button, the text flows into the window.

4. You should see an "overflow" icon in the Link box. With the Text tool selected, simply click and drag to create another text box.

5. With the Pointer tool, click on the Link box and drag to the new text box. Your text flows into the new box.

6. To unlink the text, simply click on the Link box with the Pointer tool and drag it into a blank space.

Imported Text

FreeHand supports imported text from many programs, but not all of these programs create text in exactly the same way. You may not get consistent results, even with the same text type.

In general, you can import Rich Text Format (RTF) and ASCII text from any program that supports these formats (almost every program that can generate text supports ASCII).

RTF provides significant benefits, however, when you want to keep the same or similar formatting. The fonts, size, style, and overall layout are retained. In addition, RTF retains margins, a number of tabular features, indents, alignment, and color. Even letter spacing and baseline shift are supported.

ASCII format provides simple, unenhanced text. Although this may seem to be a drawback, if you're going to do all your text manipulation in FreeHand anyway, this is all you need.

Before you start thinking about the user manual or lengthy article you want to create in FreeHand, stop and listen to this: FreeHand, as powerful as it is, is not a page-layout program, and should not be considered as such. Even though multiple pages can be created, it is not recommended that you do so.

FreeHand is designed to be an illustration program. Its strong text-handling capabilities are a big plus, particularly when creating ads, posters, and graphical information that includes text. Longer documents and documents that require a lot of text manipulation should be manipulated in page-layout programs, such as QuarkXPress and Adobe PageMaker.

Text Attributes

There is more to a text block than simply text. Considerably more attributes apply to text than to other graphic objects. Fortunately, many of these attributes are already familiar to you from your experience with word processors.

Font, Size, and Style

Controls for font, size, and style for a segment of text are available in several places in FreeHand. Regardless of which method you use, you first need to select the text you plan to alter. If you want to uniformly make these settings for the entire text block, just select the text block with the Pointer tool. If you only want to make these format changes for a specific portion of text, use the Text tool to highlight the appropriate segment within the text block. Afterward, you can set font, size, or style from the Type menu or from the Type palette. Figure 3.9 shows the Type palette.

Figure 3.9

Font, style, and size can be set in the Type palette.

Color

Like any other object in FreeHand, you can set color for text fill and stroke, but there are a few details to be aware of. Dragging and dropping a color sample from the Color Mixer or Color Lists palettes onto the text block sets the color of all text within the text block. The same happens if you select the text block with the Pointer tool and drag and drop a color sample on the object fill rectangle in the upper-left corner of the Color List palette. To set the text's stroke color, you select the text block with the Pointer tool and drag and drop the color sample on the object stroke rectangle in the upper-left corner of the Color List palette. You cannot set stroke color by dragging and dropping a color sample on the text block.

You can also select specific text you want to color by highlighting it with the text tool, then either dropping the color sample in the fill or stroke rectangle, or dropping the color sample on top of the highlighted text. In addition, you can set a color and pattern for the text block background. First select the Text block with the Pointer tool. Select the Fill icon in the Inspector, and choose the desired fill option. You assign a color or pattern to the background. You cannot, however, set different patterns for each letter's fill stroke.

Tip

Just because you can do something in FreeHand doesn't mean you should! A perfect example is stroking text. Applying a stroke ruins the look of all but the largest text, and interferes with delicate letterspacing values that are a part of each type style. This is one case where you should force yourself to list reasons why to do this, rather than why not.

Using the Text Inspector

The Text Inspector has four separate modes (see Figure 3.10). The Character icon selects elements such as one character or a range of characters. The Paragraph icon controls settings for parameters affecting entire paragraphs, including indents, paragraph spacing, and "widow and orphan" attributes. The Spacing and Hyphenation icon also is a paragraph-related function that controls the overall spacing between characters and words. The Alignment icon lets you adjust the alignment of paragraphs.

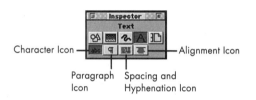

Character Icon — Alignment Icon

Paragraph   Spacing and
Icon   Hyphenation Icon

Figure 3.10

The Text Inspector's icon choices.

The Character Icon

Settings that are grouped under the Character icon include leading, kerning, range kerning, hyphenation, and some control of hyphenation parameters as they affect specific words (as opposed to the paragraph as a whole). You can also control baseline shift—moving text above or below the standard baseline. Figure 3.11 shows the Text Inspector with the Character icon selected after an entire text block is selected.

Figure 3.11

The Character icon options in the Text Inspector.

Leading

Resizing a text block with the top or bottom handles also affects the leading for the entire text block. You can adjust leading more accurately by using the

103

Text Inspector. You can alter the leading of the entire paragraph (select it with the Pointer tool) or change the Leading value of individual lines using the Text Inspector shown in Figure 3.12. The pop-up menu part of the Leading field (see Figure 3.12) lets you determine the exact unit of measure for leading values.

Whenever possible, use the fixed leading option, which gives an absolute distance between lines. Extra enables you to select a positive or negative number, which is added to (or subtracted from) the point size; the sum of the point size and the number you have entered will be the leading. Percent is the least desirable, unless you have a mixture of type sizes from line to line. It establishes a percentage of the point size as the leading. Unfortunately, this is not easily measurable.

Kerning and Range Kerning (Tracking)

Re-sizing a text block with handles along the left or right sides of the text block changes the range kerning for the entire text block. You can also set range kerning for a selection of characters by entering a specific percentage value in percents of an em in the Text Inspector, as shown in Figure 3.13.

Figure 3.13

When you have text highlighted, the Character icon of Text Inspector includes a field for range kerning.

If the text block has not been re-sized with the side handles and an insertion point is set between two characters within a text block, the range kerning field shown in Figure 3.13 changes to kerning. The difference is that kerning applies to the space added or subtracted between two specific characters, and range kerning applies to multiple characters.

Tip

Do you wonder how much space you're adding or subtracting when you work with type? An em is the width of the nominal point size. An em in 10-point type is 10 points wide; an em in 24-point type is 24 points wide. Entering a value of −10% between two characters will move them 2.4 points together.

Inhibit Hyphens/Keep on Same Line

One important way to control the look and readability of paragraphs is to restrict hyphenation. Occasionally you will want to keep two or more words on the same line, even if it means breaking up the paragraph in a less-than-optimal way.

If the text box is selected with the Pointer tool and the Inhibit Hyphens button is selected, no hyphenation will be allowed in the entire text box. When a range of words is selected with the Text tool and Inhibit Hyphens is selected, only the selected range will be restricted from hyphenation. Keep in mind that hyphenation works automatically only if it has been selected with the Spacing and Hyphenation icon. If you select this and then click on Inhibit Hyphens for the entire text block, you defeat the purpose of automatic hyphenation.

A small change you will probably make often is to select two words and then click on Keep on Same Line. The words (or characters) will always remain together. Do not select this option when the text block has been selected with the Pointer tool because of unpredictable results.

ADJUSTING CONTROLS FOR SELECTIONS OF TEXT

1. Place a block of text and break it into two or three paragraphs with the Return key (Macintosh) or Enter key (Windows).

2. Set the font to Times Roman and the size to 12 point using the Type palette.

3. Set the leading to 14 point Fixed. Now check the Extra and Percentage options to see how the value changes.

4. Change the point size to 11 point and go back and check the Extra and Percentage options.

5. Select two words on different lines. Click on the Keep on Same Line button and notice how the text reflows.

6. Type the word "Type" in 72 point Times Roman.

7. Highlight the entire word with the Text tool and select range kerning. Type −2. Notice how all the letters move closer together.

8. Place the cursor between the T and the y. Notice that there is already built-in kerning. Change the kerning to −12.

The Paragraph Icon

All the elements in this menu affect either an entire text block (select it with the Pointer tool), or individual paragraphs (when the Text cursor is placed in the paragraph). A range of characters does not need to be selected. Figure 3.14 shows the Text Inspector when the Paragraph icon is selected.

Figure 3.14

The Text Inspector with the Paragraph icon selected.

Paragraph Spacing

Some say there are two ways of creating space between paragraphs: the right way and every other way. Even though doing it correctly is easy, most people use some other method. The most popular is to add an extra hard return between the paragraphs, then format the leading of the empty paragraph to equal the amount of space needed.

Paragraph Spacing enables you to add the exact amount of space you want between paragraphs by entering the amount of space you want above or below the paragraph.

Paragraph Indents and Hanging Punctuation

The Paragraph Indents field lets you indent the overall paragraph from the left or right of the text block by whatever amount you enter.

First Line Indent will indent the first line of the paragraph, the same as when a tab is used. To outdent the first line from the text box, enter a negative number. To create a hanging indent (as opposed to a simple outdent), enter an indent for the paragraph, then a negative indent to the first line.

Closely related to paragraph indents is the advanced typographic feature known as hanging punctuation. FreeHand knows that hyphens, periods, commas, colons, semicolons, and quotation marks should "hang" outside the text block if this button is checked. Quotation marks will hang to the left or the right.

SETTING UP HANGING PUNCTUATION

1. Import or type some text, creating three separate paragraphs.

2. For the first paragraph, place the Text tool in the paragraph and type an indent of 1 pica.

3. In the second paragraph, indent the paragraph 1 pica from the left, and enter a hanging indent of 1 pica in the First Line Indent box. (Enter -1 pica.)

4. For the third paragraph, enclose the paragraph in quotation marks and click on the Hanging punctuation button.

 Tip

To move one word to the next line without generating a new paragraph, simply press and hold down the Shift key as you press Return (Enter in Windows). This special line break is called a soft return. The text continues at the beginning of the next line, but paragraph attributes such as spacing and hanging indents are not applied.

Lines Together

The Lines Together option enables you to specify how many lines at the start of the paragraph must remain with the balance of the text. This avoids unsightly widows of one line at the bottom of a page or a column. Common entries for this field are 2 or 3.

Rules

This option, located at the bottom of the Text Inspector, automatically places a line equidistant between two paragraphs: one for which the rule is applied and the paragraph below it. The lines may be centered or take on the paragraph's justification attribute (flush left, right, or centered). Rules may be configured up to 100 percent of the last line or column width. Figure 3.15 shows the pull-down menu for the rules options and the Paragraph Rule Width dialog box.

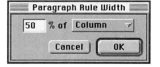

PLACING RULES BETWEEN PARAGRAPHS

1. Access the Text tool and click on the paragraph that will be above the rule.

2. Select the ruling style "Centered" from the pull-down menu.

3. Click on Edit and type 50 in the percentage window. Select Column from the pull-down menu.

4. Switch to the Pointer tool and select the text block. From the Stroke Inspector select a rule weight, then uncheck "Display border" from the Object Inspector.

5. The rules flow with their attached paragraphs.

6. Change the ruling style to "Paragraph," click on Edit, and type 100 in the percentage window. Select Last Line from the drop-down list. Notice how the paragraph rule changes.

The Spacing and Hyphenation Icon

All elements in this menu can change the entire text block (by clicking on it with the Pointer tool) or individual paragraphs (by placing the Text cursor in the paragraph). It is unnecessary to select a range of characters.

Word- and Letter-Spacing

When fonts are designed, the space between letters is built into them. In addition, a standard word space is included that is part of the character set (when you press the spacebar you get a custom-designed space). The Spacing % values enable you to override the designer's original setup when you alter the Opt percentage from 100 (see Figure 3.16). You can input minimum and maximum percentages so that lines can justify on both margins without excessive hyphenation.

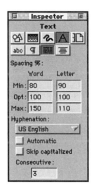

Figure 3.16

Spacing options give you full control over the justification of lines of type.

Hyphenation

Hyphenation began with the early scribes—only they had it easier than we do. At the end of the line, these ancient writers would insert a hyphen to indicate that a word continued on the next line. With this minor addition, all their text could justify on both margins. Only in the past two centuries have actual rules for hyphenation existed.

When you installed FreeHand, you selected a specific dictionary (or dictionaries) to include with the program. The first drop-down menu lets you pick the desired dictionary to use for the current document.

A check in the Automatic box allows FreeHand to make hyphenation decisions for you, based on the rules you installed with the program. Skip Capitalized turns off automatic hyphenation for all capitalized words (if you want to hyphenate them, you can still do it manually using the discretionary hyphen [Command-Hyphen on the Macintosh and Alt-T C D under Windows]). The Consecutive box specifies how many hyphens are allowed in a row. Limit this to two to prevent unsightly stacks of hyphens at the text's edge.

The Alignment Icon

Alignment controls can be used on the entire text block or on individual paragraphs, depending on whether you selected the block or simply placed the cursor in a paragraph. A range of characters does not need to be selected.

Although we often think that a paragraph can only be justified, flush left, right, or center, there are many more variables related to justifying text than simply the placement of margins (see Figure 3.17).

Ragged Width and Flush Zone

These settings define how much of a line must be filled by the text before some other action, such as justification or hyphenation (specified by the spacing and hyphenation parameters), begins.

Ragged width affects non-justified text only. You type the percentage of the total line length that each line of text must fill. If the line cannot achieve that length, including applying whatever automatic hyphenation you have allowed, it will add word- and letter-space to fill the line to the minimum length required.

The Flush Zone percent defines how long the last line of a paragraph must be, with relation to the entire paragraph length, in order to justify. The lower the number the less of the total line length the last line will have to occupy. A setting of zero in this Zone will force justify the last line.

Alignment

Simply select left-aligned, centered, right-aligned, or justified. Before you choose one of these options, consider all the changes you made to the text block (or paragraphs) in other fields in the Inspector. The result of choosing centered text may look ridiculous, for example, if range kerning and leading are small.

Automating Text Styling

Just as you can automate the selection of attributes for graphics in styles, you can include many of the attributes of text in Text styles. Text and graphics styles appear in the same style palette, and they function similarly.

After you have defined (set up) a paragraph the way you want it, you can create a style based on these settings simply by placing the Text cursor in the paragraph and selecting New from the Style palette. A new style will be created containing all the attributes of the paragraph (see Figure 3.18). If you need to tweak something in the paragraph style, you can edit the style using much the same process as that of editing graphics styles.

A paragraph style also can be based on a parent style; when an attribute of the parent style is altered, the changes transfer to all the styles based on the parent style.

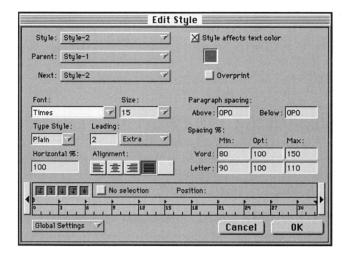

Figure 3.18

The Edit Style dialog box resembles the graphics Edit Style dialog box.

Special Text Functions

A unique and often-used capability of FreeHand is flowing text within an object, around an object, or along its path. You can even spell check this text and change the contents of a text box into graphic objects to manipulate text as shapes rather than characters.

Converting Text to Paths

There may be times when you need to change a short segment of text to graphic objects by dropping all the attributes unique to text, and just keeping the graphic shapes (and their graphic-related attributes). The FreeHand command Convert to Paths in the Type menu does just that. To change a segment of text, simply select the text block with the Pointer tool, then select Convert to Paths. What had been considered letters with text attributes such as font and size are now graphic objects.

One example of when this capability is welcome is when you plan to distribute an electronic copy of your file to others who may not have the font you used when creating the graphic. By using Convert to Paths, FreeHand eliminates the need for the font when the conversion is done. An excellent example of when such a conversion would be helpful is when FreeHand files are used as Shockwave images on the World Wide Web. You can read all about it in Chapter 5, "Shockwave for FreeHand."

After a text segment has been converted, you can ungroup the new graphic and edit the objects like that of any other graphic path, but you cannot change the words. What you can change is the shapes of letters to create special type treatments, the shape and size of the objects (with the transformation tools), and the fill pattern of the characters.

Keep in mind that holes in letters, such as the center of the letter "O" are created by punching a hole in one object with another, so the background will show through. When you punch a hole in an object with another object and the paths of both objects never cross, the two remain two separate objects. Keep in mind that until the objects are split, you may not be able to perform certain procedures on them because they are really two joined objects.

The Convert to Paths command only works on text that is an installed TrueType or PostScript font. If the text you'd like to convert is in a screen font form, FreeHand will not be able to convert the segment to paths.

Binding Text to a Path

Another text special effect that is worth a serious look is making a line of text follow the path of another object. With FreeHand, you can make text follow any path, such as the shape of a circle for an emblem as shown in Figure 3.19.

Figure 3.19

The text following the path of a circle.

The procedure for binding a segment of text to a path is as simple as selecting the text block and the target path with the Pointer tool, and selecting Bind to Path from the Type menu. Remember that every path has a start point and a direction. Although you can't see it very easily, FreeHand will flow text onto a path according to these parameters.

If you plan to bind a text segment to a path, do not convert the text to paths until after you have bound the text to the desired path. If you convert to paths first, you will have to manually place the individual letters. The following exercise shows you the best sequence for binding text and then converting it to paths.

BINDING TEXT AND CONVERTING IT TO PATHS

1. Open the file FreeHand/Ch3/BALLOONPATH from the disc included with this book.

2. Select the font Balloon D Extra Bold, which came with the FreeHand CD.

3. Type the word "Balloons" (it's an upper-case font).

4. Choose the path and the word with the Pointer tool.

5. From the Type menu, select Bind to Path.

6. From the Text Inspector's Character icon, kern 12 between the O and the N and 8 between the N and the S, in percent of an em.

7. From the Type menu, select Convert to Paths.

8. From the Fill Inspector, select Tiled, and click on the Stars Pattern in the Style menu.

9. Ungroup the characters and elongate the top part of the S.

When a segment of text is bound to a path, the first letter will be placed at the path's start point. The rest of the text will follow in the direction of the path. For a shape such as an ellipse, the direction is clockwise. The text remains visible, but the path that you bound the text to becomes invisible.

After you bind text to a path and then select the new combined object, you will see the standard selection handles, but you will also notice a hollow triangle in the object. This triangle marks the beginning of the path. You can drag the triangle to adjust where along the path the first letter starts.

If the direction the text follows along the path is just the opposite of what you want, reverse the path's direction before binding the text to the path. To do this, select the path with the Pointer tool, then choose Reverse Direction from the Arrange, Path Operations. When you bind text to the path, it will be in the desired direction.

Playing with Text that is Bound to a Path

1. Draw a circle about 4 inches in diameter.

2. Type the word "Balloons" (using the Balloon typeface).

3. Holding down the Shift key, select the circle and the word, then click on "Bind to Path" from the Type menu.

4. Alter the starting point of the word by moving the triangle around the path.

5. Create a new circle and a new word and select just the circle. From the Arrange menu, select Path Operations and Reverse Direction.

6. Select the circle and the type, then bind the type to the new path.

Flowing Text Inside a Path

FreeHand is capable of flowing text within a path, essentially filling a shape with the selected text. One example of many is shown in Figure 3.20.

Even when you flow text inside a path, you can still link with other text blocks by using the Link box. The object's handles can also be used to resize the shape and the text block within it. No side, top, or bottom handles exist, so changes to kerning or leading must be made in the Text Inspector.

To un-flow text from a path, select the combined object and choose Remove From Path in the Type menu.

FLOWING TEXT INSIDE A PATH

1. Draw a circle about 2 inches in diameter.

2. Import the LOREM.RTF text from the disc.

3. Choose the circle and the text block and click on Flow Inside Path from the Type menu.

CD ROM

Text Wrap

To wrap text around an object, select the object and the text and choose Text Wrap from the Arrange menu. Select the icon that looks like text wrapping around an object (the one on the right). Decide how much space you want between the text and the edges of the object and enter the values in the appropriate boxes. Figure 3.21 shows the Text Wrap dialog box.

F i g u r e 3 . 2 1

Making text flow around an object, regardless of its shape, is a simple two-step operation.

115

Figure 3.22

Text flowed around an oval with
a 3-point standoff distance.

Spell Checking

The earliest FreeHand versions did not include a built-in spell checker. The spell
checker included with the latest version of FreeHand is as powerful and easy
to use as spell checkers in advanced word processors. To check a document,
simply select Spelling from the Type menu, and use the Spelling window
pictured in Figure 3.24.

Figure 3.23

Accessing the FreeHand spell
checker.

Initiating a spell check is as simple as clicking on Start. When a word is found
that the spell checker does not recognize, the Spelling window will change
slightly to provide suggestions (see Figure 3.24).

Figure 3.24

The Spelling window when an
unrecognized word is found.

All the functions in this window are standard spelling checker controls. The
unrecognized word appears in the bottom-left corner of the window and is
labeled Word Found. The line below the Word Found line gives you the
context in which the word was used. The spelling checker will check the stream
of text in all linked boxes.

Chapter 4

Special Effects in FreeHand

*N*ow that you have learned to build graphics, you'll want
to add some special effects and perform functions more
quickly. This chapter covers special effects techniques you can
incorporate into your next project. Please read and note the
cautions. Not all effects can be used in all printing situations. Many
of the commands used in this chapter are found in the Operations
palette (see Figure 4.1), in the Window/Other menu.

Figure 4.1

*Path to the Operations palette
and the palette. Note the
variety of tools available.*

Transparency

One of the most often-used features of FreeHand that can be classified as a "special effect" is its transparency function. With the exception of objects that have no fill at all, FreeHand objects cannot be truly transparent. Transparency would occur in the printing process when one color is printed on top of another (the Overprint box is checked in the Fill Inspector or Path Inspector palette). Because of the nature of our monitors, we are unable to see this interaction on-screen. FreeHand does, however, provide tools that create the illusion of transparent objects.

FreeHand's Transparency tool is so easy to use that you only need to place one object over another. The transparency effect will apply to the upper object, which will make the lower object appear to partially show through the upper. Both the lower and the upper objects must be selected, and then you must select Xtras, Path Operations, Transparency or from the Operations palette. When you select this menu command, the window shown in Figure 4.2 appears.

Figure 4.2

*The greater the value in this
box, the more the lower object
shows through.*

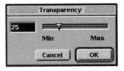

CREATING TRANSPARENT OBJECTS

1. Open the file FreeHand/Ch4/TRANS.FH5 on the disc included with this book.

   CD ROM

2. TRANS.FH5 contains two collections of objects. Each collection demonstrates different types of Transparency.

3. Select all objects in the area labeled Collection 1.

4. Select Transparency from the Xtras : Path Operations menu, and set the value to 50. Note that all the objects behind the star appear to show through except for the drop shadow. The drop shadow is made up of numerous grouped objects, so they are not used in the Transparency process.

5. Select all the objects in the area labeled Collection 2.

6. Issue the Transparency command again with a setting of 50. Notice that all the objects behind the top-most object emerge. The colors, however, that were chosen have different interactions.

 Tip

If you are trying to use Transparency, and it does not seem to work, check for the following:

- Are both objects selected?

- Is either of the objects grouped? If so, ungroup the grouped object. Basic objects such as rectangles and ellipses are grouped when they are first created.

- Is either of the objects joined with another object? If so, split the joined object. The most common situation in which this becomes a problem is when a hole has been punched out of an object with the Punch command. If the paths of the two objects never crossed, the punched object is really two joined objects.

The secret to the transparency effect is that FreeHand finds the overlapping portions of objects and creates a new object that is defined by the intersection of the two objects. FreeHand also automatically sets certain attributes for the new object, such as stroke (turned off), and the fill color of the new object

119

(a blend of the two objects' colors). The new object that FreeHand creates is then overlayed on top of the other two objects to give the transparent look. If for any reason you want to change or do away with a transparency effect you added, it is as simple as adjusting or deleting the objects FreeHand made for you.

Note

FreeHand's transparency effect is wonderful for screen presentations and for work done with CMYK colors. It doesn't work with everything though. Because FreeHand does not allow you to blend two spot colors, it can't mix them, either. If this method were to be used in the preparation of files for printing, the results would be disasterous.

Blends

The Blend command is used in a couple of ways. One of the most common can be seen in a sample document that came with your FreeHand package. The file's name for Macintosh users is Cowden, in the Sample Artwork folder. Windows users should look for the file named cowden.fh5 in the Sample directory. The file contains a picture that uses blends to create color transitions for soft shadows and other lighting effects.

Another use for blends is to create a repetitive sequence of evenly-spaced shapes (see Figure 4.3). The first and last instances of the objects must be placed precisely; the Blend tool will then evenly space objects in between at the press of a button. If you want to change the number of steps, simply select the blended object, access the Object Inspector, and type in the new number.

Figure 4.3

You provide the first and last object in the sequence. Blend shapes and colors all the objects in between.

Blend uses a start object and an end object to create new objects between the original two objects. Blend takes several factors into consideration when creating and placing the intermediate objects. The first is evenly spaced placement for the intermediate objects. This command also determines the amount of change it must make to gradually alter certain objects' attributes as each intermediate object is created. If the first and last object have different shapes, Blend creates objects that slowly transition from the shape of the first object to the shape of the last object. Figure 4.3 provides a perfect example of this.

Another factor Blend takes into account is fill color. If the first and last objects have different fill colors, Blend calculates colors for the intermediate objects that smoothly transition from the start color to the end color, provided the colors are process colors, or a spot color and white. Two different spot colors cannot be blended.

Blending for Color Effect

Blends can create color transitions that you can use as lighting effects for elements such as soft shadows. In the following exercise, you will use blending to create a soft drop shadow behind a simple object. The process used in this exercise involves creating, positioning, and setting attributes for two objects that are at extreme ends of the blend sequence.

USING BLENDS TO CREATE LIGHTING EFFECTS

1. Open the file FreeHand/Ch4/SHBLEND.FH5 on the disc included with this book.

CD ROM

2. Open the Layers palette.

3. Select the rectangle and clone it.

4. With the cloned object still selected, click on the layer in the Layers palette named Drop Shadows. This moves the object to the Drop Shadows layer.

5. Click on the Foreground layer check mark (at the far left) in the Layers palette. This step hides the original rectangle so that it won't be in the way as you work.

6. With the cloned object still selected, open the Transform palette, select the Move icon, and move the object by the following amounts:
X = 5
Y = -5
The drop shadow will be slightly dropped and to the right.

7. Set the fill color for the rectangle in the Drop Shadows layer to white, and turn off stroke.

8. With the cloned object still selected, select Inset Path from the Path Operations sub-menu. Set the values in the Inset Path dialog to the following values:
Steps = 1
Inset = -4
Miter Limit = 1
This object will become the background of the drop shadow.

9. Clone the object that you just expanded. If you're not sure what you just expanded, keep in mind that the inset was a negative number; after Step 8 it became an outset (expansion). However, the object loses the "Inset Path" value, which is one path inside another. This is a nifty way to make an element larger, centered on itself.

10. With the new cloned object still selected, again select Inset Path from the Path Operations sub-menu. Set the values in the Inset Path dialog to the following values:
Steps = 1
Inset = 8
Miter Limit = 1
This object will become the dark portion of the drop shadow.

11. Change the fill color for the new cloned object to Dark Gray, which you will find already created for you in the Color List palette.

12. Select both of the objects now in the Drop Shadow layer.

13. Select Blend from the Path Operations sub-menu.

14. Click on the Foreground layer in the Layers palette to display the original rectangle. You should now see the original object with a drop shadow behind it.

Blending for Even Placement of Objects

Occasionally you may need to space a sequence of objects equally apart between two end objects. To do this type of placement, you usually have to get out the calculator and pencil and do the math yourself. If this isn't your idea of a fun time, the Blend command provides a solution that allows you to avoid all these calculations.

In the preceding section you saw how Blend created a smooth color transition by making slight color adjustments to each new object it created between a start and end object. You can use this feature to place objects, too. If the only difference between the first and last object is physical location within the document, the incremental changes Blend will make on the intermediate objects will simply be location. The next exercise shows you how to use Blend to evenly space a sequence of objects. Although this exercise doesn't take advantage of Blend's interesting color calculations and morphing capabilities, it still is a useful feature when you need precise placement.

USING BLEND FOR PRECISE PLACEMENT OF OBJECTS

1. Open file FreeHand/Ch4/SEQBLEND.FH5 on the disc included with this book.

CD ROM

2. Click on the object in SEQBLEND.FH5 and Clone it.

3. Move the object clone to the area labled "Place End Object Here".

4. Select both objects, then select Ungroup from the Arrange menu.

5. Choose Blend from the Path Operations sub-menu.

6. More than likely, Blend created too many intermediate objects. You will reduce that number to three. To do so, open the Inspector palette and click on the Object icon. The first option is Number of Steps. For three intermediate objects, enter 3 in the blank.

If nothing happens when you select the Blend command, check to see that both the objects to be blended are selected. (Both must be selected for the blend to work.) Are both objects independent objects, or is one of them a grouped object? Many of FreeHand's basic objects, such as rectangles and ellipses, are actually grouped objects. If they are grouped objects, un-group them and then proceed with the blend.

Multi-Color Fills

Closely related to blends are graduated and radial fills. Chapter 1 explained how to create simple graduated fills, graduated tints (graduate through a range of the same color), and graduated process colors. You also were introduced to linear (a constant progression) and logarithmic (a fast progression from one color to another) graduation. Here you will learn to control the progression of a simple graduation and the use of multiple process colors in a graduation (see Figure 4.4). Multi-Color fills can add excitement to documents and allow you the greatest possible control over the effect of a fill.

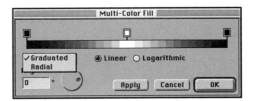

In the first exercise, you will control the speed of graduation for a simple black-to-white effect.

USING MULTI-COLOR FILL TO CONTROL A GRADUATED FILL

1. From the Window, Other menu, open the Operations palette. Be sure the Color List and Color Mixer are open.

2. In the Color Mixer, create a black tint palette by dragging the black color square from the Color List into the Color Mixer's tint menu.

3. Open the Multi-Color Fill Xtra from the Operations palette.

4. Drag the white color square from the Color List into the rightmost box on the Multi-Color gradient and the 50 percent tint from the Color Mixer menu into the middle square. This defines pure white and the 50 percent mark.

5. Drag the 50 percent tint about two-thirds down the graduation bar to define the speed of graduation.

6. Create a rectangle on the page and click on Apply in the Multi-Color Fill dialog.

7. Change the angle to taste. When you want to test any change, click on Apply. Click on OK to exit the dialog box.

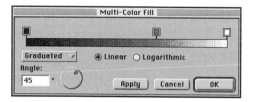

You can enter a rainbow (or more!) of colors in the Multi-Color Fill Xtra. To prepare for the next exercise, type your first name on one line and your last name on the next line in 72 point Balloon type.

APPLY MULTI-COLOR FILL TO INDIVIDUAL AND JOINED ELEMENTS

1. Convert the type to paths, then ungroup (each name should now form its own group).

2. Open the Multi-Color Fill dialog. Be sure the Color Mixer is also open.

3. Reset the angle to 0° if it is not already there.

4. From the Color Mixer, drag a cyan color patch into the left square in the Multi-Color dialog, a magenta patch into the middle one, and a black patch into the right square.

5. Now drag a yellow color patch between the magenta and black squares.

6. Adjust the squares so that the bar is evenly divided. Click on OK.

7. With the Pointer tool, select your first name. Open the Multi-Color Fill palette and click OK. Each letter will contain the fill.

8. Select your last name. From the Arrange menu, choose Join Objects. Access the Multi-Color Fill palette and click OK. The fill graduates across your entire last name.

9. Experiment with the fill at different angles. Click OK to exit the dialog box.

Power Duplicate

Power duplicating with the Edit menu's Duplicate command allows you to create one object and duplicate it as many times as you need. This saves you the work of having to create an object multiple times. FreeHand's power

125

duplicating feature also automatically places subsequent copies of an object in a regular pattern that you specify. Figure 4.5 shows an example of how power duplication can be used.

Figure 4.5

A star duplicated 10 times; each copy is rotated by 30 degrees.

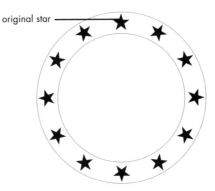

original star

DUPLICATING OBJECTS

CD ROM

1. Open file FreeHand/Ch4/PWRDUP.FH5 on the disc included with this book.

2. Select the star at the 12 o'clock position. Open the Transform palette, and choose the Rotate icon.

3. Select Clone from the Edit menu.

4. Set the following values in the Transform palette.
   Rotation Angle: 30 degrees
   Center X: 0
   Center Y: 0
   Center is set to 0,0 because the origin for the document is set to the middle of the circle.

5. Select Duplicate in the Edit menu 10 times.

FreeHand not only duplicates the object, but also duplicates the placement process. As a result, it is important that the first copy is made with the Clone command. This makes the copy in the exact same position as the original. The Transform palette is used to place the copy precisely; the remaining objects are duplicated and placed with the Duplicate command.

Power Duplicate can be used for more than placing objects in a circle, although any other operation must involve a regular repeatable sequence. Another slight limitation is that Power Duplicate only allows one transformation task. Only the last transformation will be duplicated if more than one transformation is used.

Pasting Inside

You may find that you want to fill an object in a way that FreeHand cannot accommodate with any of its object fill features. To meet these needs, FreeHand allows you to create graphics that you can paste inside of other objects. When one object is pasted within another, the inner object is clipped by the edges of the outer object. In Figure 4.6, an object is filled with patterns and colors that will make the outer object take on the appearance of a flag.

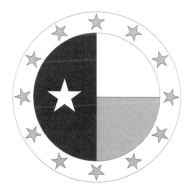

Figure 4.6

A star and the three rectangles are pasted inside the first object.

Objects are pasted inside of another object by first selecting what will be the inner object and then positioning it over the target object. When you paste it inside, the interior objects will have the same orientation and location, so be sure to position them in the exact location. Afterward, select Cut from the Edit menu to delete the interior objects from the screen (they are loaded into the Clipboard). Select the target object, and select Paste Inside from the Edit menu.

Objects pasted inside of another object can be extracted by selecting the outer object and choosing Cut Contents from the Edit menu. You often may need to do this to make changes to the interior objects before you paste them back inside the outer object.

Tracing

We have all seen elaborate graphics in magazines and newspapers that illustrate complex ideas, procedures, and systems. These illustrations are usually called informational graphics and often are immensely intricate and show accurate perspective; at some point you may have wondered "How in the world did they do that so well?" Although illustrators who create these graphics are incredibly skilled, they almost always rely on an age-old technique that you probably learned as a child: they trace the image.

Frequently informational graphics illustrators use digitized copies of actual pictures or hand drawn sketches to set up the relative placement and perspective of a drawing quickly and accurately. They then trace the image. Tracing does not guarantee a high quality final graphic, but it is the best way to begin complex drawings that require intricacy and perspective. You will still need to practice to develop your own technique, but this book can introduce you to the basics of this process.

The Trace tool traces edges it finds in an imported digital image. This tool can be a big help, but it does not have the intelligence of a human. As a result, you will usually create traces that need some touchup.

Tracing is not limited to the use of the tracing tool. You can use scanned images to guide you through constructing a graphic manually. Although this can be a time-consuming process, you can get precise placement and proportion.

Typically, the process you use with the Trace tool is as follows:

1. Import a digitized image using the Place command in the File menu.

2. After FreeHand reads in the file, click somewhere in the document to set the placement of the imported image. The point where you click sets the upper-left corner of the image.

3. Set the new placed image on the Background Layer. The image can be used on any layer, but if you plan to trace the image manually, the best layer typically is the Background layer. Anything placed in the Background layer is grayed out, which makes it easier to see the strokes and points that you will place over the image.

4. After the image is imported and placed, select the Trace tool in the Toolbox. The Trace tool must be told what area is to be traced. Click and drag the cursor within the document to create a bounding rectangle.

Click placement and drag direction must be coordinated so that the bounding rectangle encloses the area to be traced.

The instant you let go of the mouse, FreeHand goes to work tracing the image.

Tip

After you have traced the element (which should have been imported onto the Background layer), the traced image is automatically selected. Immediately move it to its own layer, then lock the Background layer so that you will not accidentally select the original image when you are cleaning up the image.

Regardless of the layer on which you place the image, it is a good idea to have the paths you created from tracing on a separate layer above the layer holding the original image. This allows you to hide the image layer if you want to see the traced paths and not the original image.

TRACING IMPORTED IMAGES

1. Open the file FreeHand/Ch4/TRACE.FH5 on the disc included with this book. The trace images are located in the background layer in this document.

2. Make sure the Foreground layer is selected in the Layers palette.

3. Select the Trace tool in the Toolbox.

4. Use the Trace tool and select an area around Object 1 that will allow you to trace all of Object 1.

5. Note that the Trace tool did not make a perfect duplicate of the original image. To get a better look at the new paths, hide the Background layer from the Layers palette.

6. Now click on the checkmark next to the Background layer to reveal it again.

7. Object 2 has two copies of the same shape. Your assignment is to manually trace one of them by placing points and adjusting handles. Keep in mind that point type selection will be an important part of the exercise. With the second copy, try to re-create the object using standard FreeHand objects and tools. There is no right or wrong way to do this step. The point is to experiment and learn.

Trapping

When we look at abutting colors on our monitors the colors are absolutely beautiful. But when we look at some printed pieces, unsightly white paper shows through. This is because the printing process is imperfect. Even if the (perfect) computer file is imaged correctly, no printing press on earth can hold perfect registration. Paper can stretch and shift—and movement of a few thousands of an inch can result in an ugly white area.

The solution to this problem is a process known as trapping. This is simply a means of overlapping colors appropriately so that there is no show-through of the background paper when it is printed on the press.

Trapping in a production situation is entirely optional, but if you choose to use it, it must be consistent within your document. If you choose to trap in your page layout program, you must also trap your illustrations. The alternative to trapping using your own computer is to pay the printer or service bureau to do the trapping for you. This is the best approach when many complex traps need to be executed (such as abutting graduated tints). For straightforward graphics, though, you should do the traps yourself.

In the past you laboriously had to apply strokes to each element, remembering what had to trap to what. FreeHand's trapping automation frees you from a lot of drudgery. However, it's still good to know the principles:

- The object in the upper layer (or the most recently created object) is known as the "object;" objects on lower layers (or created earlier) are known as "backgrounds."

- Lighter colors get larger with relation to darker colors. (Darker colors could become smaller.)

- To determine which colors are darker, read the sidebar information and reference the file FreeHand/Ch4/COLORWHEEL.FHT on the disc included with this book.

Which Color Is Darker?

Trapping, generally, is the process of making the relative size of a lighter color larger with respect to the darker color it abuts.

Chokes and spreads are determined according to the relative value of the foreground color to the background color. The standard color wheel can easily help you define those relationships. It is included on the Studio Skills CD-ROM in the file FreeHand/Ch4/COLORWHEEL.FHT.

Three pairs of colors are on the color wheel, with one primary and one secondary color to a pair: yellow/green, cyan/red, and magenta/blue.

Fully-saturated primaries (red, blue, green) are darker than fully-saturated secondaries (cyan, magenta, yellow). If we travel around the wheel from green to blue, all colors in between will be darker than green and lighter than blue; green would spread and all the other colors would choke in relation to it (they would spread in relation to blue).

Colors of the same sort (primary or secondary) at the bottom of the wheel are darker than colors higher on the wheel. Yellow is lighter than cyan or magenta; and red is darker than green and lighter than blue.

Less-saturated colors (those closer to the center of the wheel) are lighter than colors that are more fully-saturated.

TRAPPING SPOT AND PROCESS COLOR IMAGES

1. Open the template file FreeHand/Ch4/TRAPPING.FHT. On the top are three spot images: a blue square, a yellow triangle, and a red circle. On the bottom are three process color images: a cyan square, a yellow triangle, and a magenta circle. In the center is a red rectangle with a yellow line running through it.

2. Open the Operations palette.

3. Using the Pointer tool, draw a marquee around the top circle, square, and triangle to select them.

4. Select the Trapping Xtra from the Operations palette.

5. Set the Trap width to 3 (you'll need to type it—this is an extreme width so that you can see what's happening—the maximum selectable width is 1). A normal trapping width is more like .25. Now click OK.

6. Notice how the traps are applied. The red and yellow objects became larger in relation to their darker backgrounds. Select Undo and make the square yellow and the triangle blue.

7. Re-trap the elements. Notice the difference in trapping. Both red and blue objects became smaller in relation to their lighter backgrounds.

8. Select the bottom circle, square, and triangle and select the Trapping Xtra.

9. Set the Tint reduction value to 40 percent. This will make the trapping overlap less obvious when using process colors.

10. Apply trapping. Notice that the stroke applied by the trapping procedure changed color to reflect how the colors will blend. Also note that cyan is lighter than magenta, so the trap was made to the inside of the circle.

11. Select Undo and change the square to yellow and the triangle to cyan.

12. Re-trap the elements. Notice how the traps change.

13. Select the yellow line and the red rectangle; now apply trapping.

14. Zoom in and select the outer area. The Object Inspector tells us that this has become a Composite Path.

Note

Strokes that have been trapped appear to have a pattern applied to them. This is not really a pattern, but is FreeHand's visual notation that the strokes will overprint.

Trap-free Trapping

When working in CMYK, you can, to a large extent, create trap-free documents. To do this the object and the background need to have common colors. If the object and the background have at least one common color (C,M,Y,or K) trapping is unnecessary because the common color will fill between the background and the paper. In almost every case, black should be set to overprint. That way it is unnecessary to trap it.

Manipulating Color

Sometimes we want to be more precise in matching colors. Matching a color from a TIFF file occasionally is much more important than knowing in advance just what that color is. Perhaps you need a (CMYK) color to stay in a family. Unfortunately, it's impossible to darken or lighten it appropriately using the palette. FreeHand's Color Xtras make these responsibilities easy.

Eyedropper

To match colors from imported TIFFs or elements in blends, when it is impossible to simply select the object and see what the color is, you can use the eyedropper tool. Select the target color with the eyedropper and drag it to the object you want to color match. To make the color selectable, drag it to the color well of the Color List or the Color Mixer (then import it to the Color List as a permanent color). You can also make modifications to the color in the Color List.

THE EYEDROPPER AND COLOR MATCHING

1. Open the file FreeHand/Ch4/COLORWHEEL.FHT on the disc included with this book.

2. Select the Eyedropper from the Xtra Tools palette.

3. Select a color from the wheel. Press and hold down the mouse button, then drag the color over the title type. Release the mouse button.

4. Check to make sure the Color List and Color Mixer are open.

5. With the Eyedropper tool, click on the type and drag the color swatch to the Color List. All the color percentages are immediately visible.

6. Select another color from the wheel and drag it to the color well of the Color Mixer. Drag the swatch to the Color List. It is now available for application, just as if you had mixed it.

Color Saturation and Darkness

There is a difference between the saturation of a color and its darkness. Saturation is reduced by the addition of the opposite color on the color wheel (red is desaturated by cyan). Darkness is affected by the addition of the opposite color on the wheel (if the color is fully saturated) or by an increase or decrease in the percentages of all elements of color, if it is not completely saturated. Darken, Lighten, Saturate, and Desaturate are all found under Xtras/ Colors. Keep in mind that these features do not work with spot color.

133

CHANGING COLOR SATURATION AND DARKNESS

CD ROM

1. Open the file FreeHand/Ch4/COLORDEPTH.FHT on the disc included with this book.

2. The colors in the first column are for visual reference. With the Eyedropper, drag samples to the Color List. Note their percentages.

3. Perform the function listed in each column several times (until you see a visual difference in the colors).

4. Drag a sample to the Color List and compare the percentages of color with the original samples.

Extra Tools

FreeHand includes some tools that can be categorized as "just neat stuff." These tools are so much fun and create such wild effects that you'll just want to play with them to see what happens. Whether they really serve any purpose for the type of work you do is another matter.

Fractalize

The Fractalize command, available from the Operations palette (see Figure 4.7) and from the Extras, Distort menu, creates geometric shapes along the edges of a selected path, based on the figure's shape. There is no ability to define the fractalization.

Figure 4.7

Fractalize selection in the Operations palette.

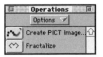

Xtra Tools (see Figure 4.8) can do things that would otherwise be nearly impossible, such as obtain three-dimensional views of two-dimensional objects, create quadratic curves, and simulate a "fisheye" view. You can soften the edge of a graphic quickly and easily by smudging it—even draw a variety of spirals automatically.

Figure 4.8

The Xtra Tools palette.

3D Rotation

The 3D Rotation tool, shown in Figure 4.9, rotates 2-dimensional objects in three dimensions. Both modes of this tool include the "Rotate From" selection, which can be along a rotation point of the X, Y, and Z axes. In the distance setting, the minimum value is 100 points (which gives a distorted view). The default is 504 points.

Expert mode offers more control over the tool. It adds a "Project From" field, which could be thought of as the location of the perspective vanishing point (where the receding lines converge). The Expert palette provides constant XZ (vertical rotation angle) and YZ (horizontal rotation angle) feedback, so you know exactly what is happening with the image at all times.

Figure 4.9

3D Rotation includes several origin points around which you can rotate an object. Easy and Expert Rotation palettes, with their pop-up menus.

Arc

The Arc command has three modes, plus an option to flip an arc. This little tool is essentially built to create quadratic curves (1/4-ellipse shapes). The three modes are standard, open, and concave (see Figure 4.10); each of these arcs can be flipped.

Figure 4.10

Arc creates different types of quadratic curves.

The Fisheye Lens

The Fisheye Lens enables you to create images that look like they are wrapped around a three-dimensional sphere or sucked into one. The effect can be either convex or concave (see Figure 4.11). Set the parameters and drag the Lens tool around the object you want to "spherize." Figure 4.12 uses an owl to illustrate this effect.

Figure 4.11

The Fisheye Lens dialog box.

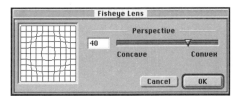

Figure 4.12

The first owl is normal, the second has a 75% convex fisheye applied to his face, and the third a 75% concave fisheye face.

Smudge

The Smudge effect, shown in Figures 4.13 and 4.14, enables you to soften the edges of objects—even smudge from one color to the next. This really is a fast way to create a soft shadow. The outside color defaults to white, but the "smudge to" color can be anything. If the object to be smudged has a stroke, that can be smudged to a different color than the fill. The smudge will be

smoother if it is unstroked. Holding down the Option key (Macintosh) or Alt
key (Windows) smudges the object from the center.

Figure 4.13

*The Smudge tool lets you alter
fill and stroke colors.*

Figure 4.14

*Pentagon smudged in one
direction and from the center
(with Option or Alt key held
down).*

Spiral

The Spiral tool enables you to draw spirals that rotate clockwise or counterclockwise, and have consistent or expanding space between the spirals, based
on the number of rotations or the width of each rotation (see Figure 4.15).

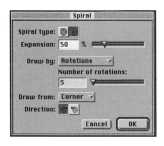

Figure 4.15

*Spiral dialog box by number of
rotations and the resulting
expanding and non-expanding
spirals.*

Figures 4.16 and 4.17 show spirals resulting from different settings in the Spiral
dialog box.

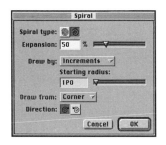

Figure 4.16

*Spiral dialog box for
incrementing expanding spiral
and the resulting spiral.*

Figure 4.17

Spiral dialog box for incrementing non-expanding spiral and the resulting spiral.

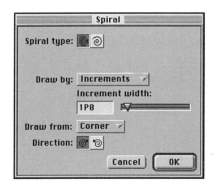

These features are so much fun that the best way to learn to use them is to just play around with them for awhile. Undoubtedly, one or two of these will come in handy, and you may even use it on a regular basis.

Shockwave for FreeHand

*T*he Internet's popularity over the past few years is largely

because of the World Wide Web, which is only one of

several types of Internet information standards. However, the

Web's user-friendly graphical interface has created such a stir

because it is often described as the universe of network-accessible

information: an embodiment of human knowledge. Its electronic

pages can contain images, text, and hypertext links that lead to

other pages with images, text, and more hypertext links. Given this

structure, and its "World Wide" accessibility, you can see why the

Internet is now an information resource for everyone.

Within the past year, a number of companies have been developing and introducing new technologies and products that allow Web-page developers to include sound, animation, and many more multimedia on the Internet.

It should come as no surprise that Macromedia is one of the companies at the forefront of this new movement. Macromedia developed Shockwave, currently the leading solution for Web interactive multimedia. It has been adopted by many Web site developers to add dynamic multimedia and interactivity, including sound and animation, to their Web sites.

Macromedia created versions of Shockwave for many of their products, including Shockwave for FreeHand. Web page authors can create illustrations in FreeHand and embed them in Web pages. These illustrations offer much more than conventional Web page graphics. FreeHand Shockwave images allow Web surfers viewing the image to use the magnifying glass to zoom in or out (to 26,500 percent!), including the capability to zoom to a defined area. Another familiar tool, the "grabber hand," allows you to pan back and forth. Both tools (and the standard pointer cursor that turns to a pointing hand when it's over a hotlink area) can be displayed in the Shockwave toolbar, so that users can access these features without having to remember commands.

These new capabilities have tremendous potential for technical illustration. Shockwave for FreeHand also allows the graphic developer to incorporate Web page links within the graphic. This allows the person viewing the page to click on certain sections of the graphic to navigate to other Web pages.

The interesting thing about Shockwave for FreeHand is that you can start using it almost immediately. Creating images for the Web pages isn't much different from creating regular FreeHand graphics. Now you can take your finest existing artwork and re-purpose it for Web-based electronic distribution.

Software Components

Macromedia has created special software for FreeHand that creates Shockwave documents. A special viewer has also been created that lets Web browsers display these Shockwave documents. Both of these new programs are designed to be extensions of FreeHand and Web browsers such as Netscape. The software is available at no charge from Macromedia's Web site, http://www.macromedia.com/shockwave/

Authoring Shockwave Files

To create FreeHand Shockwave files all you need is FreeHand; normal FreeHand files are ready to use. To use all the Shockwave capabilities, you will also need two Xtra files from Macromedia. Installing this software is as simple as dropping the two Xtras in FreeHand's Xtras directory and re-starting FreeHand.

Note

The extensions needed for Shockwave for FreeHand are also located on the disc that came with this book!

URLs Xtra

The first of the two Xtras files to use with Shockwave for FreeHand is a URLs editor, which helps you create the link addresses that can be assigned to objects of any shape within the graphic (image maps). Clicking on a particular object will call up other pages just like clicking on regular links within a web page. The URLs Xtra palette is accessed from the Windows, Other submenu (see Figure 5.1).

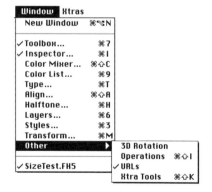

Figure 5.1

Access path for URLs Xtra.

Figure 5.2 shows the URLs editor with some sample URLs. The URLs can be applied to a FreeHand object by simply dragging the URL onto the object (just like you would do to assign a color from the Color List).

Figure 5.2

Each URL listed in the URLs editor is a link to a Web page on the Internet.

At the top of the URLs window is a pop-up menu with commands for managing the URL list. The commands include New, Duplicate, Edit, Find, and Remove.

URLs can be added to individual objects, including individual objects within groups (Option-Click [Macintosh] or Alt-Click [Windows] to select a single object within the group). They may not, however, be added to Grouped objects.

When a URL is added to the list it must be applied to an object before closing the URL window, closing the FreeHand document, or sending the FreeHand application to the background. Any URL that has not been applied to a FreeHand object will not be saved with the document.

The Duplicate command creates a copy of the selected URL. This can be handy when you need to add a series of URLs to different pages at one site. Duplicate a URL and just make the needed changes to address another page. Remove deletes the selected URL.

The Find command selects any objects that have the specified URL assigned to them. You can also click on an object, and the URLs editor will select the URL that is assigned to that object. If no URLs are assigned to the object, <None> will be selected.

To make changes to a URL that has been added to the palette, click on the URL and select Edit from the Options menu of the URLs palette, or just double-click on the URL. Make the desired changes, then press Enter when you are finished.

Deleting a URL is as easy as clicking on it and selecting Remove from the Options menu of the URLs palette. This command removes the name of the URL from the list and deletes the link in any FreeHand object associated with it.

Note

Shockwave supports both relative and absolute URLs. Absolute URLs contain the entire path name and file name for the document. Relative URLs contain a partial path name relative to the current file location on the server, not the HTML file in which they are embedded.

Afterburner

The second Xtra that you'll need to use the most powerful capabilities of Shockwave and FreeHand is the compression utility, Afterburner. This extension reduces FreeHand file sizes to minimize the amount of time it takes to transfer files over the Web. Afterburner also allows you to lock a document you've created so that it can't be downloaded, opened, and edited in FreeHand. This utility is accessible from the Xtras menu (see Figure 5.3).

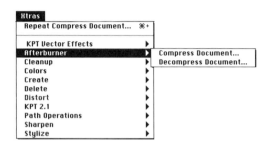

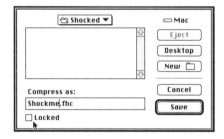

F i g u r e 5 . 3

Afterburner lets you compress and lock FreeHand files for the Web.

 Tip

If you're going to lock the files you upload to your Web site, be sure you keep a copy of the original FreeHand file. Not only will Web surfers be unable to open the locked file—you won't be able to open and edit it either.

FreeHand documents do not have to be processed through the Afterburner Xtra to be used as a FreeHand Shockwave image. However, this utility will make every file smaller in size, which reduces the time it takes to transfer over the Internet (see Figure 5.4).

Figure 5.4

Afterburner decompresses and opens a copy of the compressed document.

If you intend to use FreeHand 5.0 and 5.5 files that are not processed through Afterburner, you must name the file with an .FH5 suffix. Files created with FreeHand 4 can also be used, but their suffix must be .FH4. Even though the Macintosh OS does not require filename extensions, extensions are necessary to work correctly in a cross-platform environment such as the Web. Afterburner automatically adds an .FHC extension, or replaces the previous extension with .FHC. Files compressed using the Afterburner Xtra are automatically recognized and decompressed by the browser's plugin when the file is opened or viewed by Shockwave-compatible browsers

To name a document opened with Afterburner decompression, choose "Save" or "Save As" from the FreeHand file menu and give it a new name. (You're probably better off keeping the old file intact, just in case.) The document must be saved with a new name before you recompress it.

Viewing Shockwave for FreeHand Files

To view FreeHand Shockwave files when browsing the Web, you first need a Web browser that supports the Macromedia Shockwave for FreeHand plug-in. Netscape Navigator 2.0 supports this plug-in. By the time you read this, other browsers should also support Shockwave. (Microsoft Internet Explorer 3.0 and America Online have announced Shockwave support.) The only thing you have to do to install the plug-in is drop the file into the Plug-in directory for your Web browser and restart the browser.

Preparing FreeHand Documents for Shockwave

Before you can send out your fabulous FreeHand drawings to the Web universe, you need to prepare them for their journey as Shockwave files. Some of the steps discussed in this section aren't required, but will make the files' trip more comfortable.

Add File Extensions

FreeHand files created with the Windows version of FreeHand that are not template files already have the .FH5 suffix. Macintosh users need to add a three-character suffix. The three possible file extensions that can be used depend on the originating program:

- .FH4 for FreeHand version 4
- .FH5 for FreeHand version 5.0 and 5.5
- .FHC for FreeHand documents processed through the Afterburner Xtra

Set the Unit of Measure

All FreeHand Shockwave documents should have Points set for the document's unit of measure. To do this open the Document Inspector.

Set the Document Resolution

The resolution for the document should be set to 72, which is also set in the Document Inspector.

Set the Document Dimensions

It is important to limit the size of the document to whatever dimensions are needed by the actual graphic. This process involves a few steps:

1. Choose Select All from the Edit menu.

2. Get the dimensions of the new grouped object by looking in the Object Inspector. An example is shown in Figure 5.5.

Figure 5.5

The numbers that you will need are the values for W and H. In this example, the numbers are w = 300 and h = 100.

3. Move the grouped object to the lower left corner of the page.

4. In the Page Inspector, change the page size to Custom. If the object is taller than it is wide, make sure the Portrait page icon is selected; otherwise select Landscape.

5. Change the page dimensions to either the same dimensions as the grouped object, or if desired, somewhat larger (see Figure 5.6).

Figure 5.6

In this example, the numbers are x = 340 (width) and y = 140 (height). These dimensions create a 20-point space on all sides of the object.

Optimize the Document

You can minimize the time it takes to download your FreeHand Shockwave document by customizing the file a little. You may have created the most unusual and fantastic Web page ever using Shockwave for FreeHand, but if it is too complex and takes too long to download, most people may never sit long enough to see it.

Fonts

Web surfers who will view your FreeHand Shockwave art use different computer platforms with different operating systems, and—most importantly—different installed fonts. For this reason, it is a good idea to use only the most common typefaces. When you want to use a wider variety of typefaces, you can convert text to paths. But if you must convert text to paths, do so sparingly. Text converted to paths is interpreted as a graphic and not as text, which adds substantial paint-up time (the time the graphic takes to display on your screen) and complexity to the page.

File Size

Here are a number of ways to reduce file size to minimize transfer time:

- Delete any objects that are not visible in the final graphic.

- Delete unused colors. Use the Unused Named Colors command, in the Delete submenu of the Xtras menu.

- Delete unused or invisible layers.

- Delete items in the Background layer, especially images imported for tracing purposes.

- Simplify complex objects with the Simplify command in the Cleanup submenu of the Xtras menu.

- Minimize the use of Paste Inside.

Embedding FreeHand Shockwave Graphics in HTML Documents

FreeHand documents for the Web are similar to FreeHand documents for print. Before they are useful, they need to be embedded in a document. For the Web, those documents are created in HTML. Code is entered, using any of several authoring tools, directly into the HTML document.

Part of the process of converting a FreeHand document to a FreeHand Shockwave graphic is to size the image. As you read earlier, you check the height and width of the image and then set the document dimensions to be the same (or slightly larger). You will need those two numbers for embedding the graphic into HTML documents.

The HTML tags you will need to specify look something like this:

```
<A><EMBED SRC="EXAMPLE.FH5" WIDTH=400 HEIGHT=100></A>
```

In this example, an image named EXAMPLE.FH5 has a width of 400 points and a height of 100 points. Since the HTML document is unable to look at the graphic and see what size it is, this command tells the document how much space the graphic will need.

147

Web Server Settings

For a FreeHand Shockwave to be available on the Internet, it must be posted on a Web server. The server must be configured so that it knows how to transfer the document correctly over the network. Required settings include the following:

```
Action: BINARY
File Suffix: .FH4, .FH5, .FHC
File Type: TEXT
MIME Type: image/x-freehand
```

Unavailable Features and Limitations

Although Shockwave for FreeHand is designed to take advantage of FreeHand's power and flexibility with images, there are several features that work in FreeHand but are unavailable in Shockwave:

- Shockwave for FreeHand does not support EPS pages. This format is not space-efficient and there are Macintosh-specific screen representations. Images cannot be presented on the Web.

- Only the last page of a multiple-page document will be displayed (the one that was visible when the document was saved). Other pages may be viewed by panning. Keep in mind that multiple page documents produce large files and many people will not pan a document, so they may miss important information you have to share with them.

- PostScript lines and fills are not supported.

- Externally linked TIFF files do not display; embedded TIFF files do.

- Text effects, tab leaders, and range kerning are not supported by HTML.

Part II

Fontographer

With the introduction of the Macintosh, the art of typesetting became available to anyone who could afford a new computer. An explosion occurred in the number of fonts that were available and with software that arranges type on the page. The most popular and powerful typeface software is Fontographer, which allows you to manipulate existing fonts or create your own fonts.

Fontographer's drawing tools work just like FreeHand; the program lets you manipulate each letterform as an element with points and paths. Transformation tools are also included in Fontographer that let you modify individual letters, groups of letters, or an alphabet. You can even import FreeHand drawings into a font to make special logos and dingbat characters.

Chapter 6

Fontographer Basics

*F*ont, in its original meaning, was very different from its current usage. Like almost all typographic terms, its origins were from letterpress printing, the printing technology brought to western civilization by Gutenberg. A font was a complete set of characters for a given type size and type style.

By the 19th century, a specialized terminology was used for type. Most of this has been retained by our publishing software. For example, typesetters, using what were called California typecases, had a specialized setup that would help them assemble the individual letter slugs into lines of type. In this system there were two cases: one held the capital letters and one held all the small letters. Because the case for the capital was on top of the case for the small letters, they came to be known as upper- and lowercase letters.

As you learn Fontographer, you will learn many of these old terms. A problem, though, is that modern digital usage often changes the meaning substantially. A font, for example, is no longer restricted to a single size. Now a font is a complete set of characters for a given type style; this set can be up to 256 characters.

Digital production has eliminated many older mechanical methods, but the terminology remains. Although new computer software makes typesetting much easier, a great deal of study still is necessary to become fluent in the language of type design. Fortunately, Fontographer gives you every tool you need to create professional type fonts. Fontographer enables you to modify fonts that are already on your system or to create entirely new ones. You can replace unused characters with logos or dingbats that you want to have easy access to, and you can create special characters with precise control. You have access to an unlimited number of typefaces because if you can design it, you can create it in Fontographer.

Copyright Infringement Issues

If you create a font, you've pretty much created a work of art. Even if it is not art, it is something you have spent a great deal of time working on, for purposes specific to your work. You probably don't want others to copy your work without due consideration. You should follow the same "Golden Rule" when you need to modify existing fonts.

When you customize a font, you're adding your own ideas to a giant set of someone else's ideas. A good rule of thumb is if it makes you money, carefully consider your actions. The use of a modified font in a garage sale flyer might not be the Eighth Deadly Sin, but the same font used in a nationwide sales proposal risks copyright infringement.

Remember who might have an interest in the font you're modifying. Standard fonts such as Times New Roman might technically be the intellectual property of a type foundry, but their use is so widespread that no one will bother to notice. A display font, however, is a different story. The Pensword Armoury or Adobe Systems might not be so forgiving of your personal interpretation of Angouleme or Myriad!

The History of Typefaces

Movable type was developed and made commercially viable by Johann Gutenberg in the 15th century. Gutenberg adapted concepts used by the Chinese for centuries, but with one crucial difference. His invention was not only adaptable and portable (at least by standards of the time), it also filled the growing need of religious and commercial interests for mass-produced books. His press revolutionized the dissemination of information in Europe at the time. Within 30 years of his invention, there were more than 300 type houses throughout the Continent.

The availability of books at a reasonable price revolutionized our civilization. Before Gutenberg, the purchase of a book required hiring a monk to hand-paint a copy, which normally took several years. Every book was a hand-painted work of art, but with Gutenberg's invention, popular fiction became common-place. Copies of the old masters became readily available, and education with books reduced the need to travel and live with a master. Information and education was made possible by readily available type, the printing press, and inexpensive paper.

What comprises "type" is as simple to understand as the operation of the old typewriters: key-activated levers and springs press slugs of metal cut with reversed letters to create an imprint upon a sheet of paper. The "face" of these slugs provides the shape of the characters that appear on the page. A collection of these loose slugs, aligned in rows with the proper spacing between them, forms the basis for a traditional "printed" page.

Typefaces

The design and use of typefaces quickly became as widespread as the press itself. Wherever there was demand for type, a workshop, or foundry, would be set up to meet the demand. Its metalsmiths and punchcutters produced unique variations of standard letterforms. The first typefaces generally copied lettered script and illuminated Medieval manuscripts; however, a need for legibility and standardization led to the development of "normal" Roman characters still in use today. These typefaces were called Roman because they were modeled after the hand-carved letters in the victory columns of the Roman Caesars.

Typefaces were extremely complex works of craftsmanship. After they were drawn, the typefaces had to be carved out of metal or hardwood. Molds were made. The resulting typeface was then cast from the molds. Every different type size had to be hand cut. It could take from a year to several decades to develop a new typestyle. As a result, there were not many different styles. However, those that were developed were exquisite.

Even modern typefaces take their inspiration from the meticulous type foundries of the early Renaissance. Popular and durable modern fonts such as Caslon, Frutiger, and Garamond incorporate elements from classic fonts. Often subtle variations of these classics incorporate the flourishes that would be added by distinctive tool marks of the quill pen and other handwriting tools. These flourishes became very stylized after they were converted to carved metal.

Later developments included Italic type, capitalized here because it was the interpretation of Northern Italian handwriting of the 16th century. The first man to do this was named Aldus, hence the name of Aldus software and its characteristic graphic (his profile).

Most typefaces available from foundries today are digitized for high-volume mass-production of printed books. The Macintosh and the emphasis it put on fonts drastically changed the typeface industry, making it available to the home user. Whether users are creating a simple leaflet or a business proposal, they can typeset their own work with any of the professional-level page layout programs. With a program like Fontographer, modern digital designers have access to all of the fonts that were so laboriously produced as recently as the 1950s.

Freedom from the "tyranny of metal" imposed by lead slugs enables you to combine typestyles that existed only in metal thirty years ago. All the typefaces from the explosion of photographically created typestyles in the 1960s, '70s, and '80s can also be easily digitized. Fontographer enables you to scan, trace, re-create, and modify any typeface you find. Plus, you can create wildly innovative fonts from scratch. With Fontographer, freelance designers now have access to an industry and art once available only to those with the skill, tenacity, and vision to produce original metal typefaces.

The Fontographer Interface

Fontographer contains many of the same tools used in FreeHand for images. The same software programmers wrote both programs. A quick overview is given here to keep the old concepts fresh; the new items will be explained in more detail.

Windows

Four windows are available for type design in Fontographer, which gives you control over the most important elements of font design: which characters are included in the font, how they look when printed, how they look on-screen, and how they are spaced in relation to one another. Grouping each activity into its own window provides font designers with a sensible Fontographer interface.

Character Set

The first of these, the Character Set, is shown in Figure 6.1. The Character Set window contains all the letterforms in use by the ASCII character encoding system for the font that is open. The assignment of letters to each of the boxes in the Character Set window can be altered for special projects. Figure 6.1 shows a standard English language character set, which displays 72dpi versions of each letter already created by the designer.

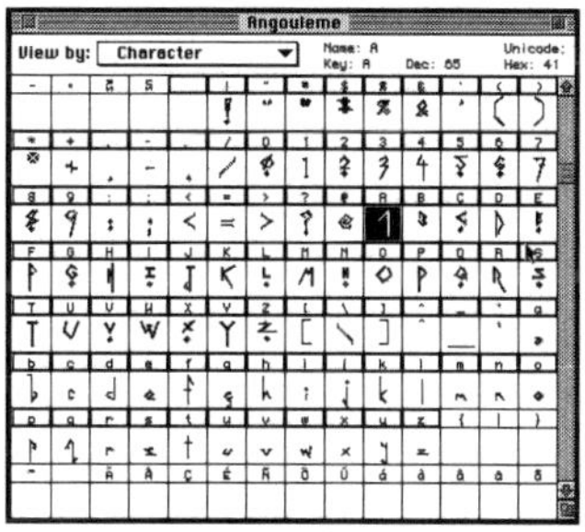

Figure 6.1

Character Set window for the font Angouleme.

155

The Character Set window also contains a subwindow for each character in the character set you are using (see Figure 6.2). The character encoding can be Mac, Windows, Adobe, and several others. Each subwindow shows the saved version of the bitmap in the bottom portion of the window. The top bar shows the character, the keystroke combination, the character width, or several other options as shown in the Figures (6.2, 6.3, and 6.4).

Figure 6.2

A portion of the character set window of Nuevo Litho font showing view by character.

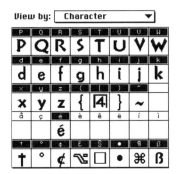

In this view the bar at the top of each character window shows the character that should print in normal Mac or Windows ASCII. If you add special characters, the bar does not change. Notice that the § character still shows in the bar of Nuevo Litho even though the character has been changed to an open ballot box.

When you use View by Keystroke, the character windows show the keyboard shortcuts for the characters (see Figure 6.3). For example, on a Mac, the character ° is indicated by SO8 in the bar above the window. This stands for Shift, Option, 8.

Figure 6.3

A portion of the character set window of Nuevo Litho font showing view by keystroke.

Many other options help you distinguish different characters. The pop-up menu shown in Figure 6.4 lists all the ways in which you can view character sets. Most of these, such as the Width option (shows how wide each character is in em-units) are rarely used. Keystroke and character are the views most commonly used.

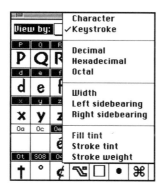

Figure 6.4

The View by pop-up menu.

Outline

The Outline window, shown in Figure 6.5, displays each character as an outline. This is where you create and modify letters in Fontographer. Each Outline window is like a separate FreeHand page containing the paths necessary to describe the character.

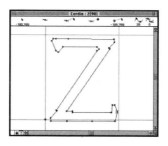

Figure 6.5

Outline window for letter "Z" in font Cordia.

Bitmap

The Bitmap window is used to inspect and modify bitmaps used by video displays to draw individual letters on-screen. Fontographer can automatically generate the bitmap images for a font by using a standard set of rules that converts the outline to the best possible bitmap for each letterform (or character outline) in the set. These bitmaps have to be generated for specific sizes. This is rarely used because Adobe Type Manager automatically generates custom bitmaps for the various sizes used in a document. If you are using ATM, you only need one bitmap, usually 12 point. The Bitmap window is shown in Figure 6.6.

Figure 6.6

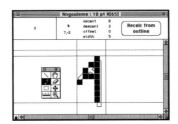

Bitmap of 10-point Angouleme "A" with modification tools.

Occasionally you need to pay special attention when generating bitmaps. If you are developing a font for use primarily on the Web, you can save headaches by making sure that the bitmaps you will be using at a particular size are actually readable. With just a little work, smaller bitmap fonts can be made much more legible on-screen.

Metrics

The fourth window, shown in Figure 6.7, is the Metrics window. The designer uses this window to place samples of text against each other to check the spacing and kerning of each letter. Spacing and kerning are easily modified by dragging simple sidebearing and kerning bars.

Figure 6.7

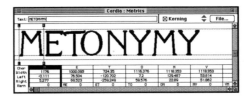

The Metrics window with sample text.

The built-in letterspacing of the font is shown at the bottom of the window. These numbers are in Fontographer's em-units. The character bar is the width of the character in em-units. Left lists the em-unit space set on the left side and right lists the space on the right.

Left and right spacings are usually set in the Character window. The Metrics window mainly is used to adjust kerning. By typing two or more letters in the bar at the top of the Metrics window, you can easily adjust the kerning of any letter pair you desire. By clicking on any of the letters that follow the first letter, a vertical line with a K on the top appears. Dragging it left or right adjusts the kerning built into that letter pair. The amount you adjust the kerning is noted in positive or negative em-units at the bottom of the window.

Figure 6.8 shows the Metrics window of "T" and "o" in Nuevo Litho with the desired kerning.

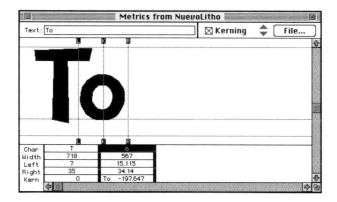

Figure 6.8

Kerning letters in the Metrics window.

Floating Palettes

Fontographer, like FreeHand, uses floating palettes to make access to the most-used tools easy to reach on your workspace. Most of the tools and many of the keyboard shortcuts are the same. Fontographer applies most of the power of FreeHand to each of the 256 possible characters. The Toolbox and Layers palettes are used with the Outline window; the Bitmaps window has its own palette of tools. Figure 6.9 shows the Tools and Layers palettes in the Outline window.

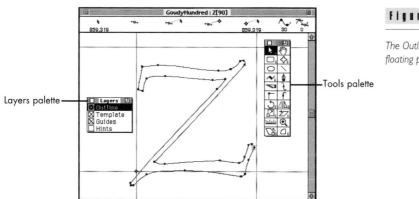

Figure 6.9

The Outline window with the floating palettes.

The Toolbox

The Fontographer toolbox, shown in Figure 6.10 is almost identical to the FreeHand toolbox.

Figure 6.10

The Toolbox.

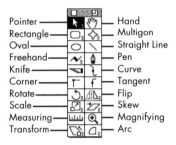

The Pointer, Rectangle, Oval, Straight Line, Freehand, Pen, Knife, and Magnifying tools work the same in Fontographer as they do in FreeHand. The transformation tools—Rotate, Flip, Scale, and Skew—are also identical to FreeHand's. Refer to Chapter 1 for more information about these tools. Although the panel that controls the specific transformations is different, the concept and behavior of the tools is the same. Any tool that has two little arrows pointing down in the lower right corner has a dialog box with options that can be opened by double-clicking.

The Hand tool enables you to adjust the portion of a character that you are viewing in the window. Place the Hand tool in a portion of the window and click and drag to a new location.

The Multigon tool functions much like FreeHand's Polygon tool. Double-clicking on the tool's icon opens the panel that controls the features of the multigon.

The Curve, Corner, and Tangent point tools replace the Bezigon tool in FreeHand. They are used to create points on new paths or add points to existing paths. These tools are similar to the point types of the same name in FreeHand (a tangent point is called a "connector point" in FreeHand).

A curve point creates a path that flows from point to point in a smooth curve because the handles lock onto the same tangent. A corner point is where two straight paths meet or where two curves meet with different tangents; a tangent is where a curve meets a straight line on the tangent of the curve. See Chapter 1 for more information about these tools.

One of the most useful tools on the floating palette is the Measurement tool. It enables you to click and drag across an Outline window to digitally measure the length of a segment or the width between two lines.

The Layers Palette

The Layers palette allows you to control what is visible in the Outline window (see Figure 6.11). After a font has been traced, for example, the Template layer, which contains the grayed graphic you used as a guide, can be turned off to reduce visual clutter. Any layer can be turned on or off by clicking on the box at the left of the layer.

Figure 6.11

The Layers palette.

The Guides layer is extremely useful. It enables you to drag guides out of the horizontal and vertical lines at the origin point. These guides are seen in the Outline windows of all characters. This makes it easy to maintain a consistent x-height, for example. They can be turned on and off as needed.

The Bitmap Palette

The Bitmap palette, shown in Figure 6.12, contains a whole-figure movement tool that shifts the entire bitmap along the grid pattern. The Straight Line, Hand, Measuring and Magnifying tools work the same as those in the Outline window Toolbox. The Pencil tool adds pixels in the bitmap image, and the Eraser tool deletes pixels. The Marquee tool selects areas of the bitmap image. The Move tool allows you to fine tune the position of the bitmap image relative to the outline image.

Straight Line — Hand
Pencil — Eraser
Marquee — Move
Measuring — Magnifying

Figure 6.12

The Bitmap palette.

Modifying Existing Fonts

The name of the program, "Fontographer," implies an association between letterform manipulation and the art of photography—an apt comparison. You take a snapshot of a font and, with a little bit of darkroom magic, use it to print your own version. Just as photographers can apply numerous special effects to their prints to make them more artistic, you can alter the shapes of letters, draw your own, and even create a font that reflects your feelings. For the latter, your result might be a little skewed, or might be a little blurry, but that may be the intended effect.

Another interpretation of this program's name is its similarity to a typographer, a professional type designer and typesetter. Fontographer has immediate appeal for these craftsmen, who are often unknown to the normal desktop designer. This program is a pure delight for typographers because of its unprecedented access to font structures.

Opening a Font

Fontographer can open both TrueType and PostScript fonts and present them as drawing objects with origin and Bézier Control Points (BCPs). The origin is the zero point of all measurements in the Outline window. It is normally marked by a vertical and horizontal line, but it is movable. The symbol for the origin point can be seen in Figure 6.13. BCPs are the same points you use in FreeHand, and come in the same types (curve, corner, and tangent). To begin with a font, you need to look no further than your own System Folder.

Figure 6.13

✤

This origin point symbol can be dragged to any location in the Outline window. All measurements will be made from it.

OPENING FONTS

1. Select the Open Font... command from the File menu.

2. From the dialog box, navigate to and open the System Folder.

3. In the Fonts folder should be at least ten basic Apple fonts, as shown. Select New York and click Open.

Fontographer will read the TrueType font and display it in a standard Character Set window. If you scroll up and down, you will see that most of the characters have already been defined, including most of the foreign accented letterforms. If you double-click on any of these letters, the Outline window for that letter will open with the Tools and Layers palettes.

Modifying a Font

Fonts can be modified by individual characters or as a whole set. Changes can be as simple as altering control points or creating fractions to applying transformations to character sets, or blending the character sets of two fonts. Fontographer's controls make formerly complex modifications easy and simple.

Perhaps you don't want to use a normal italic (slanted to the right) to emphasize a particular document. With Fontographer, you can use the Skew or 3-D Transform Tool to alter the font so that it becomes a left-sloping oblique. (To be correct, an italic only applies to fonts built on the early Renaissance handwriting. Fonts that are simply slanted digitally should be called oblique). Figure 6.14 shows a New York "G" before such a transformation.

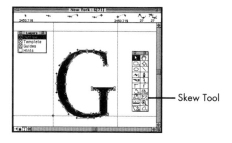

Skew Tool

Figure 6.14

New York "G" character with all points selected for skewing.

TRANSFORMING CHARACTERS

1. Open the New York character set, if it is not already open.

2. Double-click on the capital G. The Outline window opens, with all points on the G selected.

3. From the Element menu, select Transform.

4. Select Skew from the pop-up menu for the first transformation. Enter 12 in the Horizontal field, and leave all other transformations as "Do Nothing."

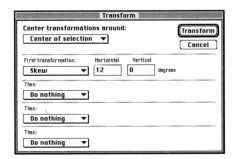

5. Click on Transform.

Figure 6.15 shows the same letter after the transformation, with a little rotation thrown in to clean up the alignment.

Figure 6.15

"G" character skewed and rotated to a rough "left" oblique.

The other transformation tools work the same way, and you can apply more than one transformation to a letter at a time by selecting them from the pop-up menus that follow the first transformation. You can also apply transformations to more than one letter at a time. In the Character Set window, select the characters you want to transform and follow the same steps.

Further Customizing

Letters are not the only thing you can customize in Fontographer. Characters that you know you will never use can be changed into custom versions of other letters to add embellishment to documents and text.

You can replace a normally unused character, such as the section character (Option-6 or §), with an open ballot box.

CREATING A BALLOT BOX CHARACTER

1. Double-click on the O6 or § character box.

2. In the resulting outline window, Select All and delete. (See the figure.)

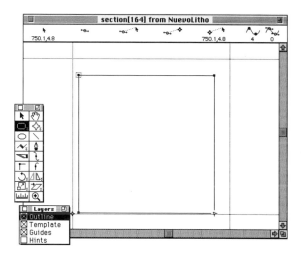

3. Select the rectangle tool and draw a square by holding down the Shift key as you draw.

4. Select all, clone the square, and select Transform from the Element menu (see the following figure).

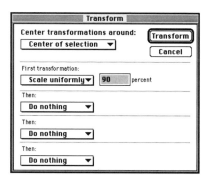

5. Set the Transform dialog to Scale uniformly at 90 percent from the Center of Selection. The result is shown in the next figure.

6. Select Correct Path Direction from the Element menu. Now (after you generate your new font) your font will set a ballot box for checking with the simple Option–6 keystroke.

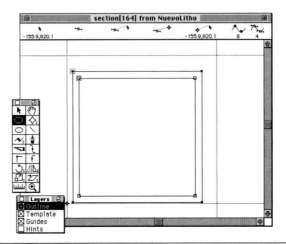

You can also create collections of "dingbats" by copying a specific drawing into the clipboard, opening a font, and pasting in the symbol. You can add a collection of favorite dingbats into a new font file and create your own definitions for each letter. Select this "custom" font and you can access your own repository of logos and symbols tailored to your needs.

Any drawing done in FreeHand can be copied and pasted into the Outline window. The only rules are that you must use closed paths with no blends or fills. Fontographer will take those paths and make the equivalent of a joined path to create your character. Paths with fills can only be used with Type 3 fonts.

Blending Two Fonts

The Blending command in the Element menu is almost too easy. If you have a font already open, you can blend it with another font simply by selecting a second font and then specifying the percentage of weight between them (see Figure 6.16). After you've made your selections, click on OK. Fontographer blends the two fonts together. Figure 6.17 shows the blend of GoudyHundred and TreacyfacesSample, using the capital J as an example.

The Blend Fonts panel.

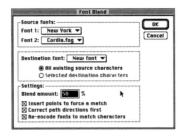

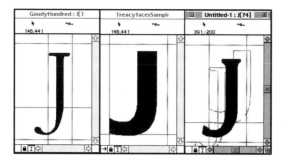

Figure 6.17

The original letterforms and the resulting blend.

When blending, you must take into consideration the nature of the final product. Fonts are a highly developed artform. After centuries of use, everyone knows subconsciously what a font should look like. Extreme modifications turn letters into nonsense (see Figures 6.18 and 6.19); others product funny results. Just because you can blend Pensword's Linia with the Mac System Font Palatino doesn't mean you have to!

Palatino 48-point
Linia 48-point

Figure 6.18

48-point samples of the original typefaces.

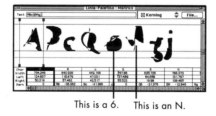

Figure 6.19

This blended font will need considerable fine-tuning to be useful.

This is a 6.   This is an N.

The Copy Reference Command

One of the most useful capabilities of Fontographer is the use of previously designed characters as the basis for new characters. The Copy Reference command in the Edit menu makes such a powerful feature a simple cut and paste operation.

A copied reference is exactly that —a reference to the original character. What makes this different is that changes made to the original are automatically updated in the character built from the reference. References are used routinely in several operations. Any character with a diacritical mark (such as "é, ô, ü) is most easily done by placing that mark over a referenced character. That way if the original is modified the accented character is too.

CREATING CHARACTERS WITH ACCENTS

1. Go to the character view of any font and find a missing character that would require a mark. For example, the aacute (á).

2. Select the lowercase "a" character and choose the Copy Reference command under the Edit menu.

3. Open the empty á character Outline window and paste.

4. A lowercase "a" will appear in the window, as shown. If you select it, a gray line appears around it. It behaves like a grouped object (as shown in the figure) and the paths cannot be modified.

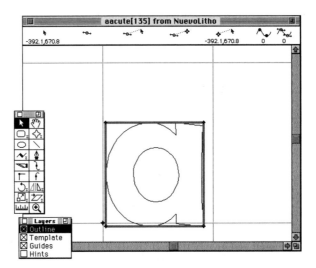

5. With the Corner tool, draw the accent shape. Use the following figure as a guide.

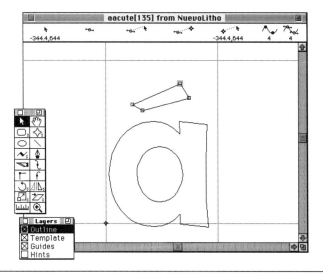

Fractions work the same way, but you have two references and resize them after pasting them into the outline window (see Figure 6.20). Most fonts do not include fractions, but the empty character windows can be found in front of the numbers in the Character Set window.

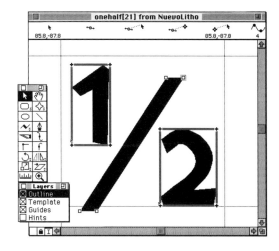

Figure 6.20

Fractions aren't included in most fonts, but you can create your own.

Creating Ligatures

A ligature is two characters that have been combined into one. Most fonts have a few, such as the fi or fl. In both of these cases, the top of the second letter interferes with the top of the first letter. The ligatures solve this problem elegantly. For script faces, however, there are many more possible ligatures that are rarely added to the fonts.

CREATING A DECORATIVE LIGATURE

1. Open Times Italic from the System Folder.

2. Open a blank Outline window and copy and paste a capital T and a lowercase h into the window. Arrange them as you see in the following figure.

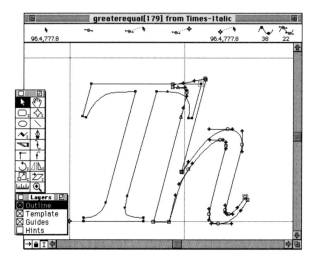

3. Use the Remove Overlap command from the Element menu. This will combine the two paths into one as shown in the following figure.

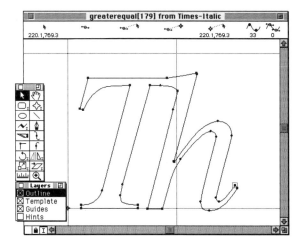

4. Use the drawing tools to make a bulge where the T and h meet (see the figure). You can make room to draw a path that punches a hole in the bulge. It may take a lot of minor adjustments, however, to adjust the shapes to your liking.

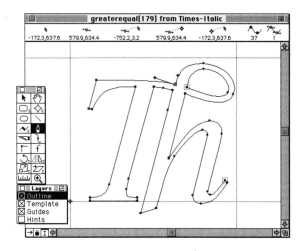

Note

Obviously, you have to be fairly motivated to spend the time necessary to add fractions and ligatures that look professional. Although these tasks aren't that difficult, you have to deal with 256 characters, which takes quite a bit of time. Do not be surprised if your new masterpiece takes several months of work on a part-time basis. The joy of using a font that exactly matches your style is worth the effort.

171

Setting Spacing and Character Width

Although Fontographer simplifies the process of making new fonts, some parts of this artform/craft are pretty complicated. Character width and letterspacing are two examples. Both require extremely delicate adjustments. Fortunately, Fontographer's designers added Auto Space and Auto Kern commands to the Metrics menu for these minute adjustments. You should not expect either of these commands to produce a perfect font, but they are great time-savers for applying default settings to a newly developed font.

You can make a unique font by modifying an existing typeface and not have to worry about these complex adjustments. By simply restricting the modified characters to the guides in the Outline windows, your new font should be spaced properly. All you need to do is choose a font to modify that has the same general character width and x-height.

If you are an experienced type designer and are eager to test every Fontographer feature, you should give the spacing and kerning capabilities a workout in the Metrics window. After you have the font spaced the way you think will work, use it for a few weeks. Chances are good you will find some problems. This process of testing and fixing can last for months. Do not despair!

Setting the Basepoint and Font Attributes

When you decide on the attributes of a font you first need to determine the location of character pieces in the em-square. Everything in Fontographer is based on the em-square. Originally, the em was a blank space the width of a capital M. The modern definition is the square of the type size. An 18 point em, for example, would be a square 18 points tall and 18 points wide.

The reason Fontographer bases everything on the em is simple: the em varies in proportion to the type size, but calculating it is consistent. In other words, it is always the square of the point size no matter what that size.

Fontographer divides the em-square into units. The norm is 1,000 units. The first thing to determine is the location of the baseline, which is the line that all the capital letters rest on. Lowercase letters have ascenders (bdfhkl) and descenders (gjpqy). The baseline is set to allow the room needed for the descenders.

Traditional fonts allowed approximately a third of the em-square for the descender; many modern fonts leave less than a quarter of the em-square. Old-fashioned script fonts (especially Art Nouveau style fonts) used up nearly half of the em.

The Basepoint

The baseline is set by typing numbers in the ascent and descent field in the Font Information dialog box under the Elements menu (see Figure 6.21). Typically, those two figures add up to 1000. A 700 Ascent and a 300 descent would make a fairly "normal" font.

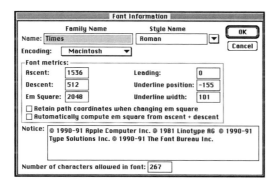

Figure 6.21

The Font Information dialog box.

Every Outline window has a vertical line at the origin. The origin is the 0 measurement of the em-square. The basepoint is the intersection of the origin line and the baseline, shown in Figure 6.22.

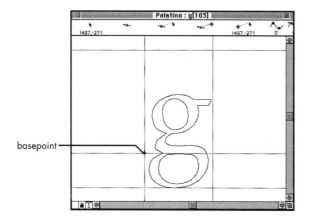

Figure 6.22

The basepoint.

X-height

The next major decision concerning the overall look of your new font is the x-height. The x-height is the height of the lowercase x. This letter is used because it is the only lowercase character that is flat at both the top and bottom. The x-height can radically affect your design.

Small x-heights look old-fashioned. Classic faces such as Caslon, Baskerville, and the like have an x-height of about 25% of the em-square. Fonts from the mid-20th century have an x-height of around a third. The more "modern" the font the larger the x-height. Some display fonts from the 1970s have x-heights of 80% of the em-square or more. Several examples are in Figure 6.23.

Figure 6.23

These are all 36-point lowercase characters, but notice the dramatic variation in x-height.

The easiest way to set the x-height is to drag a horizontal guide out of your baseline in the Guides layer. Make sure that curved or pointed character tops or bottoms extend past the x-height and baseline. Otherwise they will look too small. You should open a classic font like Times or Helvetica and examine how the character shapes fit the em-square and x-height. Figures 6.24 and 6.25 show letters from Times and the guide marking the x-height.

Figure 6.24

The x from Times Roman. A guide has been placed at the top of the character to help with the sizing and placement of other letters.

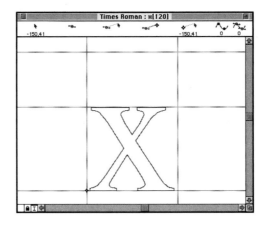

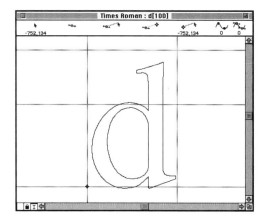

Figure 6.25

The Times Roman lowercase d. The guide placed in the x character Outline window appears on each letter, showing you the x-height of each character.

Customizing Fonts

*F*ontographer can make the creation of a custom font as simple as selecting a menu item and pressing OK. This ease of use, however, is only possible after you set up the framework for one of Fontographer's most powerful features: Auto Trace. Creating a font from scratch requires the design of at least 62 letterforms (and this number is only for the most rudimentary alphabet!). You also need the patience to compensate for the computer's occasional misinterpretation of your artistic vision, and a good sense of humor to realize that this can be fun.

If you've made it through the creative work and you're ready to begin designing that groundbreaking font, you can use one of several ways to create it. Many graphics programs enable you to draw pixel by pixel (such as xRes) or with points and paths (your old friend FreeHand) and then import those images into Fontographer. The old-fashioned but common practice of drawing each letter on paper and scanning it in is another alternative. Whichever method you use to produce templates for each letter, the Fontographer can then Auto Trace them. If necessary, you can bypass Auto Trace and use the drawing tools in the Outline window to manually trace the shape of each letterform, or you can modify the paths that you imported from FreeHand.

Typeface Design

Stanley Morrison, the designer who produced that essential typeface, Times New Roman, said typography is "the most conservative of all the crafts." Good typeface design is summed up in a simple phrase: type is design. It's hard to describe what a good typeface choice is without delving into the mystical: It flows with the page, it works with the subject, it enhances the fluidity of the artwork. Good type design is something you will learn to recognize when you see it (assuming that you spend time studying and learning about typographic excellence).

Typeface design involves making practical choices to convey a simple statement. Times New Roman suggests conservatism and trustfulness. Garamond suggests a classic elegance with a presence that Times simply does not have because of overuse. Memphis suggests order and precision; Lithos is classical proportion and elegance in a modern fashion sense. The use of a face "out-of-type"—somewhat like casting Arnold Schwarzenegger as the Pope—knocks people out of their complacency. Too much of a shock, however, can ruin the effect and bury the message.

Ergonomic and aesthetic considerations are also part of type design and use. An exciting, interesting, "artsy" font might give you a blazing headache when read on a page such as this one. But if this font were used for the heading of each chapter, it can give vigor and liveliness to the page and make the book more enjoyable.

One of the best ways to learn what typefaces can do is to look at the type in everyday life. See what design choices were made for various media. If a layout for a certain ad looks good, ask yourself why. Make mental notes about what looks good; pretty soon you will be making those choices automatically. Everyone sees hundreds of typefaces every day. Simply begin to observe type and it will help you train your eye.

Creating New Characters

To create a font, you must first tell the computer how you want the letters drawn. With pencil and paper, you only have one choice: your hand and imagination. Fontographer accepts three methods: importing characters from a painting program, from a graphics program, or scanned handdrawn artwork imported as TIFF files.

Regardless of the method, you need to consider several issues before you begin drawing. Are you creating a serif, sans serif, script, or purely decorative font? Do you need a face that is strong and bold, delicate and elegant, fashionable and exciting, subtle and intriguing, or some other form? How will the typeface be used: for a specific project, as body copy, headlines, logostyle, or for a corporate typeface? Do you need to associate your new font's design with a historic style, such as Art Deco, Victorian, Classical Greek, or 20th century Modern? Would your font work better if it were extremely condensed or expanded? Do you require something light, bold, oblique, psychedelic, sophisticated, or humorous?

Often, the best approach to solving these uncertainties is to find fonts that are already being used in a similar situation and use them as mental guidelines for your decisions. Keep in mind that professional-quality fonts look professional; lack of professionalism is equally as obvious.

Character Sets

When you begin the process of creating a font, don't forget that there are more letters in an alphabet than just "A, B, and C." Fontographer has a specific list of the minimum characters necessary to construct a paragraph of text: A-Z, a-z, and 0-9 (or 62 characters). This setup is only used by Fontographer to determine the spacing between individual characters. This minimal character set does not include punctuation, or items such as „.?/'':;{[}] (a limited example). Nor are the symbols included, which includes @#$%Áª£¢°¤|¥, (or any of the accented characters.) About half of these somewhat non-essential characters are placed on what the PC euphemistically calls the upper ASCII set. Mac users have the normal set of 256 characters.

The standard character set is already laid out for you in the Fontographer character grid. The grid includes and identifies such characters as the ampersand (&), the em-dash (—), the en-dash (–), the hyphen (-), the left double-quote ("), the right double-quote ("), and the right single-quote, or apostrophe ('). These symbols and the other characters can be arranged in several layouts for different computer systems, including the Mac, Windows, UNIX, and Adobe character sets.

Note

These characters should never be thought of as simple punctuation marks. For example, the difference between the hyphen and the em-dash is not simply a matter of length. A hyphen is not only shorter than even an en-dash, but it also sits higher above the baseline and is often angled with serifs at the ends. When the font is complete and you sit down to compose a document of text, the difference will be glaringly obvious if not done right.

Remember that you are the designer and you have control over the look and professionalism of your typeface or font.

The grid also includes other characters used in foreign languages. Whether you should include these characters depends on the application for the font. The more detailed the font, the more time it will take to create, but the more uses it will have. Quite a few foreign symbols are simply normal letters with added accents. The time it takes to create a "cosmopolitan" font actually is much less than it seems because you can copy and paste basic letter parts to create a wide variety of accented letters.

General Font Design Procedures

No matter which program you use—FreeHand, Photoshop, xRes, Fontographer, or something else—you first need to understand how to build each letter on the same set of guidelines. If you do not, you will end up with a mess that will take forever to fix in Fontographer. Even if you are creating a caps only decorative font with no numbers, you still need to draw 26 separate items that must fit together in close and complex relationships. More than that, these 26 (or 62, with lowercase letters and numbers) shapes must form a coordinated set. A font must display a united look, a single feel, and a focused style.

Fontographer automatically creates several guidelines when you open a new font and decide on your ascent and descent measurements (in the Elements menu, Font Info). If you are using FreeHand you will have to click on a corner of the guide and then drag out this guide and lock it into the Guides layer of the Layers palette. You will need to do this with each guide. Guidelines you need to consider include:

- Baseline: A line to sit the characters on.

- Left side line: A line to mark the left-most side of characters.

- Ascender: A line to mark the top of the ascenders of the lowercase bdfhkl.

- Descender: A line to mark the bottom of the lower case gjpqy.

- X-height: A line to mark the height of the lowercase x.

- Cap height: A line to mark the tops of the capital letters (this is usually 5 to 10 percent lower than the Ascender line).

These six guidelines are absolutely necessary unless you are creating an all caps font (eliminate the x-height and ascender lines values). Fontographer automatically places the first four of these values. The other two need to be dragged out in Fontographer, also. (Imagine you have a square around one of the letters and you are dragging it by clicking on one of the corners.)

Several other guidelines help a great deal by placing the extremities of letters that curve or have points. These curves or points (as in AVO and so on) are expected to project approximately 4 percent beyond the normal guidelines you just set. These lines are measured as a percentage of the em-square. Remember that all type is sized relative to the em, which is defined as the square of the point size. The optional guidelines are as follows:

- 4 percent below the baseline.

- 4 percent above the x-height.

- 4 percent above the cap height (unless that is the same as the ascender).

- 4 percent left of the left side guide.

Do you notice that something is missing—the right side guide and 4 percent right of the right side guide. These cannot be drawn because every character in a professional font has a different width—all 256 of them. The only exceptions are accented vowels (such as å á ã ä â à) and fonts that use monospaced numbers (most fonts do for accounting reasons).

When you begin your latest font project, you should draw first the letters that help you define the widths of the rest of the letters. Letters that help most are x, O, o, l, h, and P.

- The x defines the x-height.
- The O forms the base of CG and Q.
- The o is the base shape of bcdepq.
- The l starts the h which is the base of kmn.
- The P starts the B and the R (which starts the K), and so on.

Using a Drawing Program

Fontographer uses Bézier curves and control points much like FreeHand. If you draw a letter in FreeHand, you have already encoded much of what Fontographer needs to create the font outlines. All you need to do is copy and paste the graphics you drew in FreeHand into Fontographer. Of course, it is not quite that simple because you have to copy and paste 62 times (at least).

Perhaps you were wondering "Why would I want to draw a font in FreeHand when Fontographer was created by the same programmers with many of the same tools and commands?" The answer involves two reasons. The first is that you might be so accustomed to FreeHand that you know all the keyboard shortcuts by habit. (Fontographer has a different set of keyboard shortcuts.) Second, your work style might rely heavily on FreeHand's powerful filters, such as Punch, Union, 3D distort, and so on. Except for these two reasons, you are better off drawing directly in Fontographer.

If you are working in a drawing program (such as FreeHand or Illustrator) you need to remember Fontographer's importing restrictions. Even if these programs export files in several file types, Fontographer will only import certain file types. All shapes should be closed paths with no fills, colors, or fancy strokes. In addition, there can be no overlapping shapes, masks, blends, or composite paths.

IMPORTING AN EPS FILE

In this exercise you will import an EPS file into Fontographer for use in a font set. This can be very useful when creating font sets that contain characters. You can create art in a 2D drawing application and then import the art you create into Fontographer.

1. Open a new font in Fontographer.

2. Open the outline window for R.

3. From the File menu, select Import and EPS.

4. Select the file Fontographer/Ch6/R.eps from the disc included with this book. Click Open.

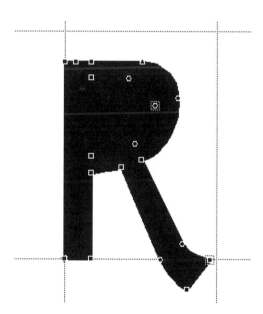

5. If the EPS file imports as a solid black shape like the character R shown above, select Correct Path Direction from the Element menu. If it looks normal, as in the following figure, this step isn't necessary.

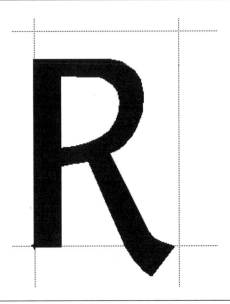

Using a Painting Program

It is virtually impossible to create a useable font from handdrawn letters created in a painting program. There is no way to set the guides, and the bitmapped letters take much more effort to draw well. In addition, everything has to be drawn with a hard edge or it cannot be traced. However, a painting program works well if you are looking for a rough handdrawn font.

The capital D in Figure 7.1 is from an original font named Scriptum Precursor, which was created as a test font to become familiar with the Fontographer working environment. The template image was done freehand on a graphics program with no control points or drawing objects at all. The template was used to manually trace the letter with points from the Tools palette and construct a handwritten D.

 Tip

Keep in mind that Fontographer can only import PICT and EPS files. In fact, it refuses to import a TIFF. To get around this limitation, use the Clipboard or Scrapbook which both use the PICT format. Copy art to the clipboard to paste it into a Fontographer window.

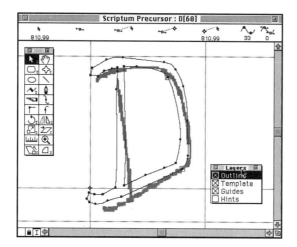

Figure 7.1

A capital D created with a "traced" PICT template.

Tracing Scanned Art

Many artists feel that the only way to have complete control of the fonts they want to create are to draw them on paper in ink. Afterward, the characters can be scanned into the computer, saved in a format (such as PICT), and then imported into Fontographer's Template layer.

 T i p

Remember that samples of old fonts are a good source of scanned templates to begin a design.

To keep things consistent when you import templates, remember that all the characters need to be scanned with the same area of pixels. The easiest way to do this is to move the same size path or selection box from letter to letter. Then all the characters will be a consistent size when Fontographer squeezes them into the Template layer of the Outline window.

In Figure 7.2 you can see a cropped scan of the letter K taken from a font called NuevoSans, which was handdrawn for scanning. It is saved as a PICT and stored in the Scrapbook (along with the other 61 basic characters).

185

Figure 7.2

A cropped scan of the letter "K" imported into Fontographer.

This character was cut-and-pasted from the Scrapbook to the Outline window of the new font, which is called NuevoSans with an Ascent of 700 and a Descent of 300. Auto Trace was then selected from the Element menu. Figure 7.3 shows the result. Auto Trace followed the bitmap well, but the scan was seriously flawed.

Figure 7.3

Auto Trace in the process of cleaning up a handdrawn figure.

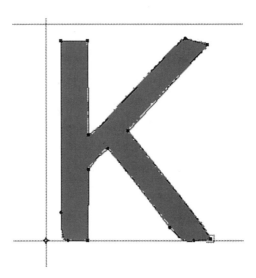

 Tip

As you can see in Figure 7.4, the PICT was placed in the Template layer. When the K was selected, four handles appeared, connected by a thick gray line running from handle to handle. Delete the imported bitmap by deleting the template layer. If you leave the bitmap in the font the font's size will be huge. Even if each PICT is only 20K, that is over 1.2 MB worth of unnecessary data after scanning.

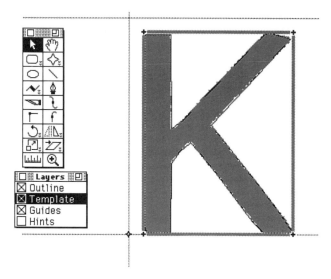

Figure 7.4

Delete the scanned bitmap from the font.

After the PICT is deleted, the resulting paths, shown in Figure 7.5, are close to the original concept, but still need some work.

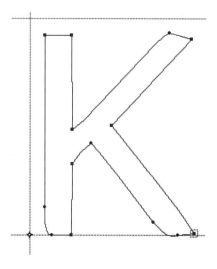

Figure 7.5

The rough outline of a new font that still needs work.

The finished, cleaned up letter (without letterspacing or kerning) is shown in Figure 7.6.

Figure 7.6

*Cleaned up and almost
ready to be generated.*

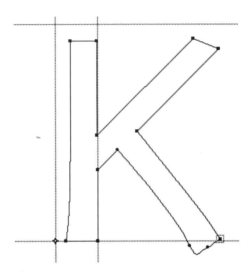

The Auto Trace Command

Auto Trace is extremely easy to use with any font. After the templates have
been read into the Template Layer, simply select the characters you want to
create and choose Auto Trace from the Element menu selection.

Click the mouse and away you go! If the templates are exactly what you're
trying to achieve, you can constrain Fontographer to outlining exactly what you
have drawn. If, however, there are degrees of freedom in the final product (that
is, you need to make some changes), or you would like a more "flowing" end
result, allow for a looser trace. The Advanced Options (see Figure 7.7) give you
greater control over Fontographer's interpretation of your templates.

Figure 7.7

*Auto Trace's Advanced Options
allow for pin-point specifications.*

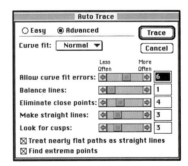

If you have more time, or want to customize your templates in a stylized way—
perhaps you need to "clear up" some mistakes, or want to ignore the boxes
(artifacts) left over from the scanning process—you can hand draw over the

template (see Figure 7.8). Hand drawing in Fontographer is almost exactly like drawing in FreeHand: in both applications you are outlining all the edges of the letter, including the interior curves.

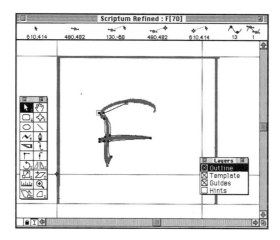

Figure 7.8

Hand drawing in progress. Use the Magnification tool to zoom in to fine-tune the curves.

Tip

If you are creating a font that is symmetrical and has a particular style throughout its alphabet, save time and effort by using the "below 32" character boxes to hold bits and pieces of letters. For example, the caps of letters such as "A" and the feet and crossbars of letters such as "F" and "t" are used frequently in different letters. Copy and paste each part into the new character box, make a few joins with the Drawing tool, and the letter will be complete. Figure 7.9 shows the final serif to a capital H being pasted into the Outline window.

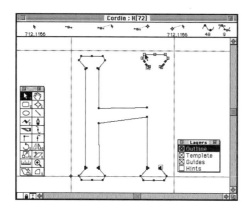

Figure 7.9

A "building block" serif being moved into place to complete the left stem of the "H."

Kerning

Kerning is a specific amount of space allowed between a specific pair of letters. If you look closely at a line of text, the spaces are rarely the same when drawn inside a word. (In other words, if you type the letters Ty the space between the "T" and the "y" is different from typing the letters Tg. Notice the space difference between the "T" and the "g.") Many different pairs of letters need special spacing. For example, pairs such as LT, AW, To, and the fragments shown in Figure 7.10 require special kerning.

Figure 7.10

The differences in spacing, or kerning, between letters. Notice how the "e" is set much closer to the "a" than to the "n."

The Fontographer Metrics window (see Figure 7.11) handles these subtle kerning differences. When you select each character, the sidebearing and kerning level values are displayed graphically and numerically.

Figure 7.11

The Metrics window with a sample of text being checked for spacing.

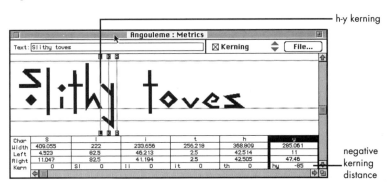

Figure 7.11 illustrates another example of spacing between letters. In a decorative font such as Angouleme, the amount of white space that exists between each outlined character can be widely divergent. In this example, the highlighted "y" has left and right sidebearings that are fine as an average distance between it and other letters. However, when a "y" is paired with the "h," the letter must be kerned to the left to keep the two letters from appearing "loose." This "negative" kerning distance is highlighted in the diagram.

Occasionally, letter pairs require positive kerning to keep them from touching each other. Regardless, the goal is to make the area of white space between all letter pairs consistent.

When checking for spacing, it is important that you also define the "space" character itself. This special "character" is character number 32, which is the "empty" box before the exclamation point. Most "spaces" are not all that large—some designers use the width of the capital I to set them! A width of 10 to 20 percent of the em-square should work fine; in other words, if the em-square is 1,000 units (the total of the Ascent and Descent) then the space character should be between 100 and 200 units wide.

The best way for a beginner to space a font is to use the Auto Space command in the Metrics menu. Bad spacing is the easiest way to ruin a font, and Fontographer's Auto Space feature works very well. To begin, try the default setting of 50, then print out some samples to see if you like the spacing. If it doesn't look great, re-run Auto Space at different values. After you fix the letterspacing, you should run Auto Kern. Auto Kern automatically creates the majority of kerning pairs in your font. 500 to 1,000 kerning pairs is considered normal.

When these base values are set, it is easy for you to manually adjust problem pairs yourself. Open the Metrics window and type various letter combinations. If you see any problem, click on the right-hand letter of the bad pair. A vertical line with a K on top appears. Simply move the letter right or left until the custom space for the letter pair looks good visually. Many professional typographers use more than 1,000 kerning pairs. You need to decide how many are necessary for the usage you intend.

Generating Your New Font

When everything is set the way you like it, it's time to generate your font. When you save your font, Fontographer writes a Fontographer database and places a .fog extension on the file. This database contains all the data necessary to generate files for any font format, including PostScript, TrueType for either PC or Mac, UNIX fonts, and others. For example, to create a Mac PostScript Type 1 font, Fontographer generates the screen font (in its suitcase) and the printer font. On a PC, PostScript Type 1 requires a PFB file and a PFM file, which Fontographer generates automatically.

Figure 7.12

The Generate Font Files panel.

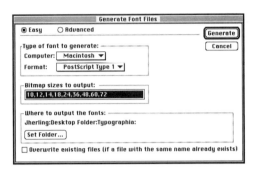

Fontographer lets you create a PC-compatible version of your font as easily as a Macintosh version. You can now easily port a font from your home Mac to your office PC. You must first decide, however, if you should generate a PostScript Type 1 or TrueType version of the font. If your font will be part of a professional printing setup, you will need to create PostScript Type 1 fonts. For home or secretarial office work on a laser printer, TrueType fonts work well.

PostScript is, at heart, a printer code, but it contains the same Bézier control information that Fontographer contains, so none of the information in your font is lost. PostScript also offers a wider level of detail and a dynamic character hinting mechanism. PostScript fonts need a PostScript driver to work, though, and you will need to generate at least one bitmap (on the Mac) so that the font can be displayed on-screen correctly. Adobe Type Manger can generate all the custom screen bitmaps from one font. All professional printers and any professional laser printer (1200dpi and above) work much better with PostScript. In fact, TrueType can often choke top-end PostScript imagesetters.

TrueType uses a proprietary method of generating curves in characters. The quadratic equations it uses have several advantages, but top-end machines do not handle them well. However, this typeface format is widely used on Windows machines and as a printer code and a display code, eliminating the need for on-screen bitmaps.

Hinting

Hinting is an option found in the File menu's Generate Font Files dialog box. Hinting modifies small font bitmaps (under 10 points or so) to make them more legible on-screen. The coarseness of a monitor's resolution can chew up normal bitmaps so much that they are completely illegible. Hinting changes these bitmaps radically, so much so that often the hinted screen image will no longer look like a specific font, but will still be readable. If you are curious about hinting, the Fontographer User's Guide has excellent illustrations.

PostScript Type 1 and TrueType Fonts can create hinting (TrueType's hinting is a little more powerful). Fontographer's recommendation is to always turn hinting on and avoid manually constructing your own hinting. Hinting requires a great deal of programming knowledge plus the ability to understand the PostScript page description language.

Some Final Comments

Creating fonts is considered by many to be the highest form of graphic design. To create a font of the same caliber as Garamond, Helvetica, or Gill Sans requires more skill, experience, and time than you might think.

However, Fontographer will let you customize fonts that you use daily in a matter of a few fun-filled hours. The interface is so similar to FreeHand that working in Fontographer comes naturally to anyone with FreeHand skills.

Your new fonts will work well on your computer and with your printer, and they can be installed like any other font. However, problems could develop when you use the font in documents that need to go to a service bureau or printing company. These firms will need a copy of your font. As a result, you need to make sure that your changes, additions, and modifications are part of a renamed font that you can legally call your own.

Keep in mind that it is illegal to simply open a font and rename it. Although it is true that a type style cannot be copyrighted, the software that describes that style can and is copyrighted. Scanning a printed version of a font will usually introduce enough changes to allow you to make a font your own. It is not ethical to create a renamed scanned copy, but font companies do it all the time. To keep everything legal and ethical, make sure you work with your own scans and scanned paths. In addition, draw your own shapes and use a unique name for your font. Do not simply steal someone else's creativity.

The easiest and best way to use Fontographer is often to make your own dingbat font containing logos, drawings, and various special shapes that you use all the time. If you print out a character map, this type of symbol font will be extremely handy. If you want to create a professional font, however, Fontographer is arguably the best font creation software on earth.

Part III

Extreme 3D

Extreme 3D provides three-dimensional modeling, animation and rendering capabilities formerly available only in complex modeling applications. Extreme 3D is a full-featured modeling and animation program that allows you to create high-quality renderings without a lofty price tag. The application uses an intuitive interface that makes the creation of complex models as easy as working in FreeHand.

Extreme 3D includes spline-based, CAD-accurate modeling and time- and frame-based animation. With a click of the mouse, you can import files from all the other products in the studio and create complex models and animation. Extreme 3D also lets you create three-dimensional renderings from two-dimensional FreeHand and xRres art, and even from Fontographer font families.

Extreme 3D Basics

*E*xtreme 3D is a three-dimensional modeling, animation, and rendering application that provides all the tools and options necessary for professional level production work. Extreme 3D works like many of the other 3D packages, but also includes unique features such as the Twist tool and native FreeHand file import capability.

Extreme 3D ties in well with the other products in the Macromedia line because it can import and export files from and to applications easily. If you have used other 3D products in the past, you should find the workspace and user interface familiar. If you have not used a 3D application, you will need to learn how to navigate through a 3D environment.

To orient yourself in the 3D world of Extreme 3D, you need to understand its new surroundings and the tools you use to move around. With practice, orientation in a 3D world is fairly simple. Think of the views you see in the workspace as windows you can use to look into the scene from various perspectives.

The Major Components of Extreme 3D

Three integrated components make Extreme 3D a professional-level modeling application: spline-based modeling, time and frame-based animation, and production-quality rendering. Each component gives Extreme 3D a powerful set of features that allows users to produce production level results easily and quickly.

Spline-Based Modeling

Extreme 3D uses a spline-based modeler, enabling you to edit surfaces as curves by moving their control points, just as you can modify shapes in FreeHand. By using the modeling tools within Extreme 3D, you can create complex shapes with relative ease.

Extreme has a high degree of precision (accurate up to 15 decimal places.) With this degree of accuracy, Extreme 3D performs much like more expensive modeling programs. Trimming, point-level surface editing, and deformation tools (twist, bend, taper, non-uniform scale, and skew) are easy to use when you know the basics of the application. By using some of the other 3D functions, such as linking, pre-set primitives, and interactive texture maps, you can create highly complex and realistic scenes.

Time and Frame-Based Animation

Extreme 3D's animation score is time- and frame-based. A frame is an individual still image in an animation. The point in time in an animation where a change starts or ends is called a keyframe. You determine how the scene starts and how the scene ends and the computer will fill in the frames between the keyframes.

In Extreme 3D, each property that can be edited—from the shape of a model to its surface material to its location—can be animated. Using the deformation tools, you can have an object change its shape and size over time.

By using watch linking, you can have an object, light, or camera follow (or track) another object throughout the animation score. This gives you more control in maintaining the center of attention.

Extreme 3D's modeling capabilities feature advanced data filtering (you determine what objects and tracks you want to see), visual feedback, and interactive keyframe manipulation. When previewing animations, you can choose from using the current render style for realistic visualization or use the bounding box render style for quicker real-time performance.

Production-Quality Rendering

An important feature of any 3D application is how well it renders the scenes you create using the models you make. To make a scene more realistic, Extreme 3D permits you to add a variety of lights and shadows, fog, and a mixture of surface materials. The time it takes for a final render is determined by what objects and properties are needed to be shown in the scene or animation. The computer will take more time to create a believable image depending on the rendering mode selected and how many objects are in a scene.

Rendering is the process by which the computer creates a view of a scene you have constructed using models, textures, and lights. Prior to rendering, you build a scene with objects and other simplified elements on-screen. To achieve the most realistic look of these objects, you later have to have the computer create a final rendering.

You can change the mood of a scene by adding fog or creating turbulence. You can map images to objects' surfaces or use the basic material shaders. Material shaders allow you to change the texture and look of the surface of an object. By using the basic material shaders, you can create an infinite number of materials. This also helps to reduce memory requirements associated with more complex texture maps.

In addition to efficient material shaders, this program also provides sophisticated texture mapping tools that can be used to create original materials from bitmapped images imported from other applications. For example, you can apply a texture map of a label created in FreeHand to a three-dimensional can created in Extreme 3D.

One of the greatest features of Extreme 3D is its distributed rendering system. Rendering is one of the most time consuming parts of working in 3D. With distributed rendering, you can spread a rendering process across multiple computers if you work in a networked environment. This environment can include both Macintosh and Windows computers.

Extreme 3D can render images up to 8192 by 8192 pixels (the PICT file format on the Macintosh limits the maximum resolution to 4090 by 4090 pixels). At this resolution, Extreme 3D can produce art suitable for professional high-resolution output to print or video.

Extreme 3D's renderer also supports other high-end features such as visible spotlights, including cone lighting.

The Workspace

Extreme 3D creates a world to work in, similar to what a 2D application might refer to as a document or page. The world is the space in which you create 3D models or animations. Within this world, you can navigate by choosing preset views, or by creating custom views. When you open a new file, you are presented with the Workspace—the area visible through the project window.

The 3D world in Extreme 3D is practically boundless, and objects can exist in your world that do not show up in your Workspace. Imagine looking through the window of a house. As you look into the house you can see almost all the objects in one of the rooms but you are unable to see into other rooms in the house, or even the other sides of the objects in the room. This limitation is the same for Extreme 3D: you may not be able to see all the objects that exist in a scene. You can, however, change your view of the world so that you can see other objects that may be hidden from your viewpoint. If you look out the front window in your home, objects in your backyard would not be visible. However, you could move to a position where you can look out the back window. By doing this you have changed your viewpoint and therefore changed what is visible to you.

The Views

In the Workspace you have several ways in which you can view a scene. Different views affect distance, position, and angle. These views show you new perspectives in projects, especially animated projects. Different views of animated scenes enable you to move around the subject or follow it from the viewpoint of other objects, as the camera does.

When viewing items in a 3D world, you need to be aware of the various distances between objects, the camera's distance from the objects, and the orientation of all the objects in the scene relative to your position. When you change your orientation, the relative position of objects to one another does not change, only your orientation to those objects.

Extreme 3D has a collection of preset views and the capability to customize views to user-defined settings. The available views are Front, Back, Left, Right, Top, Bottom, Three-Quarters, and Home. The first six provide a direct look at the Workspace from the direction named. The Home view is the default view in Extreme 3D: choose Home from the View menu to return the view to this default. The Three-quarter view is a view tilted downward from the upper left. Figures 8.1, 8.2, and 8.3 show the Three-quarters view compared to Front and Right views in Extreme 3D.

To change views in Extreme 3D, simply select the view you wish to jump to from the View menu. You can also use keyboard shortcuts to jump between multiple views quickly and easily.

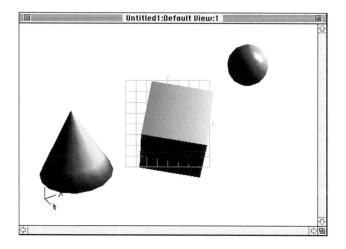

Figure 8.1

Three-quarters view.

Figure 8.2

Front view.

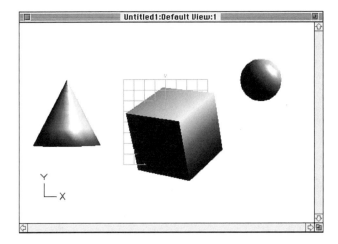

Figure 8.3

Right view.

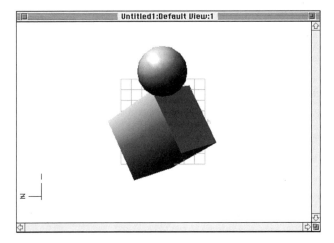

Custom Views

Creating custom views enables you to change your viewpoint with accurate and predictable results. Custom views can save time and effort when you are working on animations, especially when you repeatedly need to return to a specific angle or position.

One way of changing a view is to enter in values directly. Within the Views window, you can set the position, orientation, and scale of a custom view. This will allow you to control the distance to the object, perspective, and other parameters.

CREATING A NEW VIEW

1. Choose Views from the Windows menu. This will open the Views browser.

2. Choose New View from the View menu. The default name will be "Untitled View."

3. With the view selected in the Views browser window, type the new name "out front looking down" and press Enter or Return.

4. For a view that is out front and looking down, enter -60 for the X orientation, 10 for Y position, and 20 for the Z position.

Another way to change a view is to use the Hand tool. The Hand tool enables you to move your view up and down, and left and right. By using modifer keys, which are listed as follows, you can change the rotation and the scaling.

■ Command (Mac), F4(PC)—Press this modifier key while dragging in the Workspace to rotate the view around the x and y screen axes relative to the tool's preferences (the look-at point is the default). Drag up and down to roll the view away or toward you. Drag left and right to rotate the view to the left or right.

■ Option (Mac), F3(PC)—Press this modifier key while dragging in the Workspace to rotate the view around the y and z screen axes relative to the tool's preferences (the look-at point is the default). Drag up and down to rotate the view clockwise and counterclockwise. Drag left and right to rotate the view to the left or right.

■ Control (Mac), F2(PC)—Press this modifier key while dragging in the Workspace to resize the view relative to the tool's preferences (the look-at point is the default). Drag up and down to rotate the view clockwise and counterclockwise. Drag left and right to rotate the view to the left or right.

Using a View from Another Extreme 3D File

You may have created a stock view that you use in most of your production projects. In some cases you may need to re-create this view in a different Extreme 3D project. By using a stock view, you can re-create the same vantage point in new files without disturbing the original file from which you've taken the view. This can save you time when creating several renderings from the same viewpoint. You create the view in one file and then copy it to the new files as it is needed.

COPYING VIEWS

1. Open the file that contains the view you would like to transfer. Make sure that the Views browser window is open.

2. Select the view you would like to copy from the views list and choose Copy from the Edit menu.

3. From the Scenes pop-up in the Windows menu, select the name of the file into which you will paste the view.

4. Click inside the Views list of the Views browser and choose Paste from the Edit menu.

The Elements of a View

Three elements make up the view that you see in a 3D world: the eye point, the look-at point, and the view distance. Each of these items affect the position and orientation of what you seee when creating a 3D model or animation.

The eye point

The eye point is your viewing position and orientation in the Extreme 3D world. Imagine that the book you are reading right now is your three dimensional scene. The point at which your view begins—your eyes—is the eye point. This is simply the point from which you are looking at the objects in your 3D scene. Figure 8.4 gives an example of the eye point.

Figure 8.4

The eye point.

eye point

The look-at point

The look-at point is the focus or center of the view (see Figure 8.5). The exact point where your eyes are focused on this book or the object in the view is considered the look-at point.

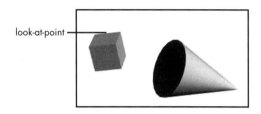

Figure 8.5

The look-at point.

The view distance

The View Distance refers to the distance between the eye point and the look-at point (see Figure 8.6). How far your eye is from the point that you are looking at in this book is called the view distance.

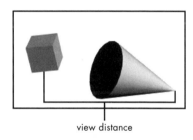

Figure 8.6

The view distance.

Perspective

In real life, objects that are father away appear smaller than actual size. In trying to accurately imitate the 3D world, Extreme 3D allows you to change the perspective.

When using the settings for perspective in Extreme 3D, the size of the objects in your scene will change as the distance to them increases or decreases. When you change the perspective of a scene, the scale, orientation, and position of objects in the scene remain the same. These changes enable you to create a variety of realistic effects.

The concept of using the view settings in three dimensions is often hard to explain, but is easy to illustrate. Figures 8.7 through 8.10 show you a single object as it appears in four of the standard views.

WORKING WITH VIEWS

1. Create a new scene and add three objects.

2. From the View menu, choose Perspective and Very Wide. Notice how distorted the scene becomes. Objects that are farthest away become much smaller. This is similar to photos that are taken with a wide angle lens.

3. From the View menu, choose Perspective and Orthographic. With this perspective, no matter how far away an object is, it is shown as the same size.

Figure 8.7

View Narrow PICT.

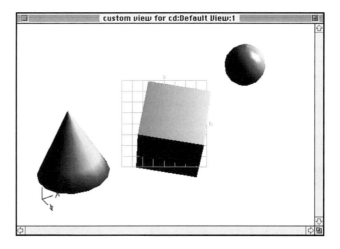

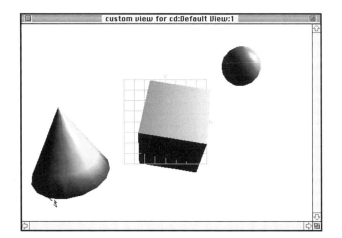

Figure 8.8

View Moderate PICT.

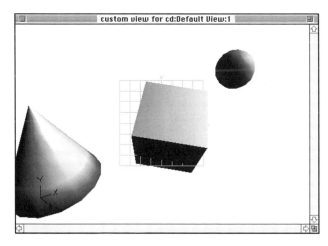

Figure 8.9

View Wide PICT.

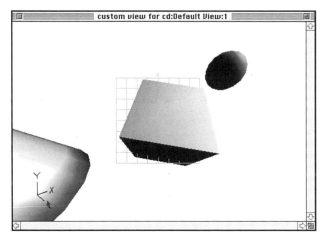

Figure 8.10

View Very Wide PICT.

Orienting Yourself in Extreme 3D

Most graphic applications have two dimensions: height and width. A 3D application also has depth. Each of these dimensions is expressed as coordinates on an axis. The axis for height is x, width is y, and depth is z. Figures 8.11 and 8.12 show a visual representation of the x, y, and z axes in two and three dimensions. The z axes only appears in three dimensions.

Figure 8.11

Axes in a two-dimensional grid.

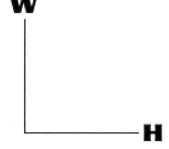

Figure 8.12

Axes in a three-dimensional grid.

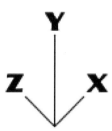

One of the most confusing ideas related to orientation can be the point from which you started moving your objects. If you customize your view and then forget to save that viewpoint or the orientation of the objects to be used as starting points, you may have a hard time finding the viewpoint again.

To help keep track of position and bearing, Extreme 3D has a few tools that move objects for you and also provide feedback on the position of objects you move. Visible grids represent the working plane and the ground plane, and the heads-up axis and object axis provide information about the orientation of objects.

The Working Plane

The working plane is a visible grid that extends out infinitely in the 3D world. When you create a new scene, the working grid is a flat-on view—similar to the 2D world of FreeHand. Any drawing that you create in Extreme 3D will be parallel to the working plane; any objects you move are moved parallel to the working plane. Figure 8.13 shows the grid as it appears in a default project window. The default placement for the grid is the center of the three-dimensional world (0,0,0).

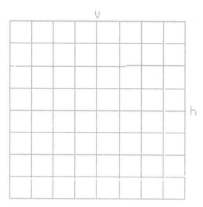

Figure 8.13

The working plane.

Turning the working plane on and off

To turn the working plane on and off, choose Show Working Plane from the Object menu. This will put a checkmark next to this item in the Object menu, which indicates that it can be seen. The author recommends keeping the working plane on while you modify or reposition objects because the plane provides instant visual feedback. The working plane will always stay in the default position unless you modify it. This makes it a valuable reference point if you have made several changes to the orientation of your view.

Positioning the working plane

In some instances, moving the working plane might be necessary. You can move the working plane by clicking and moving it as if it were any other object in the scene. Another way to move the working plane is to select it and then use the arrow keys to nudge the working plane up, down, right, and left in small, preset increments.

209

Moving the working plane enables you to have a helpful reference point for your scene. One way this capability can come in handy is if you want to place an object on a kitchen countertop. You could move the working plane parallel to a countertop within your scene so that object can then be placed or moved in reference to the countertop.

 Tip

If the working plane needs to be nudged (repositioned) more than a few taps of the arrow key, drag it close to the desired position and then use the arrow keys to position it more precisely.

Orienting the working plane

The default position for the working plane is parallel to the screen. Occasionally you may need to adjust its orientation. Press and hold down the Option or Command key (for Macintosh), or the F3 or F4 key (for Windows) while dragging the cursor away from the working plane. (Figure 8.14 shows the working plane halfway through a move.) The orientation of the working plane should be adjusted if you need to build your 3D scene from a different viewpoint. Using the working plane in this manner will enable you to reference a static point in your custom view.

Figure 8.14

The working plane while moving.

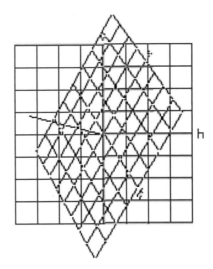

The Ground Plane

Unlike the working plane, the ground plane is not moveable; it is the floor of your 3D world. The ground plane will always be positioned in your scene at the 0 coordinate of each axis—the center of your 3D world. Figure 8.15 shows the ground plane in the project window. The ground plane can be toggled on and off by choosing Show Ground Plane from the Objects menu.

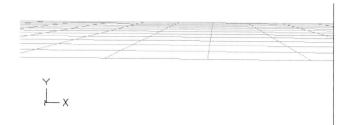

Figure 8.15

The ground plane.

The Heads-Up Axis

The heads-up orientation axis shows you the orientation of the current view in Extreme 3D's three-dimensional world. The direction of each of the world coordinates are represented by the corresponding letter names: x, y, and z. Figure 8.16 shows the heads-up orientation axis in the project window.

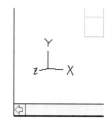

Figure 8.16

The heads-up orientation axis.

The Object Axis

Every object that you create in Extreme 3D can display its own object axis (see Figure 8.17). This axis is useful when determining watch links, where one object tracks (or watches) another object. The object axis also shows you an object's position and orientation. When an object or objects is selected, you can see the object axis for each of the objects. By viewing the object axis you can quickly determine if an object is rightside up, or upside-down, along with the orientation of its other axis points. When you select more than one object, you can see the axes for all the objects.

Figure 8.17

The object axis.

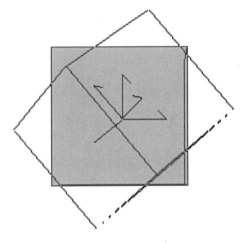

The Status Bar and Tool Space

The Status Bar at the bottom of the screen provides information about Extreme 3D tools, menu items, and controls, along with information about how to use each of these items. When the cursor is over a tool, the Status Bar displays the name of the tool. If a tool is selected and the cursor is in the Workspace, the Status Bar tells you how to use the tool. Whenever several steps are required to use a tool, the Status Bar displays each step in order. When a step is completed, the next instruction displays. The Show Status Bar menu item in the Window menu toggles the Status Bar on or off.

The Tool Space is the area just above the Status Bar (see Figure 8.18); Extreme 3D provides numerical feedback regarding what the tool is doing or lists information that it needs to complete a task. You can also enter in this Tool Space area specific dimensions for objects when you have a tool selected. For example, if the Rectangle tool is selected, you can enter the height and width of the rectangle into the Tool Space, rather than drag across the Workspace to define a rectangle. To be able to enter values in the Tool Space, press the Tab key.

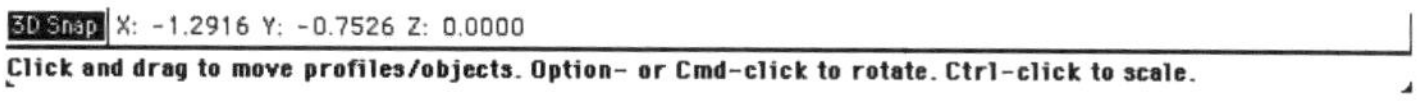

```
3D Snap  X: -1.2916 Y: -0.7526 Z: 0.0000
Click and drag to move profiles/objects. Option- or Cmd-click to rotate. Ctrl-click to scale.
```

Figure 8.18

The Status Bar and Tool Space.

The Toolbox

The Toolbox is the most important window in Extreme 3D. From here you select tools to make primitive 3D models, create text, edit geometry, or create simple 2D primitives. The Toolbox is broken into four sections: tools for moving and editing, tools for drawing, tools for modifying, and the 3D geometry tools.

To use these tools effectively, keep in mind these tips:

- Double-click on any tool that has a white notch in the lower left corner to change its preferences.

- After you use a tool, the default tool is automatically selected. When you first start Extreme 3D, the Arrow tool is the default tool. To change the default tool, press and hold down the Option key (Mac) or F3 key (PC) when selecting a tool. If you have to draw a number of boxes, you can make the Box tool the default, then draw your boxes; afterward, you can re-assign the Arrow tool as the default.

- A black notch in the lower right of a tool icon indicates that the tool is part of a tool group. To see all the tools in that tool group, click and hold on the tool. The tool group will expand over the current tool.

- When you use a tool, watch the Tool Space (the informative display at the bottom of the screen). The Tool Space instructs you on what to do next. If you need to enter exact values, you can click in the Tool Space or press the Tab key.

The Center-Corner Toggle

At the bottom of the Tool palette is the center-corner toggle. This toggle changes the operation of several tools in the palette. The toggle operates in two ways: when the toggle is set to center, the first point establishes the center; dragging the cursor sizes the object about that center. When the toggle is set to corner, the first point is locked down, and dragging the cursor sizes the object's bounds from corner to corner.

213

Moving and Editing Tools

The tools in the first section of the toolbar are used more often than any other tools while working in Extreme 3D. This section includes the Arrow, Hand and Rotation tools, Rotate Point, Zoom, Working Plane, Construction Point, Construction Line, Construction Axis, and Construction Grid tools. These tools perform a variety of functions (use Figure 8.19 as a reference).

Figure 8.19

Tools for moving and editing.

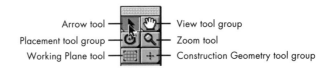

Arrow tool

The Arrow tool is used to select, open, close, edit, and move objects. To select multiple objects, press and hold down the Shift key while using the Arrow tool. To select a profile object, click on its outline. You can also select multiple objects by drawing a marquee around the objects (a visible red bounding box).

Hand and Rotation tool group

What appears to be the Hand tool in Figure 8.19 is actually a tool group that consists of the Hand and Rotation tools (see Figure 8.20). These tools are used to set the position and orientation of the current view. When the current view is set properly, you can move around the scene and see it from any position in the three-dimensional world. Note that all of the tools in this group display the hand cursor.

Figure 8.20

The Hand and Rotation tool group.

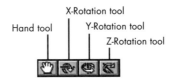

Placement tool group

The Placement tool group consists of the Rotate Point tool, the Rotate Axis tool, and the Placement tool. These tools enable you to rotate and place objects with almost surgical precision. Figure 8.21 shows this tool group.

Rotate Point tool ———— Placement tool

Rotate Axis tool

Figure 8.21

The Placement tool group.

The Zoom tool

The Zoom tool enables you to zoom in or out of the current view by changing the scale of the view. Press and hold down the Option key on the Mac or the F3 key on the PC to zoom out with this tool.

 Tip

To zoom in on a particular area of the scene, drag a rectangle around the area you want to see more closely.

Working Plane tool

The Working Plane tool is used to change the working plane's orientation in a scene. This operation requires a few steps.

1. If the Working Plane does not already show in the scene, make it visible by choosing Show Working Plane from the Object menu.

2. Select the Working Plane tool and click once in the current scene to define the center of the working plane.

3. Define the x axis (the horizontal direction) of the Working Plane by clicking a second time inside the scene.

4. Define the y axis (vertical direction) of the Working Plane by clicking a third time in the scene, and on a point included in the plane.

The Working Plane can also be aligned to an object in the current scene. To align the working plane to an object press and hold down the letter O (not the number zero) then click on the object that will align with the Working Plane.

Construction Geometry tool group

Construction geometry provides visual references to help you create objects, just like scaffolding on a building that is under construction. These visual references can be useful in your scene. A tool group is included that controls the four types of construction geometry: Construction Point, Construction Line, Construction Axis, and Construction Grid (see Figure 8.22).

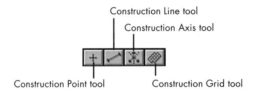

Construction Line tool
Construction Axis tool
Construction Point tool
Construction Grid tool

Drawing Tools

The second section of the toolbar includes the Text, Polyline, Line, Spline, Center Arc, Regular Polygon, Rectangle, and Circle tools. Figure 8.23 shows these drawing tools.

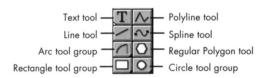

Text tool — Polyline tool
Line tool — Spline tool
Arc tool group — Regular Polygon tool
Rectangle tool group — Circle tool group

Text tool

This tool creates profiles of the invidual letters of entered text. The profiles can then be extruded to form 3D objects. Extreme 3D extracts TrueType and Adobe Type 1 font outlines. There is a limitation however: the maximum number of characters you can type is 63 at a time. To add the profiles of a character or line of text:

1. Select the Text tool and click in the Workspace where you want to place the lower left corner of the first character.

2. Type the text in the Tool Space. Press Enter when you finish.

After letters have been created in the current scene, you can edit their outlines just like any other spline or polyline object in Extreme 3D. To do this, select the first character—you can now move or manipulate the entire line of text.

All the subsequent characters are linked to the first character. If you move the first character, the whole line will move. You can also select characters as individual objects. To do this, use the Unlink tool to unlink a single character from the rest of the text.

If you make a typo, you have to reenter the entire line of text because the text is converted to outlines.

Polyline tool

A polyline in Extreme 3D is a line that has more than two points. Polylines can be used alone or combined with other profiles to create complex models or to create open or closed polygons.

To draw a polyline, select the Polyline tool and click to define its points. Double-click to complete the polyline. To create a closed polyline shape, complete the object by double-clicking on the start point.

Line tool

The Line tool draws a line on the current working plane. When you use this tool or the Polyline tool, you can press the H key to constrain the line horizontally; press and hold the V key to constrain the line vertically.

Spline tool

This tool creates open or closed splines on the working plane. A spline curve is really a Bézier curve and is one of the most often-used items during the creation of a three-dimensional scene. The spline curve shown in Figure 8.24 can be extruded, lathed, or have any other effect applied to it to create a 3D form.

Figure 8.24

Spline curve at work.

Drawing splines is like drawing Bézier curves in FreeHand: click on the Spline tool to add control points along the path; you can then drag out handles to control the angle and height of the spline curve. These handles can be edited as you are drawing the spline curve or later.

USING THE SPLINE TOOL

1. Select the Spline tool and click in the Workspace to create a starting point for the curve.

2. Click once at each spot where you would like to create an additional control point.

3. Double-click to define the end point and complete the curve.

If you want to create a spline curve that has a sharp corner in it, press and hold down the F3 key (for Windows) or the Option key (for Macintosh) as you drag out the handle.

Arc tool group

The Arc tool group consists of the Center Arc tool and the Tangent Arc tool (see Figure 8.25). Use these tools to create curved line segments on the current working plane. Use these objects as part of a profile or as a basis for 3D objects.

 Figure 8.25

The Arc tool group.

Center Arc tool Tangent Arc tool

The Center Arc tool draws a profile arc. You first set the center for the arc. The second point sets the radius and starting point; clicking on a third point sets the ending point of the arc.

The Tangent Arc tool draws a profile arc by specifying a line to which it is tangent. You set the first point of the line and arc. The second point sets the ending point of the line; clicking on a third point sets the ending point of the arc.

Regular Polygon tool

This tool can be used to create regular polygons, which is a profile of three or more sides, all of which are equal in length. To create a polygon:

1. Select the Polygon tool and click to define the object's center.

2. Set the number of sides by entering a value in the Tool Space.

3. Drag away from the center to define the radius and object's perimeter.

Rectangle tool group

The Rectangle tool group consists of the Rectangle tool and the Square tool, which allow you to create rectangular and square profiles.

Circle tool group

The Circle tool group consists of the Circle and Ellipse tools. Use these tools to create 2D circles or ellipses that can be extruded to build 3D objects.

Modifying Tools

The Materials Application tool group includes Texture Map, Mirror, Profile Modifier, Control Point, Surface Modifier, Unlink, and Link tools. Figure 8.26 shows these tools.

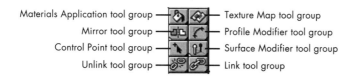

Materials Application tool group — Texture Map tool group
Mirror tool group — Profile Modifier tool group
Control Point tool group — Surface Modifier tool group
Unlink tool group — Link tool group

Figure 8.26

The modifying tools.

Materials Application tool group

The Materials Application tool group consists of the Bucket tool and the Eyedropper tool (see Figure 8.27). The Bucket tool applies the currently selected material to a 3D object; the Eyedropper tool selects a material from an object. Selecting a material from an object will make it the current material in the Materials browser window.

Paint Bucket tool — — Eyedropper tool

The Texture Map tool group

The Texture Map tool group consists of the Intrinsic, Cylindrical, Spherical, and Projective texture placement tools, and the Material Orientation tool (see Figure 8.28). These tools are used to define how a texture map is placed on an object. When these tools are used in combination with the tool space, you can alter the position and the scale of the texture maps.

Figure 8.28

The Texture placement tool group.

Intrinsic   Cylindrical

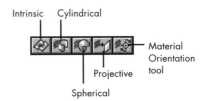

Material Orientation tool

Projective

Spherical

The Texture Map tools are used in conjunction with the Mapping Type found in the Info page of the Objects browser. The Mapping type sets the way that the mapping is applied to an object. Intrinsic mapping is also known as rubber sheet mapping: the map is stretched to map around the object. Projective mapping projects the texture map onto the surface of the object, like a slide projected onto a person standing in front of the slide projector screen.

Mirror tool group

The Mirror tool group consists of the 2D and 3D Mirror tools, which can be used to create mirror images of profiles and 3D objects. You can create mirror images by duplicating the object or flipping it across a mirroring plane.

The Offset tool included in this group (see Figure 8.29) is used when you need to create a duplicate copy of a profile that must be in a different position from the exact mirror position of the original.

Figure 8.29

The Mirror tool group.

3D Mirror tool

2D Mirror tool —  — Offset tool

To use the tools in this group, follow these steps:

USING THE 2D MIRROR TOOL

1. Using the Spline tool, create half of a heart shape.

2. With the outline selected, select the 2D Mirror tool.

3. Click on the first point of the heart outline.

4. Click on the last point of the heart outline. This defines the axis on which you mirror the outline. At this point, you may want to select both halves, then choose Objects, Join Profiles.

Profile Modifier tool group

The Profile Modifier tool group consists of the Fillet tool and the 2D Trim tool. The Fillet tool rounds the corners on profiles. The 2D Trim tool enables you to cut away parts of profiles.

USING THE 2D TRIM TOOL

1. Use the Circle tool to create a circle.

2. Select the 2D Trim tool.

3. Click on the first point on the outline of the circle that will be the start of the trim operation.

4. Click on the end point on the outline of the circle that will be the end of the trim operation.

5. Now click on the section of the outline that you want to trim.

Control Point tool group

The Control Point tool group consists of the Control Point tool and the Move Object Center tool. The Control Point tool allows you to add and remove control points on open and closed profiles as well as simplified 3D geometry. The Move Object Center tool allows you to move the object center on profiles and 3D geometry.

Moving an Object's Center

1. Double-click an object to open its geometry.

2. Select the Move Object Center tool.

3. Click the object and drag to set the new location for the center point.

Surface Modifier tool group

The Surface Modifier tool group consists of the Projection, 3D Trim, and Intersection tools. The Projection tool can be used to project an image of a profile onto a 3D object and mark it with trim curves. The Intersection tool is used to mark the intersection of two pieces of geometry with trim curves. The trim curves are just outline mapped to the side of an object.

The 3D Trim tool enables you to cut away pieces of 3D geometry that have been marked with trim curves. You click inside the trim curve to delete the surface contained by the curve. If you click outside the curve it leaves only the surface contained inside the trim curve. Figure 8.30 shows each of these tools.

Figure 8.30

The Surface Modifier tool group.

Projection tool ⎯⎯ 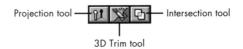 ⎯⎯ Intersection tool

3D Trim tool

Link and Unlink tool groups

The Free Link, Lock Link, Ball-joint Link, and Watch link tools let you create and edit hierarchical relationships among objects. By linking individual objects together, you can simulate complex mechanical and biological movement.

When you link two objects together, one object becomes the parent and the other becomes the child. The child object moves the same way as the parent object. Extreme 3D has four types of links:

■ Free link: The child moves and rotates independently of the parent, resulting in the parent dragging the child along with it when it moves. When the parent rotates, the child rotates around the center point of the parent.

- Lock link: The child cannot rotate independently of the parent. With this link the child will always rotate around the parent's center point. The child moves when the parent moves and vice-versa; however, neither can move independently of the other.

- Ball-joint link: The child can rotate but not move independently of the parent. When the parent rotates, the child will rotate with it around the center point of the parent.

- Watch link: The z axis of the child object stays oriented to and "watches" the center of the parent object. When the parent moves, the child will rotate to orient its z axis to the parent object's new position. Both the parent and the child can move independently of each other.

An object can have a watch link and a hierarchical link. Each object's link constraints can be modified in the Objects browser.

The Unlink tool group consists of the Unlink and Reparent tools. The Unlink tool breaks existing links. The Reparent tool moves an object up one level in the link hierarchy.

To examine the hierarchy of the objects in a scene, open the World browser by selecting World from the Windows menu. Double-click on objects in the World browser to display a list of objects contained within the scene. Double-clicking on the name of an object in the list shows all the child objects associated with it.

3D Geometry Tools

The 3D geometry tool section of the Toolbox contains the Extrude and 3D Primitive tool groups, the Sweep and Lathe tools, and the Deformation and Skin tool groups.

Extrude tool group — 3D Primitives tool group
Sweep tool — Lathe tool
Deformation tool group — Skin tool

Figure 8.31

The 3D geometry tools.

Extrude tool group

The Extrude and Bevel Extrude tools enable users to pull profiles along an extrude depth line to create 3D objects. For example, these tools can be used to turn circles into cylinders and squares into cubes. Bevel Extrude can also be used to create professional-looking three-dimensional type. Try the following exercise to gain a better understanding of Bevel Extrude's functions.

EXTRUDING TYPE

1. In a new project window, double-click on the Text tool. This will open the dialog box shown.

2. Choose the font and size (in inches) and click OK. The type is converted to outlines and it is free-linked to the first character you entered.

3. With the text outlines selected, choose the Extrude tool.

4. Click the screen and drag out a line to the length you want the type to be extruded.

 Tip

When extruding multiple outlines such as type, it is best to lock link the objects together so that you can move them as a group. With all the extruded objects selected, click on the Lock Link tool and then click on the first character or object. When an object is selected and moved, all the other objects move along with it as a group.

224

3D Primitives tool group

The 3D Primitives tools draw basic 3D objects such as cubes, spheres, and cones (see their icons in Figure 8.31).

Cone tool —— Cube tool

Sphere tool

Figure 8.32

The 3D Primitives tool group.

Sweep tool

Sweep pulls a profile along a path to create a 3D swept object. For example, sweeping a circle along a line produces a cylinder. You can do the same thing with the Extrude tool, but sweeping a circle along a spline curve will create a segment of curved tubing similar to a bent pipe.

USING THE SWEEP TOOL

1. Select the Circle tool and draw a circle.

2. Using the Polyline tool, draw a simple zig-zag shape.

3. Select the circle outline. This will be the profile or cross section of the sweep path.

4. Select the zig-zag outline. The sweeped object is instantly created.

Lathe tool

Lathe rotates a profile around a defined axis to create a 3D object.

USING THE LATHE TOOL

1. In a new project window select the Circle tool and draw a circle in the project window.

2. With the circle selected, choose the Lathe tool. Click and draw a short line to the left of the circle (see the figure). This determines the axis around which the circle will be lathed. The result is a 3D donut shape.

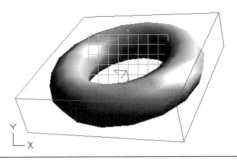

Deformation tool group

The Twist, Bend, Taper, Stretch, and Skew tools deform objects over a defined range (see their icons in Figure 8.33).

Figure 8.33

The Deformation tool group.

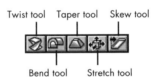

Before you deform any 3D object, its surface geometry must be simplified. When you select an object that needs to be simplified before it is used with any of the deformation tools, a dialog box appear that asks whether you want to simplify the object or deselect it. You cannot deform an object without simplifying it.

When you animate deformations, make sure the current time in the score is set to zero. If you don't want deformation changes to appear in the animation, make sure the animation toggle is off.

By double-clicking on any of the deformation tools, you can access its Preferences panel. Here you can change the axis along which the deformation occurs.

USING THE DEFORMATION TOOL

1. Access the Cube tool and add a cube to the scene.

2. Select the Twist tool and double-click it to access its Preferences. Set the preferences to deform along the object's Z axis.

3. With the cube selected, click above it and drag down to twist the object. Dragging up will twist the object in the opposite direction.

Skin tool group

The Skin tool stretches a surface between two or more profiles in a scene. The Cross-section tool stretches one profile along the shape of a second profile.

USING THE SKIN TOOL

1. Access the Circle tool and draw a circle on the left side of the screen.

2. Open the Objects window by choosing Objects from the Windows menu.

3. Under the Y axis orientation, enter a value 90. This will rotate the object 90° along the y axis.

4. Use the Rectangle tool to draw a tall skinny rectangle on the right side of the screen.

5. In the Object browser under the Y axis orientation, again enter a value of 90. This will rotate the rectangle parallel to the circle.

6. Select the Skin tool.

7. Select the circle and the rectangle outlines.

8. Press Enter or Return to skin a shape between the outlines.

Chapter 9

Customizing Materials in Extreme 3D

*T*his chapter covers advanced techniques possible in Extreme 3D, such as customizing materials, creating material effects, creating lighting effects, and animating your scene.

The Materials Editor

The settings for materials in Extreme 3D often determine the difference between amateur and professional work. Combining these attributes will create stellar effects that give renderings a professional appearance. To begin, select Materials from the Window menu to open the Materials browser (see Figure 9.1).

Figure 9.1

The Materials browser.

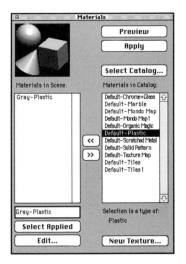

 Tip

Materials you create are saved in the current catalog. To create a new catalog, make a new folder or directory on your system, then choose it by clicking on Select Catalog.

When a particular material is selected in the browser, you can move it from the catalog to the scene, or vice versa. You edit the material in the Material Editor, shown in Figure 9.2.

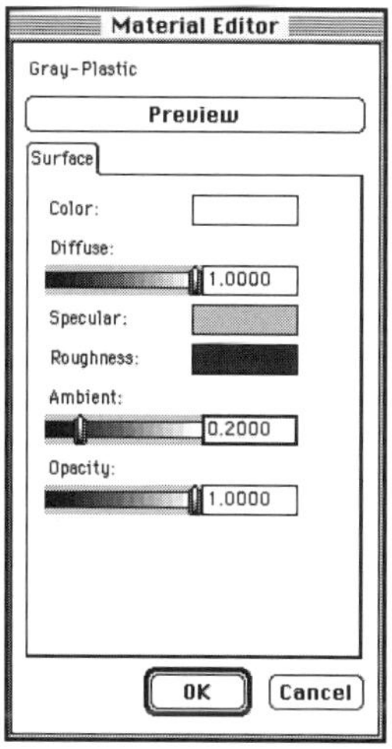

Figure 9.2

The Material Editor.

The Color Value

The surface color of any material in Extreme 3D is determined by the color property. The color seen when the material is applied to an object depends on other settings, such as the diffuse value, global ambient color, specular and roughness color of the material.

To change the color value:

1. Click once on the color chip next to the word "Color" in the Material Editor. This will open the color picker dialog box.

2. Choose a color, then click on OK.

The Diffuse Value

Diffuse sets the intensity of a material's surface color, similar to the lightness attribute in an HSL color system. When the diffuse value is set to 0.0, the material will appear black. This happens at this setting because none of the surface is reflective. When the value is higher (closer to 1.0), the surface reflects the diffused light at its maximum amount.

Ambient Color

Ambient Color simulates light in areas of an object that are not directly illuminated. It works with the diffuse value to create realistic shading effects. To

231

create shinier surfaces with high contrast, use a lower ambient value with a higher diffuse value. For a more flat or dull effect, use a higher ambient value in combination with a lower diffuse value.

Specular and Roughness Values

These values set the intensity of specular highlights—the direct reflections of the light sources in a scene—in the material. Specular and roughness colors are used in combination on the surface of a material to make it look shiny or dull.

To set the specular and roughness values:

1. In the Material Editor's window (in the specular and roughness section), click on the color chip for this value.

2. Select a color from the color picker, then click on OK.

Opacity

Opacity sets how transparent a material appears to be. This value allows you to see objects that might be hidden or underneath a solid object. Values close to 1 are opaque; values close to 0 produce transparent objects. If you render an image with an alpha channel, the alpha channel contains the transparency of an object. This is useful when creating images for use within xRes.

 Tip

Materials with opacity values less than 1 do not show their opacity until you make a final rendering. Keep in mind that the preview mode also does not show fog or light effects. To see all the effects in a scene you need to create a final rendering.

Material Effects in Extreme 3D

Material effects can be created in Extreme 3D that add clouds to an object, create a glass-like appearance, add rust to a metallic surface, or even create a believable-looking planet!

Creating a Cloud Effect

Cloud effects are used quite often in professional renderings. This effect can be created using the default-organic magic material in Extreme 3D.

CREATING CLOUDS

1. From the Materials browser, move the Default-Organic Magic material from the Materials in Catalog list to the Materials in Scene list.

2. Click Edit... in the Materials browser.

3. Set the first material's surface color to white.

4. Set the specular to white and roughness to dark gray.

5. Set the opacity to 1.0.

6. Set the second material's surface color to black.

7. Set the second material's specular color to black.

8. Set the diffuse and ambient to low values.

9. Set the second material's opacity to 0.

10. Set the value for material proportions to a value below 0.4.

Try experimenting with the filter type (smooth), Filter Complexity (Medium), and Scale until the desired effect is achieved. When you finish, the material should look something like the following example.

Creating the Glass Effect

Materials that resemble glass can be created by increasing their refractive properties. Materials such as Default-Chrome and Default-Plastic look great with a glass effect.

CREATING GLASS

1. Move the Default-Plastic material into the Materials in Scene list in the Materials browser window.

2. Click Edit....

3. Set the color of the material to a light blue.

4. Set the diffuse value below 0.3.

5. Edit specular so that it is a light color (light blue, light green) closer to white.

6. Edit roughness so that it is a darker color (dark gray or dark blue) closer to black.

7. Set the opacity to a value of less than 0.3.

8. Set the ambient to a value of between 0.1 and 0.3.

Keep in mind that an object's transparency cannot be seen unless there is another object behind it. Try placing a second object in your scene to show the transparent effect.

Adding a Rusted, Weathered Look to Metal

The rust technique can be used to add realism to metal objects—from a rusted chain found in the yard, to an out-of-service destroyer in a shipyard.

CREATING RUST

1. From the Materials browser, move the Default-Organic Magic material to the Materials in Scene list.

2. Click Edit... in the Materials browser.

3. Set the filter type to Natural Blend.

4. Set the Filter Complexity to Low.

5. Set Bump to a value of 0.6.

6. Select Linear Blend for the Bump Filter.

7. Set Material Proportions to 0.2. This determines the ratio for rust to metal. In this example it is at 20 percent rust.

8. Set the color of Material 1 to a pumpkin orange.

9. Set Diffuse of Material 1 to 0.6.

10. Set the Specular and Roughness to a dark gray.

11. Set the Color of Material 2 to a light gray.

12. Set Diffuse of Material 2 to 0.6.

13. Set the Specular to white.

14. Set Roughness to a light gray.

15. Set Ambient to 0.0.

Experiment by changing the Filter Types and Material Proportions. Change the scale if you intend to apply this technique to larger objects.

Creating a Livable Planet

To create this material, you will be adding water and vegetation to an ordinary sphere—resulting in an inhabitable planet.

CREATING WORLDS

1. From the Materials browser, move the Default-Organic Magic material to the Materials in Scene list.

2. Click Edit...in the Materials browser.

3. Set the filter type to Edge Blend.

4. Set the Filter Complexity to Medium.

5. Set Bump to a value of 0.4.

6. Select Edge Blend for the Bump Filter.

7. Set Material Proportions to 0.67. This determines the ratio for water to earth. In this example it is set at two-thirds water.

8. Set the color of Material 1 to a royal blue.

9. Set Diffuse of Material 1 to 1.0.

10. Set the Specular and Roughness to white.

11. Set the color of Material 2 to a grass green.

12. Set Diffuse of Material 2 to 1.0.

13. Set the Specular and Roughness to a medium gray.

Experiment by changing the color of the vegetation or the water. Change the Filter Complexity and Bump values to apply to various sizes of planets.

Applying Texture Maps

A texture map is a bitmap graphic that you can apply to an object. With texture maps, you can add material textures that are difficult to create in any other way. If you have a scanner, you have an unlimited source for texture maps, or you can create your own by using xRes.

To use a texture map, you need a PICT bitmap image on the Macintosh or a BMP image on the PC. Texture maps are scaled to fit a square, so it is best to start with a square bitmap. The best results are with sizes that are scaleable by 2—256 by 256 pixels, 512 by 512 pixels, or 1024 by 1024 pixels.

CREATING NEW TEXTURE MAPS

1. Move the Default-Texture Map material into the Materials in Scene list in the Materials browser window.

2. Click Edit....

3. Click the texture map to edit the texture.

4. Click Load... and find your texture map.

5. When your texture is loaded, click OK.

6. Click OK again to exit the Materials editor.

7. To tile the texture map on your object (to apply multiple copies), select Objects from the Windows menu. Click on the info tab and check the box next to Tile.

To scale the size of the texture map on your selected object, select the Intrinsic Texture Placement tool. Press the Tab key to enter the tool space at the bottom of the screen. Enter a value in the u Scale for the width and the v Scale for the height.

Using the Alpha Channel

Many professional textures have alpha channels added to the image. The alpha channel is an extra channel that holds a value for each pixel. This value, for example, can determine the opacity of an object. In xRes it can also be used as a mask. Some other ways in which you can use the alpha channel to create material effects include:

■ Composite over color will use the alpha channel to composite a texture map over the surface color of a material. The surface color will show through wherever the alpha channel is laid into the texture map.

■ Existence of surface makes the texture map and the object that it covers invisible when the alpha value is 0.

■ Luminance map creates a glowing effect in every pixel proportionate to that pixel's alpha value. The higher the value, the brighter the glow. This will give the appearance of luminance independent from light sources.

The override alpha setting ignores alpha information for a particular texture map. Use this setting when you have a texture that contains alpha information you do not want to use.

237

Creating and Customizing Lights

This section covers advanced lighting effects in Extreme 3D, including everything from changing the color of a light to controlling and animating its orientation and position. For the exercises in this section, make sure you have the Lights browser open and ready to work (see Figure 9.3).

Figure 9.3

The Lights browser.

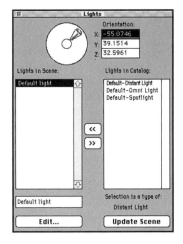

Adding Lights

Adding lights to a new scene is relatively easy. The goal in this chapter is to help you create more advanced (and difficult) lighting techniques in your work. The following sections show you professional techniques such as copying lights from other Extreme 3D files, and controlling light placement when pasting a light into a scene.

ADDING NEW LIGHTS TO A SCENE

1. Choose Lights from the Windows menu.

2. Select a light type from the Lights in Catalog list.

3. Click the left double-arrow button to move this light into the lights in scene list.

4. Name this light in the text entry field below the scene list, then press Enter (or Return).

5. Click once on the button labeled Update Scene to redraw the scene. This will show the effects of the new light you have added.

COPYING LIGHTS

1. Select the light you want to copy from the Lights in Scene list.

2. Choose Copy and then Paste from the Edit menu.

3. Name this light in the text entry field below the scene list and then press Enter.

4. Click once on the button labeled Update Scene to redraw the scene. This will show the effects of the new light you have added.

It is important to note that you can perform this function using the Duplicate command in the Edit menu. To use this technique, simply replace Edit, Copy and Edit, Paste (as shown in Step 2) with the Duplicate command. Remember, lights that you copy or duplicate have the same values and settings of the original light.

SPECIFYING POSITIONS WHEN COPYING LIGHTS

When copying and pasting lights, you can control the position of the light in the scene when executing the Paste command. To do this follow these steps.

1. Use the arrow tool to select a light in your workspace.

2. Choose Copy from the Edit menu.

3. Choose one of the construction object tools. By choosing the construction axis (or grid) tool, you can specify position and orientation.

4. Click in the work space at the point where you want the new light to be placed. This will place a construction object at this position.

5. Rotate the construction object to the desired position for the new light.

6. With the construction object selected, choose Paste from the Edit menu.

CHANGING THE TYPE OF LIGHTS

If you used the wrong type of light or just want to use a different type of light, you can replace the lights with cut and paste techniques.

1. Create a new light with your desired settings, color, and intensity.

2. Cut the light to the clipboard.

3. Select a light (or any object) with the position and orientation you want the light to have.

4. Paste from the clipboard your new light. This light will have the same position and orientation as the selected object.

You can use this technique if you have an Omni light you want to replace with a spotlight. Create a new spotlight and Cut it to the clipboard. Select the Omni light and Paste. The Spotlight will take the place of the Omni light.

Customizing Lights in Extreme 3D

More advanced techniques are available in Extreme 3D for controlling lights, including determining and changing position and orientation in a scene and changing the color and intensity of a light source.

Editing the Position and Orientation of a Light

The position and orientation of lights in Extreme 3D scenes can be controlled with three basic techniques, using tools or using values in browser windows. We will cover the steps needed to use each of these techniques below.

EDITING POSITIONS USING TOOLS

1. Choose the arrow tool and select a light in your scene.

2. Drag the light to a new position.

3. Change the orientation by entering the X, Y, and Z coordinates in the orientation section of the Lights browser.

4. Click on Update Scene to see the results.

EDITING LIGHTS USING THE OBJECTS BROWSER

1. Select the light you want to edit.

2. Choose Objects from the Window menu to open the Objects browser.

3. Place the cursor in the text entry field for the value (X, Y, or Z) you want to change.

4. Type a new value and press Enter to apply it to the light.

5. Click on Update Scene to see your results.

Editing lights with the Light Pointer

The easiest way to change the direction a light is shining is to use the Light Pointer in the Lights browser (see Figure 9.4).

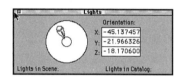

F i g u r e   9 . 4

The Light Pointer.

 T i p

If the Light Pointer appears to move in a direction opposite the mouse, this means the light is shining from the back of the scene.

USING THE LIGHT POINTER

1. Open the Lights browser by selecting Lights from the Windows menu.

2. Select a light from the Lights in Scene list.

3. The Light Pointer points in the direction the light will shine. Click on the pointer and drag it in the direction you want it to project.

4. Click on Update Scene to see your results.

Note that the numbers in the coordinates fields are updated as you move the pointer. Keep in mind that Omni lights cannot be controlled with the Lights Pointer as they have no specific orientation values to control.

Changing the Color of the Light

Changing the color of a light in Extreme 3D simulates "gel" lighting effects. The steps to change the color of a light are simple.

1. In the Light editor, click on the color chip.

2. Select a new color from the color picker.

3. Click OK.

4. To see the change, click on the Update Scene button.

241

Changing the Intensity of the Light

Editing a light's intensity will determine its brightness. Light intensity values between 0 and -20 are referred to as negative lights. A negative light uses the opposite color of its assigned light color. This is useful for intensifying shadows. Use the following steps to change the intensity of lights in Extreme 3D.

1. In the Light editor, type a value in the intensity field and click OK.

2. To see the effect, click on the button labeled update scene.

Customizing the Effects of Light

Lights in Extreme 3D can have all the properties and effects of lights in the real world. This section covers creating some of the more popular effects such as casting shadows, creating visible cones lights, and creating dust effects with spotlights.

Shadows

Shadows add to the realism of a scene. To include shadows in the final rendering you need to follow a few steps. Keep in mind that Omni lights cannot be set to cast shadows.

CASTING SHADOWS

1. Open the Lights Browser by selecting Lights from the Windows menu.

2. Select the desired light and click on the Edit button.

3. Check the Cast Shadows box in the Light Editor.

4. Click OK.

5. From the Render menu, choose Final Render Setup.

6. Check the Render Shadows box.

7. Click OK.

8. Render your scene.

Creating visible cones of light

In Extreme 3D, spotlights can be used to create visible cones of light. You can change such parameters as the radius of a spotlight's cone and how crisp, clear, or fuzzy a cone appears to be.

1. From within the Basics page of the Lights editor, set the cone angle slider to the desired angle for the spotlight's cone, and press the Tab key.

2. Adjust the cone fuzziness slider to indicate the percentage of the cone that will be softened or fuzzy.

3. Click the dust cone page and adjust the starting radius of the light cone.

   Remember, a value of 0.5 will soften half the radius of the cone from the outer edge inward. In addition, the value in the dust cone page will set the starting radius of the light cone. The larger this value is, the wider the light will be at its source. A good example of a visible cone of light is shown in Figure 9.5.

Figure 9.5

A visible cone of light.

CREATING DUST WITH SPOTLIGHTS

You can create atmospheric scenes with the addition of dust. Extreme 3D also allows you to create smoke-like swirls using the dust properties. The following steps will help you create dust and smoke in your scene.

1. Create a spotlight with a cone angle.

2. In the dust cone page of the Lights editor, set the amount of dust using the Dustiness slider.

3. Type the desired number of fall off units in the fall off field.

4. To render fall off in a scene, check the use fall off check box.

5. Set the turbulence offset to a value between 0 and 1.0.

6. Set the dust turbulence between 0 and 1.0. This will determine how evenly the dust is distributed throughout the cone of light.

7. Adjust the turbulence scale to determine how much space the concentrated swirls of dust will fill.

8. To use shadows cast in the dust as well as on objects, check dust shadows.

243

Animation in Extreme 3D

Animation in Extreme 3D is easy to learn because of the programs' intuitive animation controls, which let you set the time, length, and playback of animation sequences.

To begin creating animation, choose Animation Controls from the Animate menu. If this dialog box is already on-screen, you can bring it to the top by choosing this command; choose the command again to close the dialog box. Figure 9.6 shows the Animation Controls window.

The Animation Controls window.

The Animation Score

The Animation Score displays tracks that contain detailed information about animation in Extreme 3D. The score should be used and thought of as the animation browser. The score serves two main functions: it lists all the Extreme 3D elements, such as objects, materials, and lights, and lists the properties of each that can be animated. Properties that can be animated include the position of an object or the color value of a material. You can animate light sources and the light color changing for the light source just like you would any other object in Extreme 3D. The score also manages the animation tracks. Tracks are the timelines associated with each property that are displayed to the right of the property name in the list. Figure 9.7 shows the Animation Score window.

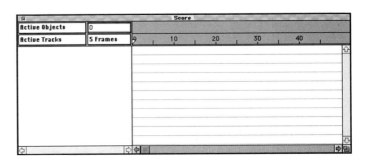

The Animation Score window.

USING THE ANIMATION CONTROLS

1. Create a new scene and add a cube, using the cube tool, to the left side of the scene.

2. Open Animation Controls from the Animation menu. Click the End value box and enter 30. This will give you 30 frames of animation.

3. Click the fast forward button in the animation controls to go to the 30th and last frame.

4. Move the cube to the right side of the screen.

5. Click the rewind button and then click play. You will see a wireframe of the cube move from the left side of the scene to the right side.

Animation Paths

Animation paths represent the position and movement of a selected object as a spline curve in the workspace. When displayed, the animation path can be selected, opened, and edited in the same way as all splines. To see the path in the previous example, select Animation Path Show from the Animation menu.

 Tip

To convert an animation path to a profile, select the path in the workspace or in the World browser and choose Convert Path to Profile. (Use the Animation Path command to make an object's path visible in the workspace.)

To convert a spline to an animation path, select the object's position track in the score and select the profile for the new path in the workspace, then choose Convert Profile to Path. The track's current keyframes will be deleted and the new path's control points will define the path's new keyframes.

Advanced Animation Techniques

This section covers some of the advanced techniques for animation in Extreme 3D such as rotating objects (automatically and manually) and animating lights in a scene. These techniques help cut down the time you spend working on projects.

Rotating Objects

One of the most-used animation techniques is the rotation of three-dimensional objects. This technique is often used in commercial animation when logos are rotated 360 degrees around an axis.

Rotating objects manually

The Rotate point tool enables you to rotate an object around a specified point.

1. Click to define the point around which the object will rotate.

2. Click a point on the object that you want to use as a handle for rotating the object.

3. Drag the handle point around the center of rotation.

 Tip

You can also enter rotation values in the tool space to rotate a precise number of degrees. To do this, click to define the point around which the object will rotate. Afterward, type the number of degrees of rotation in the tool space and press Enter or Return.

Rotating objects automatically

The Auto Rotate command in the Animate menu (see Figure 9.8) opens a dialog box in which you can specify the axis around which a selected object will rotate. You can also input the number of degrees the object will rotate. Auto Rotate allows for degrees of rotation greater than 180 and is especially useful for objects that spin repeatedly. The Auto Rotate command will create four keyframes for every 360 degrees of rotation.

Figure 9.8

The Auto Rotate dialog box.

To change the degrees of rotation after using Auto Rotate, you must delete the object's Orientation track from the animation Score window (select it by name and press the Delete key) and choose Auto Rotate again.

Four choices are possible for the axis of rotation:

■ Object's X Axis. The object rotates around its x axis.

■ Object's Y Axis. The object rotates around its y axis.

■ Object's Z Axis. The object rotates around its z axis.

■ Working Plane's Z Axis. The object rotates around the working plane's z axis.

 Tip

To define precisely where a rotation begins, add a keyframe to the Orientation track at that point, then set the current frame to the rotation end time and apply the Auto Rotate command.

Animating Lights in Extreme 3D

Animating lights in Extreme 3D can add to the overall production quality of your animation. By tracking objects with lights, changing their properties over time, and moving lights around during the animation sequence, your animation become more realistic and exciting.

Animating the position and orientation of lights

To animate the position of a light in the current scene, follow these simple steps.

1. Select the light you want to animate.

2. Set the current time to 30 in the Animation Score (see Figure 9.9).

3. Move the light in the scene from its current position to the desired end position. You can do this by moving the light on its axis, or actually moving the light so that it is animated moving across the scene.

Figure 9.9

The Animation Score with the current time set to 30.

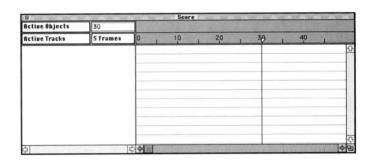

Animating lights to track objects

These steps will link objects to lights so that lights follow objects anywhere in the scene.

1. Choose the Watch Link tool from the Tools Palette in Extreme 3D.

2. Drag a line from the light object to the object that will be watched.

3. Set the current time to 30 in the Animation Score.

4. Select the target object and move it to a new position in the workspace.

Animating the properties of lights

Animating properties such as color and intensity can add realism to almost any animated light source.

1. Open the Score window.

2. Select the property track of the property that you would like to animate.

3. Set the current time to 30 in the Animation Score.

4. Use the entry field to change the keyframe data, or enter a new value in the appropriate field of the Lights Browser.

Rendering an Animation

To see the results of all your hard work creating an animation, you need to render the animation to disk. When you render to disk, be sure you check the selected options in the Final Render Setup and the Windows Setup dialog boxes.

When you render QuickTime or AVI movies, you are limited to the size of the currently selected window. When you Render to Disk from the Animation menu, the Render button is grayed out in the dialog box if you try to render a QuickTime or AVI movie. To change the size, click on the Cancel button to exit the dialog box and select Window Setup from the Windows menu. In this box you can change the Image Size.

RENDERING ANIMATION TO DISK

1. Set your window size by selecting Window setup from the Windows menu.

2. Create your animated scene.

3. Select Render to Disk from the Animation menu.

4. Enter the frame or frames you want to render.

5. Select QuickTime or AVI movie.

6. Click on the Render button.

7. A dialog box for AVI or QuickTime movie settings will appear. Click on OK for the default settings.

8. Wait. Your computer will chug and churn creating your animation frame by frame.

The amount of time it takes to render the animation depends on a number of factors, including window size, the complexity of the objects and their materials, the number of frames in the animation and the speed of the computer.

Part IV

Macromedia xRes

Macromedia xRes is one of the most powerful graphic applications available and is the latest challenger to Adobe's pixel editing program, Photoshop. If you are familiar with Photoshop or another image-manipulation program, xRes will be easy to use: the toolboxes, filters, and effects are all quite similar. However, xRes offers multiple levels of undo and a special "xRes mode" that can easily handle large images.

xRes can import rendered images from Extreme 3D that you can manipulate or prepare for use on the Internet. xRes can also be used to create texture maps in Extreme 3D or for photomanipulation in a layout created in FreeHand. This flexibility enables you to work in applications that suit your specific needs and later combine different files into a seamless final piece.

xRes Basics

Macromedia xRes is one of the most powerful image editing applications available, and is the latest challenger to Adobe Photoshop. xRes offers many of the same capabilities as Photoshop.

xRes has several advantages when compared to other graphics applications. One of the most noteworthy are two different work modes the application offers: Direct and xRes. Direct mode is used for working with smaller graphic files (20 MB or less), while xRes mode is reserved for working with files that are much larger than (20 MB or more). Unlike other graphics programs, xRes also offers multiple levels of undos. This is one of its the best features because users can go back several changes in the document if necessary. Most other graphic applications of this type only offer one level of undo.

Modes and File Formats

xRes introduces new working methods: Direct mode and xRes mode, with new file formats to optimize these two modes. Each mode has its advantages and disadvantages. Each project you are working on will determine the best mode.

Direct Mode

Direct Mode is the default work mode for xRes. This mode is used when working with images under 20 MB in size. The advantage of Direct Mode is that users can open images and modify them without having to render them before changing and saving each file. (Rendering is a required step in xRes Mode, which can cause a delay in saving a file). A drawback to Direct mode is that it lacks the sheer speed of working in xRes Mode. Because xRes Mode can handle larger images quickly, it can handle smaller images with even greater speed.

xRes Mode

xRes Mode is the premier advantage to Macromedia's image editing software. This method allows you to work with very large files in as little as 16 MB of RAM. You can open large scanned photographs and manipulate them easily with minimal time delays.

Unlike other image editors that provide this feature, xRes does not use a proxy system when working with files. A proxy system uses a lower dpi (dot per inch) resolution to represent a high-resolution image. In xRes the image resolution is not reduced or modified to increase performance. The biggest problem with proxy systems is the complications created when trying to apply filter effects to images. Because the resolution has been lowered, you will have to guess what the effect of a filter will be.

In xRes this is not a problem, because xRes uses selective processing to achieve its performance gains. This method allows you to work with very large files with as little as 16 MB of RAM. To illustrate this approach, imagine you were working on a large image with millions of pixels in it. If you ran a filter on the entire image while in xRes Mode, the filter's effect would be calculated only for the visible area of the image—the portion of the image that you could currently see in the window. Processing the remainder of the image to apply the effect is delayed. When the file is ready to be exported, xRes renders the file out into what ever the format you have chosen. xRes calculates and processes changes to the image as it renders the file rather than while you are trying to work with the image. This saves a great deal of time and offers great performance advantages over Direct Mode.

LRG

LRG is a new document format used specifically for larger graphic files. This format allows files to be stored in a series of zoom levels, which makes it easier to manipulate larger images. LRG documents will automatically open in xRes Mode. The computer only has to display the effects applied to the section of the document currently displayed at the current zoom level. Your files first need to be opened in this format before you can work with them in xRes Mode.

To open a file as an LRG file format in xRes, choose Open as LRG from the File menu and select the file you want to open (see Figure 10.1).

Figure 10.1

The Open as LRG dialog box.

To save a file as an LRG file, choose Save As from the File menu. Select LRG in the File Format section of the Save dialog box (see Figure 10.2).

Figure 10.2

The Save Dialog Box showing the LRG file format selection.

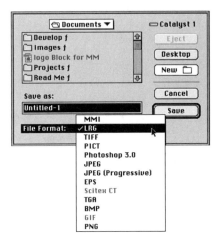

This will save the current file as an LRG. This setup is useful if you open a file in Direct Mode that is not an LRG file type and then want to save it as an LRG file so that the next time you open the file it will open in xRes Mode. LRG files are automatically opened in xRes Mode but you can switch to Direct Mode if needed.

MMI

The MMI (Macromedia Image) format is also a graphic file format new to xRes users. This format is unique in that it allows users to save a document with several different objects in it without merging the objects into one layer. In xRes Mode, an MMI file points to the objects' links within the file (saved using the LRG file format). This is similar to the way FreeHand imports images. The images are not contained within the file but are linked to files located elsewhere. If you delete LRG files that are linked to an MMI file, when you open the MMI file the deleted LRG objects will be missing.

To save a file as an MMI file type, choose Save As from the File menu and select MMI in the File Format section of the save dialog box (see Figure 10.3).

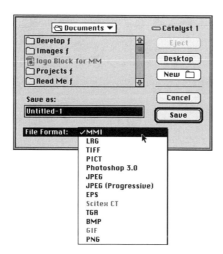

Figure 10.3

*The Save Dialog Box showing
the MMI file format selection.*

When you send files to other artists, you need to remember to include all the LRG files that are used by the MMI file.

If you need to send a file to an artist who is using Photoshop, you need to save the objects as separate objects because xRes merges all the objects when saving a Photoshop 3.0 document. To save the separate objects, select all the objects and use the Save Object command in the Objects Window submenu of each object. You will then be prompted to save each object one by one.

 **Tip**

Included with xRes is a utility called Batch Convert, accessible from the Xtras menu. Batch Convert allows you to convert a folder or directory of files from one file format to another. Before you can use xRes Mode, you must convert all of your files to the LRG file format or the GIF format before files can be placed on the Internet. To do this, follow these steps:

1. Put all the files you want to convert into one folder or directory.
2. Create a new folder/directory for the soon-to-be converted files.
3. In xRes select Batch Convert from the Xtras menu, and the file format to which you want to convert your files.
4. Choose the source folder/directory containing the files you want to convert.
5. Choose the destination folder/directory into which you want xRes to put the converted files.

Objects

Objects are individual items in a document. A document can contain many objects. Selecting an object within a document will allow you to edit the object by painting it, filling it with color, applying a filter to it, or any other editing technique available in xRes. Some object functions in xRes can be controlled through the Objects window. Figure 10.4 shows the Objects window as it appears in a document containing three basic objects.

Figure 10.4

The Objects window.

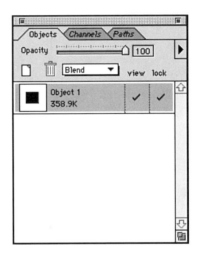

Each object created in xRes can be selected and manipulated using the Objects window. The Object Options window enables you to change the name and position of any object in a document (see Figure 10.5). To open the Objects Options window, either double-click on the object within the document window or double-click on the object's name in the Objects window.

Figure 10.5

The Object Options window.

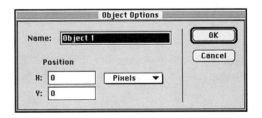

In the Objects window you can also change the opacity of objects, duplicate and delete objects, and control effects such as Add, Subtract, and Multiply.

Channels

Channels in xRes store color information in a document. Channels are most often used to select certain areas of information. When a channel is used in this fashion it is referred to as an Alpha Channel. When a selection is specified as an Alpha Channel, it can be used to mask out the selected information. Channels are also used to break up an image by color channels. This means that in RGB color mode, anything created on the canvas would have three channels: red, green, and blue. Unlike an Alpha channel, these channels are visible to the user while working with objects in xRes.

Channel Options

Several options are available for channels in xRes. Each of these options can be controlled through the Channels window (see Figure 10.6).

Figure 10.6

The Channels window.

The Channels window allows you to control duplicating, deleting, and masking of channels in addition to setting the view or mask of one or all of the channels. The only feature that cannot be controlled directly from the Channels window is setting the opacity of a channel. To do this you must open the Channel Options window (see Figure 10.7). To open the Channel Options window, simply double-click on the channel that needs its opacity changed, and enter a new value. You can also move the slider to set a new value.

Figure 10.7

The Channel Options window.

Changing the Opacity and Color Mask of a Channel

To change the opacity and color mask of a channel, double-click on the channel that you want to change in the Channels window.

The Channel Options window will open. The provided slider enables you to change the opacity of the channel. To change the Color Mask of a channel in this window, first select a foreground color in the Tools palette and then drag the cursor over the color block. Note that the cursor will change into the Paint Bucket tool. With this tool you can apply the foreground color you selected as the Color Mask for the channel.

Mask

A mask in xRes is used to protect a section of an image from the effects of a filter or brush stroke applied to a particular object. This special xRes feature is noteworthy because xRes is one of the only programs that lets you mask a specific image section in a multi-image document.

Color Mode

The color mode setting in xRes determines if the colors in the current document are in RGB, CMYK, HSB, HLS, YIQ, Grayscale, or some Custom Color set. Each type of color set provides different adjustments for controlling color in an image.

Note

For more information about color modes, see the sidebar "Introduction to Color Theory," in Chapter 2.

Paths

A path is a line (or a curve) created using the Pen tool in xRes. Paths are very useful in xRes because they can produce a more accurate selection than any other Marquee tool available in the application. A Path can produce a precise anti-aliased selection. Paths also can be created from lines and curves that cannot be produced as easily with the Marquee tools. This includes Bézier curves, which are used in many forms of commercial art and in illustration for display advertising.

Creating a New Path

xRes provides three ways to create a new path:

■ Click once on the New Path Icon in the Paths window.

■ Select New Path from the Path sub-menu.

■ Click on the Pen tool in the tools palette and start drawing.

Each time you create a new path, it is numbered in sequential order after the previous path. To change the name of the path, double-click on the current path in the Paths window and enter a new name.

CREATING A SELECTION FROM A PATH

1. In your document window, click once on the path from which you want to create a selection.

2. Choose "Select From Path" from the Paths window sub-menu.

TRACING A PATH WITH THE BRUSH TOOL

1. Select the path you want to trace with the Paths window.

2. Choose "Stroke Path" from the Paths window submenu.

```
New Path
Delete Path
Save Path...
Load Path...
Select From Path
Stroke Path
Make Clipping Path
```

261

3. Select a brush from the Brushes palette that you want to use to trace the path.

4. Choose a variant from the drop down menu in the window as shown below.

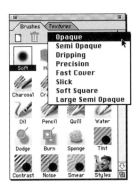

FILLING A PATH

1. Select the desired path in the Paths window.

2. Choose "Select From Path" from the Paths window sub-menu.

3. Select the Foreground or Background colors from the dialog box.

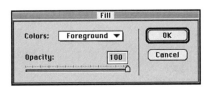

4. Set the opacity percentage using the slider, ranging from 0–100.

5. Click OK.

This process will fill the path with the color and opacity that you chose.

Clipping paths are used to mask out or clip away an area from an image. Clipping paths are used with EPS images that will later be imported into FreeHand. If you scan a photo, for example, and you want to mask out the background, you can create a clipping path to mask out this part of the image.

When you import the image as an EPS file with its clipping path into FreeHand, the area outside the clipping path will not appear.

CREATING A CLIPPING PATH

1. Select the path that will be used as the clipping path by clicking on it once in the Paths window.

2. Choose "Make Clipping Path" from the Paths Window sub-menu.

Floating Palettes

xRes has five floating palettes: Tools, Brushes, Textures, Swatches, and Picker. Each of these palettes contains tools and other objects that manipulate images in the application. Figure 10.8 shows the Palettes menu.

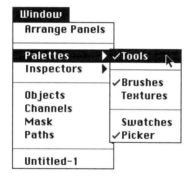

Figure 10.8

The Palettes menu.

The lines of division between the Tools and Brushes menu items and the Textures and Swatches menu items indicate tools that are combined into floating palettes. Figure 10.9 shows the Brushes palette. Notice the file tab for the Textures palette. Floating palettes in xRes are grouped in functional sets so that you can access and change related functions without having to open an additional palette.

The Tools Palette

The Tools palette holds all the tools that allow you to manipulate images (see Figure 10.10).

Figure 10.9

The Brushes Floating palette.

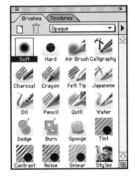

Figure 10.10

The Tools palette.

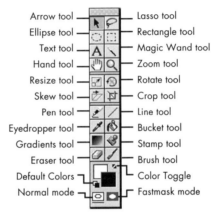

Arrow tool — Lasso tool
Ellipse tool — Rectangle tool
Text tool — Magic Wand tool
Hand tool — Zoom tool
Resize tool — Rotate tool
Skew tool — Crop tool
Pen tool — Line tool
Eyedropper tool — Bucket tool
Gradients tool — Stamp tool
Eraser tool — Brush tool
Default Colors — Color Toggle
Normal mode — Fastmask mode

Arrow tool

This tool is used to select objects in xRes. Selecting objects makes them active so that they can be moved or manipulated. You can keep objects from moving by putting a check in the object's Lock column in the Object window. Press the A key to select this tool.

Lasso tool

This tool selects irregular-shaped areas and is part of the marquee family. You can draw a selection freehand or press and hold down the Option key on the Mac or the Alt key on the PC and click from point to point for straight line segments.

Circular Marquee tool

This tool allows users to select a circular or elliptical selection area of the current document or a section of an image. To constrain your selection to a circle, press and hold down the Shift key before you make your selection. To draw a selection out from the center, press and hold down the Option key on the Mac or the Alt key on the PC as you drag out the shape of your selection.

Rectangular Marquee tool

This tool speaks for itself; use it whenever you need to select a square or rectangular selection area of the current document or a section of an image. To constrain your selection to a square, press and hold down the Shift key before you make your selection. To draw your selection out from the center, press and hold down the Option key on the Mac or the Alt key on the PC as you drag out the shape of your selection. Press the M key to select this tool from the keyboard.

Text tool

This tool lets you create text objects in the current document. To create a text object, select the Text tool and then click once in the current document. The window shown in Figure 10.11 will present options for creating a text object. You can enter your type and set its attributes such as font and styles. Pressing the letter T key will select this tool using the keyboard.

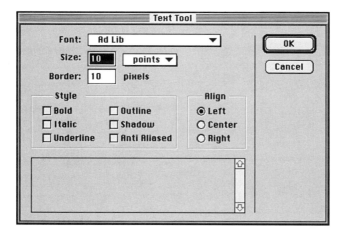

Figure 10.11

The Text window.

Magic Wand tool

The Magic Wand creates selections based on pixels with a similar color value. This tool has several options that control the amount of similarity necessary for pixels to be included in a selection. The keyboard shortcut for the Magic Wand is the letter W.

To use the Magic Wand tool:

1. Click once on the Magic Wand tool in the Tools window.

2. Click a pixel in the current document where the selection will be created.

3. Now enter the opacity for the Magic Wand tool. Use a value anywhere between 1 and 100.

If the selection is too small, increase the Magic Wand tool tolerance to create a new selection. To change the tolerance of the Magic Wand tool:

1. Double-click on the Magic Wand tool in the Tools window. This will open the Wand Options window (see Figure 10.12).

Figure 10.12

The Wand Options window.

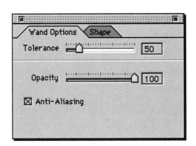

2. Set the tolerance using the slider to select a value between 1 and 100.

3. Set the opacity using the slider to select a value between 0 and 100.

Hand tool

The Hand tool lets you move the document around in the current window. If an image is so large that you cannot see all of it in the current window, use the Hand tool to move the object within the window without making any changes to the document. You can temporarily access the Hand tool by pressing the Space bar as you click and drag the mouse within the document window.

Magnify tool

This tool does just what the name suggests: you use it to magnify a section of an image in the current document window. To zoom out using this tool, press and hold down the Option key on the Mac or the Alt key on the PC.

Pressing the Z key will select this tool using the keyboard.

Resize tool

To resize an object:

1. Select the object you want to resize.

2. Click once on the object with the Resize tool.

3. Click a second time on the object and then drag the cursor. A frame appears that shows the shape and size of the selection. Release the mouse button to resize to object to the size of the frame shown on-screen.

The keyboard shortcut key for the resize tool is the letter S. Figure 10.13 shows the object width and the width of the resize box.

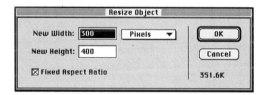

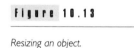

Figure 10.13

Resizing an object.

Rotate tool

The Rotate tool rotates a selected object in a document. Press the R key to select this tool using the keyboard. xRes provides two methods for using this tool. The first method involves eyeballing the amount of rotation you need.

1. Select the object you would like to rotate.

2. Click once on the Rotate tool to activate it.

3. Click on one of the four corners of its bounding box.

4. Press and hold down the mouse button, and move the mouse. This causes the object to rotate in the direction the mouse is moved.

When you use the Rotate tool in this manner, a bounding box shows how much the image will rotate (see Figure 10.14).

The other way to use this tool is much more precise.

1. Select the object to be rotated.

2. Choose the Rotate tool from the Tools palette.

3. Double-click on the object with the Rotate tool.

4. This will open the Rotate window (see Figure 10.15). In this window, you can enter a specific angle of rotation.

Figure 10.14

Bounding box shown while using the Rotate tool.

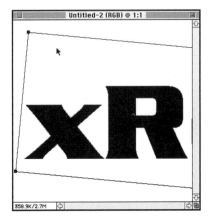

Figure 10.15

The Rotate window.

Skew tool

The Skew tool is used to skew or slant objects. Press the K key to select this tool using the keyboard.

1. Select the object to be skewed.

2. Choose the Skew tool from the Tools palette.

3. Press and hold down the mouse button on one of the corners of the object and move the mouse to skew the object.

Figure 10.16 shows a before and after of an object that has been skewed.

Figure 10.16

The Skew effect before and after.

Crop tool

The Crop tool can make mincemeat of an xRes document. If there are parts of an image you don't want or don't need, the Crop tool will quietly eliminate this riff-raff. To get to this tool in a pinch, press the C key. If you have a little more time, check out this method:

1. Select the Crop tool from the Tools palette.

2. Click and hold down the mouse button to select the area you would like to crop.

3. Move the cursor into the center of the selection. This will cause the cursor to change to a hammer. After the cursor changes, click once to crop the document (see Figure 10.17).

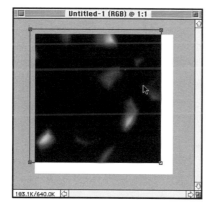

Figure 10.17

Cropping an image in xRes.

Pen tool

This tool can be used to draw paths in xRes. The quickest way to access this tool is to press the P key. If you forget this shortcut (most users do), try the following steps.

1. Select the Pen tool from the Tools palette.

2. Click once inside the current document.

3. Click a second time within the document. This produces a line between the two points where you clicked (see Figure 10.18).

Figure 10.18

Example of the Pen tool in action.

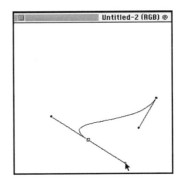

Line tool

The Line tool is used to create a straight line—horizontal, vertical, or diagonal—within the current document. Press the L key to select this tool.

Eyedropper tool

This tool can be used to select colors for the Tools palette's Foreground color.

1. Select the Eyedropper tool from the Tools palette.

2. Place the Eyedropper tool over the area of the document that contains the color you want to use and click once. This changes the Foreground color to that of the color selected by the Eyedropper tool.

3. To set the background color, select a color using the Eyedropper tool, then press the X key to toggle the colors. The newly selected color will be assigned to the background.

The I key on the keyboard is the shortcut key for the Eyedropper.

Paint Bucket tool

This tool is used to fill large selections in a document with the current foreground color. You can change the tolerance of the Paint Bucket fill by double-clicking on this tool, which opens the Bucket Options window. A high tolerance setting will fill in a broader range of color. Press the U key to select the Paint Bucket tool from the keyboard.

Gradient tool

This tool is used to create gradients in xRes. Gradients are a gradual change from one color to another. If you can't remember the keyboard shortcut for the Gradient tool (the letter G), follow these steps to access it:

1. Select an area in the current document to fill with a color gradient.

2. Choose the Gradient tool from the Tools palette and double-click on it.

3. Set the options for the Gradient tool as shown in Figure 10.19.

4. Create a gradient by clicking within the area that was previously selected.

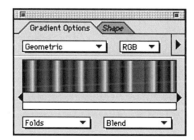

Figure 10.19

Gradient Options.

Stamp tool

The Stamp tool clones a section of the current image or document.

1. Choose the Stamp tool from the Tools palette.

2. Define an anchor point for the Stamp tool by Option-clicking (Alt for Windows) where the document will be cloned.

3. Select a destination area where the clone will be made and drag to clone the image from the source area.

To access this command from the keyboard, press the O key.

Eraser Tool

This tool lets you erase parts of an image or document. Double-click this tool to display the Eraser Options window. If you check the Erase from undo checkbox in the Eraser Options window, the tool will clone from what the image looked like before the last change. Press the E key to select this tool quickly.

Brush tool

The Brush tool lets you paint the current xRes document. Several Brush tool options are available, which are covered in more detail in the following section. Figure 10.20 shows options for the Brush tool in Artistic mode. Press the B key to select this tool from the keyboard.

Figure 10.20

Options for the Brush tool in Artistic mode.

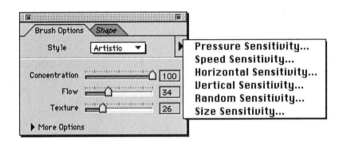

Foreground and Background color blocks

The Foreground and Background color blocks show the Foreground and Background colors currently used. You can toggle these two colors by pressing the X key. Press the D key to reset the colors to their default values, a black foreground and white background.

FastMask mode

The FastMask mode is used to create a quick mask by painting over an area.. The steps are simple.

1. Click on the FastMask mode icon in the Tools palette.

2. Press the D key to restore the default colors.

3. Select the Brush tool.

4. Paint over the area you want to mask.

5. Click on the Normal mode (next to the FastMask mode.) You now have a selection that is masking off the area you painted.

The keyboard shortcut is the A key.

The Brushes and Textures Palettes

The Brushes and Textures palettes contain options for the Brush tool. These palettes contain different types of brushes and several different textures that can be used together. Experimentation is highly recommended; the possibilities for combining these options are almost endless. Figures 10.21 and 10.22 show the palettes and some of the options available in each.

Figure 10.21

The Brushes palette.

Figure 10.22

The Textures palette.

The Swatches and Picker Palette

This palette can be used to select colors from the Swatches (which displays color chips) and the Picker (which displays available colors as a continuous gradient). Operating either of these two items is simple:

1. Move the mouse over the palette and then over the area that contains the color you want to use.

2. When the cursor is over the desired color, click once to make it the active Foreground color in the document.

Figures 10.23 and 10.24 show each of these palettes.

Figure 10.23

The Swatches palette.

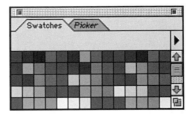

Figure 10.24

The Picker palette.

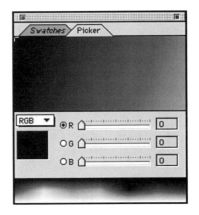

Chapter 11

Special Effects in xRes

This chapter covers intermediate techniques that can be performed in xRes, such as adding manual drop shadows, blending objects, and creating gradient effects. You will also read about the use of xRes's basic filters. A filter is an effect applied to an image to alter its appearance.

Drop Shadows

Drop shadows are used in many professional displays and commercial art pieces. They can be produced manually and with filters. However, many graphic artists still produce this effect manually because of the need for precise control. Many filters are available for creating drop shadows, but few offer the control manual and many are not as stable as the application.

CREATING DROP SHADOWS

1. Select a color. Pick a red color if you do not have a favorite.

2. Create a text object in an RGB document. The text can be anything at all but try to limit it to a few letters. Set its size to about 72 points.

3. Duplicate the text object by choosing the Duplicate command from the Edit menu.

4. Click once on the duplicate object to select it.

5. Click the default color swatches on the tools palette to set the colors back to black and white.

6. Choose the Fill command from the Edit menu and set the foreground color to 100 percent opacity and then click OK. This produces a black shadow.

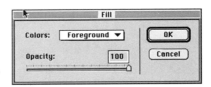

7. Open the Channels window and click once on channel number four. This selects channel 4, which is used as a mask for the type.

8. Apply a Gaussian Blur to the channel by selecting the text and then choosing Filters, Blur, Gaussian. Use a value of 6.

9. Click once on the RGB composite channel. The text now has a black drop shadow.

10. Use the Move Backward command (in the Arrange submenu of the Modify menu command) to move the shadow object behind the text.

11. Now position the drop shadow text object so that it is in the desired position for the effect.

12. In the Object window, set the opacity to 60 percent for a more subdued shadow effect.

Drop shadows can also be applied to other objects the same way the tutorial was used to apply the effect to text. Try experimenting with these steps and also with different colors to create your own drop shadow effects.

Blending Objects

Blending is another trick of the imaging trade, and the process is actually simple to create in xRes. Blends enable you to set the way the composite image will look when objects react with other objects that are layered on them. Several different blends can be performed in the application: Blend, Additive, Subtractive, Multiply, Difference, Maximum, and Minimum. Because of their different color modes, RGB and CMYK will generally have opposite effects.

Figure 11.1

A multiply blend.

The blends are created by calculating the color of each pixel depending on the settings of each object's blend mode. The easiest way to understand these blends is to experiment and see how each mode reacts with each object.

Blend modes in xRes are a little different from blends in some other applications. They all have similar effects, but xRes simplifies the process of creating a blend. Each mode is different; one way to understand this is see what effects the mode will have in xRes and then practice them yourself with a short tutorial.

Blend

Normal blend mode uses the opacity of an object when combining two objects. Normal is one of the most useful blending effects in xRes because it takes the opacity and calculates the values to give the appearance of two images fading together.

CREATING NORMAL BLENDS

1. In a new document, create a Black square.

2. Now select the Text tool from the Tools Palette.

3. Select a red color for your foreground color.

4. Create a text object in your current document

5. Position the text so that part of it is over the square, and the other part is off the square.

6. With the text object layer selected in the Objects window, choose Blend from the pull-down menu at the top of the window.

7. Set the opacity of the text object to 40 using the slider at the top of the Objects window.

Additive

The additive mode of blending adds together the pixel values for objects that are part of a composite image (any color image). In CMYK color mode adding values together darkens an image. Just the opposite occurs in RGB color mode (the image lightens).

ADDITIVE BLENDS WITH OBJECTS

1. Using the same file that you used for the previous lesson, create a new text object.

2. Set the blend for this new text object to Add.

3. Set the opacity of the text object to 90.

4. Position the new text object so that only half of it is over the black box you created in the previous exercise.

Notice that with the Normal Blend, the entire Text Object can be seen; the Additive Blend only shows the section that is over the black box. The reason for this is that white is the greater value in RGB.

Subtractive

The Subtractive Blend mode is the opposite of the Additive Blend mode. The pixel values of the top layer are subtracted from the pixel values of the layer or layers beneath it.

To see how this works, select Subtractive for the text object. Notice that the blue text over the white background is now yellow. The blend subtracts the blue text from the white background. Figure 11.2 shows the result in black and white.

Figure 11.2

The Subtractive Blend effect.

Subtractive Blend Mode can be used to decrease value or light from an RGB image or to increase value or light to a CMYK image.

Multiply

The Multiply Blend mode multiplies object pixel values together. This mode creates a darkening effect on an object. White areas in a Multiply-blended object have no effect on the composite image.

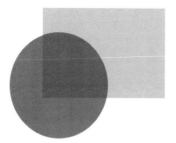

Figure 11.3

The result of a Multiply blend.

Difference

The Difference Blend mode calculates the absolute difference of composite object pixel values. If there are no differences in two objects, the composite will be black. If two identical objects are on top of one another, a glowing edge appears around high contrast, overlapping areas. To see this effect, scan a photograph and duplicate it. Apply the Difference Blend to the topmost object. If the images are not lined up precisely you will see this glowing effect. Use the arrow keys to nudge the top object pixel by pixel to change the effect.

Figure 11.4

The result of a Difference blend.

Maximum

The Maximum Blend mode calculates the maximum value of two composited object pixel values. In RGB color mode, the object with pixels that have the brighter value (closest to white) will be displayed.

Figure 11.5

The result of a Maximum blend.

Minimum

The Minimum Blend mode calculates the minimum value of two composited object pixel values. The object with pixels that have the brighter value (closest to black) will be displayed.

Figure 11.6

The result of a Minimum blend.

Custom Gradient Effects

Gradient effects appear in many forms of graphic art. Some artists use third-party filters to create gradient effects, but making these effects manually gives you far greater control and unique gradients that you can use in your art.

Options for Creating Gradients

The Gradient tool can create fills with different colors, opacity values, blending modes, shapes, and effects. These can be used in any number of combinations to create the desired effect. Figure 11.7 shows the Gradients window, which you will use to adjust the different values that make up a gradient.

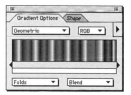

Figure 11.7

The Gradient window.

The Gradient Shape Menu

This menu is used to select the shape of the gradient that will be created. Figure 11.8 shows available shapes. When you use any of the shapes it is important to view the gradient effect in the preview window before applying it to the actual image.

Figure 11.8

The Gradient shape menu.

The Gradient Color Mode

This menu is used to select the color mode of the gradient. You can choose from either RGB or CMYK. All the gradient exercises in this section must be performed in the RGB color mode.

The Gradient Blending Mode

The gradient blending mode is where you select the blend mode of the gradient. To select a blend mode for the gradient simply choose a mode from the pull-down menu as shown in Figure 11.9.

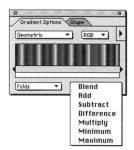

Figure 11.9

The Gradient Blending mode.

The Gradient Presets Menu

This section of the Gradients window provides numerous preset gradients. Each combines different effects, as shown in Figure 11.10.

Figure 11.10

The Gradient Presets menu.

```
Hot Pink
Pastels
Silverado
Cobalt Blue
Cafe au lait
Sunrise
Metal Burst
Kryptonite
Gradient9
Rainbow
Red Light
Purple Haze
Black->White
White->Black
Hue Cone
Starburst
Sunny Sky
Vibrant Satin
R-O-Y
Blue Wood Frame
Satin
Geometric
Holiday Cheer
Striped Diamond
Blast Off
Serendipity
Snowflakes
Steel Pipe
```

USING PRESET GRADIENTS

1. Double-click on the Gradient tool in the Tools Palette window.

2. Select a preset gradient from the presets menu of the Gradient window.

3. Set the color mode for the Gradient to RGB.

4. Now select the shape for the gradient or use its default.

5. Select the Blending Mode for the gradient. Experiment and try Add or Multiply.

6. Click and drag (using the Gradient tool) inside your document and create a line over the image, as in the following figure.

7. Release the button to create the gradient. If you do not like your first attempt, simply Undo and repeat the previous step until you achieve the desired effect.

You can also change preset gradients in the presets menu and add your own custom gradients to this menu.

The Gradient Range Sliders

The triangles at each side of the Gradients window are the Range sliders. These sliders control the limits for the areas that can and will be affected by colors dropped into the gradient color ramp. Figure 11.11 illustrates these visible limits.

Figure 11.11

The Gradient Range sliders.

The Gradient Submenu

The Gradient submenu lets you save, add, name, and delete gradients to and from the Gradient Presets menu. This menu can be used to modify existing gradient presets and then save them to the presets menu as your own custom gradient. Figure 11.12 shows these options in the Gradient submenu.

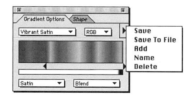

Figure 11.12

The Gradient submenu.

You can create temporary gradients that are used only for your current session or you can save to a file the full set of gradients, including any changes you may have made.

Creating and Applying Gradients in xRes

To become an ace with creating and applying gradients in xRes, you first need to understand how to create new gradients, modify existing gradients, and work with the cross gradient effect.

CREATING A NEW GRADIENT

1. Open the Gradient Tool Options box by double-clicking the Gradient tool in the Tools palette.

2. Select "Add" from the submenu for gradient tool options.

3. In the dialog box that appears, enter a name for the gradient you are creating and click OK.

4. Select a Foreground color from the Swatches window.

5. Now adjust the Range sliders so that you can fill only a portion of the gradient with the foreground color you have selected.

6. In the Gradients window click once in the area between the range sliders. This will fill the area with the foreground color you selected.

7. Reposition the Range sliders, select a new foreground color, and repeat the process of adding a color to the gradient.

8. Select the color mode for the Gradient as RGB.

9. Select the Blending Mode for the Gradient.

10. Select the shape for the Gradient.

11. Select "Save to File" from the gradient tools option submenu. Confirm that you want to save the work you have done, then click OK.

MODIFYING A PRESET GRADIENT

1. Select the Preset Gradient Sunrise.

2. Select Add from the Gradient submenu and give it a new name.

3. Change the Shape of the Gradient to Satin.

4. Change the Blending Mode of the Gradient to Subtract.

5. Select a purple color and click on the orange side of the Color Ramp.

Cross fade gradients can be used to give an object a gradual opacity. A fade from left to right on an object produces a completely opaque left side that fades to a completely transparent effect on the right side. Cross fades are used quite often to give an object a ghosty effect that appears to be fading away.

CREATING CROSS FADES

1. Double-click on the Gradient tool in the Tools Palette.

2. Select White > Black from the Preset Gradients menu.

3. Select the object you would like to apply the effect to by clicking once on it in the Objects window.

4. Select the object's fourth channel or add a channel if it doesn't exist by clicking on the add channel icon in the Channels window.

5. Select a shape for the cross-fade from the Shape menu. A line or ellipse is recommended for this effect.

6. Click and drag (using the Gradient tool) inside your document.

7. Release the button and the gradient will be created.

8. Click on the RGB composite channel and check channel 4 as the mask.

When you place this object over another, it will have a variable opacity because of the gradient in the mask channel.

Using Basic Filters in xRes

Filters enable you to apply complex effects by simply choosing menu commands. In most case filters create preset effects such as blurs, ripples, and lighting. You will find a good assortment of filters included with xRes and some additional filters provided by Macromedia and created by MetaTools. You will experiment with these filters, which are part of the Effects menu, in the following sections.

The Sharpen Luminosity Filter

This filter applies a sharpen filter to the luminosity of an image. This is used for sharpening detail with minimal affect to the color.

USING THE LUMINOSITY FILTER

1. Select the document you want to apply the filter to.

2. Choose Luminosity from the Sharpen submenu under the Effects menu.

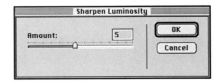

3. Set the amount of filter effect you want to apply to the image.

4. Click OK.

The Gaussian Blur Filter

This filter blurs an image so that it looks out of focus. You can use the FastMask to mask out an object in the foreground of a scan and then selectively blur the background.

APPLYING A GAUSSIAN BLUR TO OBJECTS

1. Select an object to Blur.

2. Choose Gaussian from the Blur submenu under the Effects menu.

3. Set the radius of the blur. The larger the value, the greater the blur.

4. Click OK.

The Motion Blur Filter

This filter creates the effect of motion in a document (see Figure 11.13). This filter creates an effect similar to taking a photograph of a moving object.

Figure 11.13

An effect created by the Motion Blur filter.

APPLYING A MOTION BLUR TO OBJECTS

1. Select an object to Blur.

2. Choose Motion from the Blur submenu of the Effects menu.

3. Set the angle for the blur.

4. Set the Distance the object will be blurred.

5. Set the number of copies for the filter to make when executing the motion blur.

6. Click OK.

The Noise Filters

The Add Noise and Add HLS Noise filters add random pixels to an image. These filters create a distressed look in an image and add grain to a photo. These filters are also used to break up gradients with visible banding of colors and to add interesting color effects to a simple grayscale scan.

The Colorize Filter

The Colorize Filter remaps the color of each pixel to the color ramp of the Gradient tool based on each pixel's brightness value.

To use the Colorize Filter:

1. Double-click on the Gradient tool to open the Gradients Options window.

2. Create a color ramp or select a preset from the list. Hue Cone is a good example.

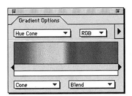

3. Choose Effects, Stylize, Colorize.

The Fisheye Filter

This filter creates an effect of looking through a fisheye lens (see Figure 11.14). This filter can also be used to create a peephole or magnifying glass effect for the selected object.

Figure 11.14

An effect created by the Fisheye filter.

USING THE FISHEYE FILTER

1. Select the area you would like to change.

2. Choose Fisheye from the Distort submenu of the Effects menu.

3. Specify an amount for the filter.

4. Click OK.

The Whirlpool Filter

This filter creates a "Swirl" or "Whirlpool" effect that can be used for swirled text (see Figure 11.15) and a drain pipe effect.

Figure 11.15

The Whirlpool filter.

USING THE WHIRLPOOL FILTER

1. Select the area you would like to change.

2. Choose Whirlpool from the Distort submenu of the Effects menu.

3. Set an amount for the filter.

4. Click OK.

To put an added spin on things, try applying the whirlpool effect after a -75 Fisheye effect.

The Emboss Filter

Use Emboss to create an embossed look on an image. This is one of the more popular filters and is found in most graphic applications. Emboss creates an image without color (see Figure 11.16).

Figure 11.16

An effect created by the Emboss filter.

USING THE EMBOSS FILTER

1. Select the area you would like to emboss.

2. Choose Emboss from the Stylize submenu of the Effects menu.

3. Set the Depth for the effect. Try a value 2-4 to start.

4. Set the Angle for the effect. 45 degrees is a typical value.

5. Set the Contrast for the effect. Try a value of 75 to 125 for good contrast.

6. Click OK.

The Glowing Edge Filter

This filter is an edge detection filter; in other words this filter affects the edges of images. This filter creates a neon-like glowing effect around an image. Glowing edge is extremely useful for many graphic artists who traditionally have created this effect manually. The main use for this effect is to create images that have either a neon or metallic appearance.

USING GLOWING EDGE

1. Select the area you would like to change.

2. Choose Glowing Edge from the Stylize submenu of the Effects menu.

3. Set the Amount for the effect.

4. Set the Radius for the effect.

5. Click OK.

The Threshold Filter

The Threshold filter sets all the pixels in an image to either black or white depending on the threshold setting. This filter gives an image a hard edge.

Using Threshold To Make a Starry Night Sky

1. On a new white image, apply the Add Noise filter with a value of 100.

2. Apply the Threshold filter (Effects, Other) with a value of 157.

3. Invert the image by selecting Invert under Modify, Color.

Using Kai's PowerTools

As an added bonus, xRes includes a set of filters designed by Kai Krause. Just a few years ago graphic artists would spend hours creating an effect that today takes only a few seconds. Custom designed filters such as Kai's PowerTools (KPT) are the main reason for this change.

As with the Gradient tool, many of the KPT filters have presets. The interface for the KPT filters is significantly different from your typical dialog box. The lower left corner describes the action that would occur if you clicked the mouse on its current location. By clicking on the question mark in the Texture Explorer you can find extensive on-screen help.

The following sections cover techniques that include the Special Edition Kai's PowerTools ME (Macromedia Edition). The Macromedia Edition is a useful subset of the complete Kai's PowerTools. These filters come with xRes, but need to be installed before they can be used.

Creating Custom Backgrounds

The exercise in this section uses KPT 3 Texture Explorer. The KPT Texture Explorer is a plug-in filter that generates infinite textures and backgrounds. The textures are generated by complex mathematics. On the right is a large source texture surrounded by smaller derivative textures that add to the mutation of the source texture. By clicking on the derivative textures, you can generate a vast amount of textures. On the left is the mutation tree, which sets the amount of mutation. To use a specific texture, simply click on the circle with the checkmark to accept that texture.

Figure 11.17

Kai's Power Tools Texture Explorer.

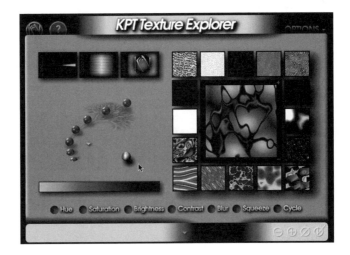

USING KPT'S TEXTURES

1. Open a new document and make it 350 pixels in height by 350 pixels in width.

2. Select the entire document.

3. Choose KPT 3 Texture Explorer 3.0 from Effects, KPT.

4. Click on the arrow in the middle bottom of the screen to open the Preset menu.

5. Select a preset to modify.

6. Adjust each parameter that appears at the bottom of the KPT Texture Explorer window. The figure shows the KPT Texture Explorer window with the settings for each parameter.

7. Click on the derivative textures to explore different looks.

8. Click on the circle with the checkmark in the lower right to use your new texture.

Creating Gradients on Text

In the center of the Gradient Designer is the preview window. This window shows you how the gradient will look with the current parameters applied to your selection. You can adjust the gradient bar below the preview window by clicking and dragging the mouse to select a new color. Or, you can choose from numerous preset gradients by clicking on the triangle in the center bottom of the screen. Click on a gradient to accept it, then click on the circled checkmark to apply it to your selection.

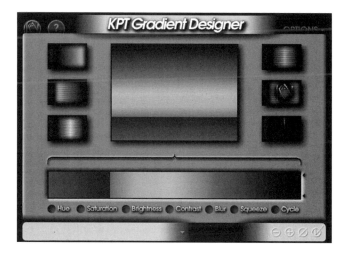

Figure 11.18

Kai's Power Tools Gradient Designer.

USING KPT FOR TEXT GRADIENTS

1. Select the Text tool from the Tools palette.

2. Create the word xRes using any font, and make the point size 150 points. Try using a font that has a wide area and is not too thin. Serpentine is a good font to use if you have it.

3. Select the text object in the document.

4. Choose Arbitrary from Modify, Rotate. Set the angle to 45 degrees counter-clockwise.

5. With the text still selected, Choose KPT Gradient designer 3.0 from Effects, KPT.

6. Select a gradient pattern to modify from the presets menu as you did in steps 4–6 of the previous section.

7. Click on the arrow in the middle bottom of the screen to open the Preset menu.

8. Select a preset to modify.

9. Adjust each parameter that appears at the bottom of the KPT Texture Explorer window. The figure shows the KPT Texture Explorer window with the settings for each parameter.

10. When you have selected a gradient to modify, adjust each one of the parameters that appear at the bottom of the KPT Gradient designer Window.

11. When all the adjustments are finished, apply the filter.

Using the Spheroid Designer

The KPT Spheroid Designer enables you to create realistic, 3D textured spheres. At the center of the KPT Spheroid Designer is a large sphere that acts as a preview. If you click and drag on this center sphere, you can rotate it to change the direction of its lighting. The spheres around it control various lights shining on the central sphere. If you click on the triangle in the center bottom of the interface, you can view and select from a large set of premade spheres—click on one to choose it. To accept the final sphere, simply click on the circle with the checkmark.

Figure 11.19

Kai's Power Tools Spheroid Designer.

WORKING WITH KPT'S SPHEROID DESIGNER

1. Choose the Circle tool from the tools palette.

2. Select an area in the upper left corner of the document approximately 1 inch from the top and 1 inch from the bottom.

3. Choose KPT Spheroid Designer 3.0 from Effects, KPT.

4. This filter works similar to the other KPT and xRes filters. At this point you should use the outside spheres to adjust what the Sphere will look like (make it to your liking). Presets are also available if you would like to begin with one of these premade filters.

5. When you have the sphere the way you would like to see it in your project, apply the filter by clicking on the circled checkmark (lower right part of KPT).

In the center of the Gradient Designer is the preview window, which shows you how the gradient and its parameters will look applied to your selection. You can adjust the gradient bar below the preview window by clicking and dragging the mouse to select a new color. Or, you can choose from preset gradients by clicking on the triangle in the center bottom of the screen. Click on one to accept it, then click on the circled checkmark to apply it to your selection.

Project

Integrating the Applications

This project is an extended exercise that exposes you to all four applications of FreeHand Graphics Studio. In this project you'll create a three-dimensional soup can. The logo and several parts of the label will be created in FreeHand, and a background from xRes will be added. You will create a special fraction in a new font, and then map all these things to a 3D model you create in Extreme 3D. This 3D modeler will also be used to animate the final product. If your company or clients want an animation for a presentation, or a three-dimensional illustration of their product for their web sites, you might find various portions of this project to be especially useful.

We recommend you work through the project from beginning to end. However, if you want to focus on a particular application, or would like to see what the finished file looks like, you can find them all on the disc included with the book. The names of files on the CD-ROM will be noted throughout the project so that you can compare your results.

Creating a Logo in FreeHand

To begin this project, you will create a logo for an imaginary soup company. The logo will consist of the name of the company, "Bigtowne," with the "i" replaced by a drawing of a tall building.

BIGTOWNE

Setting Up the Document

In FreeHand, open a new document and set up the page:

1. Turn on Rulers. Make sure Rulers is checked under the View menu.

2. Turn on the Info Bar. Make sure Info Bar is checked under the View menu.

3. Turn on the Grid. Make sure Grid is checked under the View menu.

4. Turn on the Guides. Make sure Guides is checked under the View menu.

5. Turn on Snap to Point. Make sure Snap to Point is checked under the View menu.

6. Turn on Snap to Guides. Make sure Snap to Guides is checked under the View menu.

7. Turn on Snap to Grid. Make sure Snap to Grid is checked under the View menu.

8. Show the Inspector palette. Make sure Inspector is checked under the Windows menu.

9. Click the Document icon (fifth icon) in the Inspector palette.

10. Click the Document Setup icon (second row, second icon) in the Inspector palette.

11. Click the measurements pulldown and select Inches. Notice the rulers switch to an inch scale.

If you save this document in the same folder or directory as the FreeHand application, and name it "FreeHand Defaults," the attributes you just set will be applied to every new document you open.

Creating the Building

1. Switch to Keyline view. Under the View menu, make sure Preview is unchecked.

2. Select the Rectangle tool and create a two-inch square.

3. Draw a 1.75" wide by 4" tall rectangle.

4. Using the Polygon tool, draw a triangle two inches wide by six inches tall. To simplify the process:

    a. Click in the lower left corner of the two-inch square for the first point.

    b. Click the lower right corner of the square for the second point.

    c. For the third point, click and drag above the center point of the square, six inches up from the base.

    d. To close the triangle, click again on the lower left corner of the square.

5. From the Edit menu, choose Select All. This selects the three objects you created.

6. From the Windows menu, open the Align palette.

7. Select Horizontal: Align center and Vertical: Align bottom. Click the Apply button.

The results should look like this:

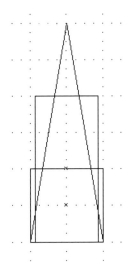

With all the objects still selected, you need to combine them, set the fill to black, and the stroke to none.

1. Select Union from the Path operations sub-menu under the Xtras menu.

2. Select the Pointer tool.

3. Notice that after using the Union Path operation, there are two extra points in the base of the drawing. Click the point near the lower left corner.

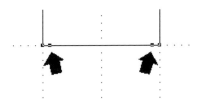

4. Press and hold down the Shift key, then click the extra point near the lower right corner.

5. Press the Delete key. This will remove these two points. It is a good habit to delete unwanted points—it keeps a drawing as simple as possible.

6. Under the Windows menu, select Color List to open the Color List palette.

7. Click the Fill icon in the Inspector. Select black from the Color List.

8. Click the Stroke icon in the Inspector. Select None from the pop-up menu.

Note

Keep in mind that you won't see any changes unless you toggle from keyline view to preview.

Adding the Windows

1. Away from the building, draw a rectangle .25" wide and .75" high.

2. Clone the rectangle by selecting Clone from the Edit menu.

3. Switch to the pointer tool and click the rectangle (avoiding the corners) and drag it half an inch to the right. If you press and hold down the Shift key after you have clicked the rectangle, you can constrain its movement.

4. Select Duplicate from the Edit menu. Duplicate will use the offset from your last movement.

5. Draw a selection rectangle around the three rectangles.

6. Select Clone from the Edit menu.

7. Click one of the rectangles, again avoiding the corners, and drag them straight down one inch.

8. Select Duplicate from the Edit menu.

9. Duplicate again.

10. Draw a selection rectangle around the twelve rectangles.

11. Select Join from the Arrange menu.

 Tip

As you use FreeHand, cloning and duplicating should become second nature to you. You can speed up the creation of multiple repeating objects by becoming familiar with these commands.

Finishing Touches

1. From the Edit menu, choose Select All.

2. In the Align palette, set horizontal alignment to center and the vertical to bottom.

3. Click the Apply button.

4. Make sure None are selected for both Color Fill and Stroke.

5. Select Punch from the Path operations sub-menu under the Xtras menu.

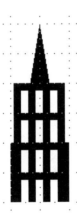

Adding the Type

1. Select the Type tool and click and drag to create a wide type box.

2. Under the Windows menu, open the Type palette.

3. Click and drag the font selector in the Type palette to select Times.

4. Click the Styles selector of the Type palette and select Bold.

5. Click the Size selector of the Type palette and select 72 points.

6. Type "BIGTOWNE" in the text box. Resize the text box by dragging the lower right corner handle to the right to see all the letters.

7. Select the Pointer tool and click the building.

8. Click one of the building's handles and drag holding down the Shift key. Resize the building to one inch tall.

9. Select the building and choose Cut from the Edit menu.

10. Double-click the text box to edit it.

11. Highlight the "I" and choose Paste from the Edit menu. If needed, resize the text box to see all the letters.

12. Select Convert to Paths from the Type menu.

13. On the Inspector palette, click the Fill icon and then select Basic.

BIGTOWNE

14. Select Save from the File menu to save your work. Name the file LOGO.fh5.

Enhancing the Logo in Extreme 3D

In a new scene in Extreme 3D, select Import from the File menu. Select FreeHand 4.0/5.x.

1. Select and import LOGO.fh5.

   Use the file Project/LOGO.fh5 on the disc if you did not create the file in the previous steps.

CD ROM

2. In the Window menu, select Window Setup.

3. Click and hold briefly on Custom Size.

4. In the Custom Size window enter 600 by 200 pixels. Click OK.

5. Click OK to get out of the Window Setup.

6. Under View menu select Fit to Window.

7. Click and drag the working plane over to the center of FreeHand logo in the upper right.

8. Under View menu select Fit to Window again.

305

9. Drag a selection rectangle around the building shape.

10. Click the Extrude tool icon.

11. Press Tab to access the Tool Space and enter a value of 1. Press Enter (Return).

Applying a Material for a Shiny Gold Look

1. Open the Materials Browser by selecting Materials under the Windows menu.

2. Select the Default-Scratched Metal material from the Material Catalog.

3. Click the top button, next to the catalog, to add the material to the scene.

4. Click the Default-Scratched Metal in the Scene Material List.

5. Click the Edit button.

6. Select Stripes for the Scratch pattern.

7. Set the Scale to 0.5.

8. Set the Surface color to a light gold color.

9. Set the Specular to a faint gray.

10. Set the Roughness to a dark gray.

11. Click OK.

12. Click the Apply button in the Materials Browser.

Adding Depth

1. Drag a selection rectangle around the remaining letters.

2. Select the new material you just created for the building from the Materials browser.

2. Select Bevel Extrude by clicking and holding the Extrude tool and sliding the mouse to the right.

4. Press the Tab key to enter the Tool space. Enter 1.0 for the depth and 0.05 for the bevel. Press Enter (Return).

5. Drag a selection rectangle around all the objects.

6. Under the Render menu, select Adaptive Smoothing.

7. Click the Final Rendering Settings. Enter 0.9 and click OK. This will give the curved letters a smoother edge when the image is finally rendered.

8. Select the Lock Link tool from the Tools palette and click the letter B object. With the objects linked, if you move one, you will move them all as a group.

Rotating the Logo

1. With the objects still selected, open the objects' info box. Select Get Info under the Edit menu.

2. Enter -20 for the X orientation value. This tilts the logo away from you.

Lighting the Scene

1. Open the Lights browser by selecting Lights from the Windows menu.

2. Click the Edit button to edit the default light in the scene.

3. Check the Cast Shadows box and click OK.

4. Enter 25, 5, and 60 for the X, Y, and Z orientation values of the light in the scene.

5. Click the Update Scene button.

6. Save your file as BIGTOWNE.e3d.

Rendering the Logo to Disk

CD ROM

You can use the file Project/BIGTOWNE.e3d from the disc.

1. From the Render menu, select Final Render Setup.

2. Check the Render Shadows box and click OK.

3. From the Render menu, select Render to Disk.

4. Under final render size, enter 1200 × 400. If the label was to be printed commercially, you could figure on needing 300 pixels per inch. This rendering is ideal for 4 inches by 1$^{1}/_{3}$ inches.

5. For the File Format to render, select Targa 32-bit file sequence. (On the Mac you can also render it as a PICT file sequence.)

6. Click OK to render the label.

7. Name the file BIGTOWNE.tga and click OK to save it.

For the next few moments, your computer will busily work to render the final image to disk.

Adding a Background to the Logo in xRes

CD ROM

1. In xRes, select Open from File menu.

2. Select BIGTOWNE.tga.

You can use the file Project/BIGTOWNE.tga from the disc.

3. Open the Channels window by selecting Channels from the Window menu.

4. In the Channels window, check the mask column of Channel #4 as a mask (you may need to scroll down to see it).

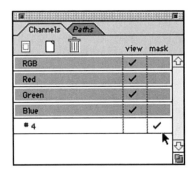

5. Under Windows menu, open the Objects window.

6. Create a new object by clicking the New Object icon in the Objects window.

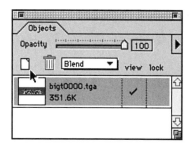

7. A New Object window will open. Uncheck the transparency box and click OK.

8. From the Modify menu, select Arrange and Send to Back.

9. To make sure the colors are appropriate for printing, change the color mode to CMYK.

Adding the Gradient Background

1. Click the Gradient tool in the tools palette.

2. Double-click the foreground color in the Tools palette to open the Color Picker window.

3. In the Picker window, select CMYK as the color mode.

4. Set the C, M, Y, and K values to 0, 100, 100, 0 respectively. This creates a bright red to use in the gradient.

5. Double-click the Gradient tool to open the Gradient Options window.

6. Select Sunrise from the presets and set the color mode to CMYK.

7. Move the mouse to the right edge of the color ramp in the Gradient options. The pointer will change to a bucket icon. Click to set the right side color to the new red.

8. To add the gradient to the new object, click and hold at the top of the image window. Press and hold the Shift key to constrain the gradient and drag down to the bottom edge of the window. Release the mouse.

9. From the File menu, select Export and TIFF.

10. Name the file BIGTOWNE.tif and click Save.

11. Check the byte order for your computer and click OK.

You now have a 4-color process (CMYK) TIFF that you can import back into FreeHand.

Creating Special Characters with Fontographer

In the following section you will replace a character in a typeface with a newly constructed character. You will be replacing the \ (backslash) character with a ¹/₃ fraction character.

Note

You should always work from a copy of a font rather than the original font to prevent ruining the entire font. Before you modify anything, Quit all, then open the System Folder. Make a copy of the font you are about to change, then use it in Fontographer.

Modifying the Font

1. From the File menu, open a sans serif typeface such as Helvetica or Arial.

2. Click the "1" character.

3. Select Copy from the Edit menu.

4. Click the "\" character.

5. Select Paste from the Edit menu.

6. Click the "3" character.

7. Select Copy from the Edit menu.

8. Double-click the former backslash character to open the character's outline window.

9. Select Paste from the Edit menu.

10. From the Elements menu, select Transform.

11. In the Transform window, select Center transformations around: Basepoint.

12. For the first transformation, select Scale Uniformly and enter 40 for the scaling percent.

13. Double-click a point of the "1" shape.

14. While holding down the shift key, click the "1" shape and slide it up the top guideline.

15. Select the Rectangle tool and draw a small horizontal dividing bar between the "1" and the "3" shapes.

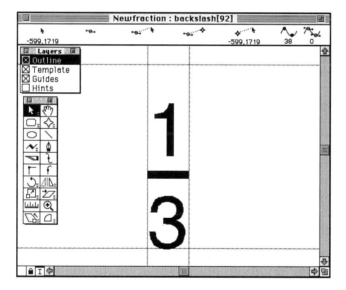

16. Close the character's Outline window.

Generating the Font

1. From the Element window select Font Info.

2. Name the file Newfraction and click OK.

3. From the File menu, choose Generate Font Files.

4. Select your computer type and TrueType within the dialog box.

5. Click the Generate button.

6. Select Save as from the File menu.

7. Enter a new name and save the Fontographer database file for future use.

8. Quit all open applications, then install your new font.

 **CD ROM**

The Fontographer database for this font is Project/Newfraction.fog and the suitcase that you can install into your system is Project/Newfraction.suit.

Creating the Label in FreeHand

Preparation

Create a new document by selecting New from the File menu. If you did not create a new Defaults file, you will have to reset all the parameters for the document. If you did save a new defaults file, skip to the heading "Customizing the Document."

Setting up the Document

1. Turn on Rulers. Make sure Rulers is checked under the View menu.

2. Turn on the Info Bar. Make sure Info Bar is checked under the View menu.

3. Turn on the Grid. Make sure Grid is checked under the View menu.

4. Turn on the Guides. Make sure Guides is checked under the View menu.

5. Turn on Snap to Point. Make sure Snap to Point is checked under the View menu.

6. Turn on Snap to Guides. Make sure Snap to Guides is checked under the View menu.

7. Turn on Snap to Grid. Make sure Snap to Grid is checked under the View menu.

8. Show the Inspector palette. Make sure Inspector is checked under the Windows menu.

9. Click the Document icon (fifth icon) in the Inspector palette.

10. Click the Document Setup icon (second row, second icon) in the Inspector palette.

11. Click the measurements pulldown and select Inches.

Customizing the Document

1. In the Inspector palette, make sure the Document icon is selected (fifth icon), then click the Pages icon (second row, first icon.)

2. Click Letter and drag down to Custom.

3. Click the horizontal page icon and enter 8.125 for the width (x) and 3.625 for the height (y).

4. Click and hold on the vertical ruler on the left side of the window. Watch the horizontal ruler and the x value in the Info Bar at the top of the screen as you drag to the right. Release the mouse at the $2^3/8$" mark. The x value should read 2.375. This creates a vertical guide.

5. Add another vertical guide at the $5^3/4$" mark. The x value would equal 5.75.

6. Create a horizontal guide by clicking and dragging out from the horizontal ruler. Watch the y value. Place a horizontal guide at 0.125.

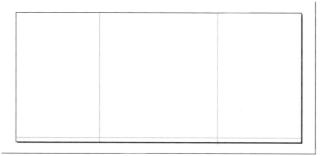

Creating the Background

1. Open the Color Mixer and click the CMYK icon.

2. Set C to 0, M to 100, Y to 100, and K to 0.

3. Open the Color List. Click the right side of the color swatch in the mixer and drag the new color to the Color List. This adds bright red to the Color List.

4. Double-click the default name in the Color List and rename it bright red.

5. Create and name two more colors: gold: C 0, M 20, Y 100, K 0; and dark red: C 0, M 50, Y 100, K 50.

Creating the Gradient

1. Using the rectangle tool, draw a box 8.125" wide and 2.625" tall at the very top of the page.

2. In the Inspector, click the Fill icon.

3. Select Graduated.

4. Click the gold swatch in the Color List and drag and drop it onto the From swatch in the Inspector.

5. Click the white swatch in the Color List and drag and drop it onto the To swatch in the Inspector.

6. Leave the Taper set to Linear and set the angle to 270 degrees.

7. Go to the Line icon to set the line color to None.

Importing the 3D Logo

1. Using the rectangle tool, create a box 3.375" wide and 2" tall.

2. In the Inspector, click the Fill icon and select None (this clears the gradient), and then select bright red.

3. Set the line width to None.

4. From the File menu, select Place and import the BIGTOWNE.tif into the document.

 CD ROM   You can use the file Project/BIGTOWNE.tif from the disc.

5. Choose Select All from the Edit menu.

6. Open the Align palette from the Windows menu.

7. Select Horizontal: Align center and Vertical: Align top. Click the Apply button.

8. Select just the 3D logo TIFF and cut to the clipboard. Choose Cut from the Edit menu.

9. Select the bright red box and choose Paste Inside from the Edit menu.

10. Slide the box to the top of the page and align between the guides.

Finishing the Gradient

1. Using the rectangle tool, click the lower left corner of the box defining the imported logo, and drag out a box to the bottom of the page and the left vertical guide. This will create a box 3.375" wide and 1.625" tall.

2. As above, add a gradient to this box. Set the From color to bright red and the To color to dark red. Set the angle to 270 degrees.

Adding More Buildings

1. Import LOGO.fh5 file that you created in the beginning of this project.

   You can use the file Project/LOGO.fh5 from the disc.

CD ROM

2. Ungroup the text and delete the letters, leaving only the building.

3. Move the building to the inside left of the lower box.

4. Clone the building and move it horizontally 0.5 inches.

5. Use the Duplicate command, under the Edit menu, four more times.

Adding the Starburst and Product Name

1. Double-click the polygon tool to open its settings window. Set the number of sides to 32. Since the slide will only go up to 20, enter 32 in the input field.

2. Set the shape to Star, Points to Manual, and move the slider to the two-thirds mark and click OK.

3. Click in the center of the label and drag the radius out to one inch.

4. Set the starburst's line color to none and the fill color to dark red.

5. Select Clone from the Edit menu.

6. Under the Xtras menu, choose Path Operations and Inset Path.

7. Set the inset value to 0.0312 and click OK.

8. Select both starbursts and select Group from the Arrange menu.

9. Move this to the center of the label, under the logo.

10. Using the Type tool, click and drag a text box the size of the starburst.

11. Set the font to Times, size to 18 point, and style to Bold Italic.

12. In the Inspector palette, click the Text icon (forth icon, top row) and then click the Alignment icon (forth icon, second row).

13. Click the Center Alignment icon (second icon at the bottom).

14. Select white for the fill color.

15. Enter the text "Premium Chicken Noodle Soup", pressing Enter (Return) after each word.

16. From the Edit menu, select Clone.

17. Select black for the fill color and use the arrow keys to nudge the black type down and to the right a bit.

18. Group the white and black type together.

19. Move the type to the center of the starburst.

Adding Other Text

1. Using the Text tool, draw a new text box about two inches wide at the bottom of the label.

2. Set the font to Helvetica, the size to 10 point, the style to plain, and the color to white.

3. Enter the text "NET WT. 11\ OZ. (312g)" in the text box.

4. Select the backslash character and change the font to Newfraction.

5. Move the new type to the lower center of the label.

CD ROM

6. Import the file Project/SLOGAN.RTF from the CD and place it on the left side of the label.

7. Import the file Project/DIRECTNS.RTF from the CD and place it on the upper right side of the label.

8. Import the file Project/INGRDNTS.RTF from the CD and place it on the lower right side of the label.

Adding Lines and Dots

1. Using the Line tool, draw a line along the lower horizontal guideline, from the left edge to the right edge. Set the thickness to 2 points and the color to black.

2. To add the row of dots across the top of the label, draw an eighth-inch circle with the Circle tool and set its fill color to the bright red and its line color to none.

3. Clone the circle and move it to the right 0.25 inches. Duplicate it 30 more times to produce a row of dots.

4. Select all the dots and group them together.

5. Move the dots to the top of the page to complete the label.

6. Save your file to your disk as LABEL.fh5.

Rasterizing the Label

With the file still open in FreeHand, select all the objects in the label.

1. From the Xtras menu, select Create PICT image. (In Windows, select Create BMP). This Xtra is very memory intensive when you use a high-resolution or the anti-aliasing options.

2. Choose Colors: Millions, Antialiasing: 2 (if FreeHand has enough memory), and set the Image resolution to 72 dpi.

3. Click Save. Name the file LABEL.pict (LABEL.bmp on the PC) and save it.

Creating and Animating a 3D Model

1. Import the can profile titled Project/CANPROFL.fh5 from the CD.

2. From the View menu, choose Fit to Window.

3. Select the profiles and drag them to the center of the working grid.

4. From the View menu, choose Fit to Window again.

5. There are two profiles—a vertical line for the label and the actual can profile. These two profiles are very close together.

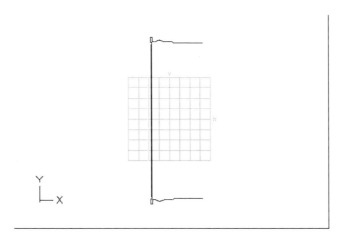

6. Using the Construction Line tool, click once on the lower right end of the can profile. Click a second time on the upper right end of the can profile. This creates a reference line around which the profiles will be lathed.

7. Click the label profile and select the Lathe tool. Click once on the lower right end of the can profile. Click a second time on the upper right end of the can profile.

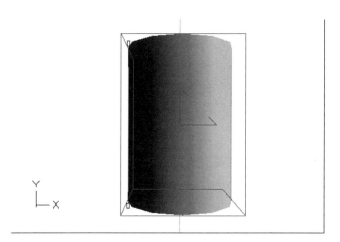

Mapping the Label

1. With the tube selected, open the Material browser and move the Default-Texture Map material into the material scene list.

2. Click the Edit button once.

3. Click the texture map to edit the texture.

4. Click the Load... button and locate your texture map (LABEL.pict on the Mac, LABEL.bmp on the PC.)

 CD ROM   You can use the file Project/LABEL.pict or Project/LABEL.bmp from the disc for the Mac or PC.

5. When the texture is loaded, click OK.

6. Set the Specular color to dark gray and the Roughness to white.

7. Click OK and then Apply.

Creating the Can Object

1. Select the can profile.

2. Select the Lathe tool. Click the construction line and then click the same construction line, but higher up than your first click.

3. With the can selected, open the Material browser and move the Scratched Metal material into the Material scene list.

4. Select Scratched Metal from the Material scene list and click Apply.

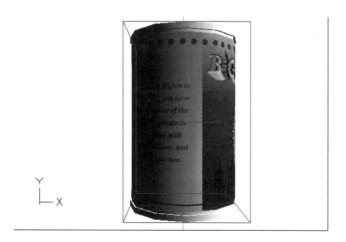

Modifying the Scene

1. From the Objects menu, choose Show and All.

2. Select both objects and from the Render menu, choose Adaptive Smoothing.

321

3. Select Final Render Settings and set the value to 0.9. Click OK.

4. Using the Lock Link tool, click the label and link it to the can.

5. Open the Objects window by choosing Objects from the Windows menu.

6. On the placement page, for the position enter 0 for the x value, 0 for the y value, and 0 for the z value.

7. For the orientation, enter 75 for the x value, -75 for the y value, and 50 for the z value.

8. Under the Windows menu, choose Window Setup. Click Custom Size. Enter 300 for width and 400 for height. Click OK.

Setting the Camera Position

1. From the Windows menu, choose Views.

2. Select Camera View. For the Orientation enter 0 for the x value, 0 for the y value, and 0 for the z value.

3. For the Position, enter 0 for the x value, 0 for the y value, and 10 for the z value. This will position the camera in front.

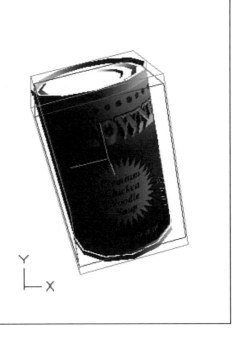

Setting the Lighting

1. From the Windows menu, choose Lights.

2. For the Default Light orientation in the scene, enter 15 for the x value, -45 for the y value, and 60 for the z value.

3. Click Edit and check the Render Shadows box. Click OK.

4. Move another Default Light from the catalog list to the Scene list.

5. For the new Default Light orientation in the scene, enter 30 for the x value, 30 for the y value, and -15 for the z value.

6. Click Edit and check the Render Shadows box again.

7. Set the light's intensity to 0.5 and click OK.

8. Click Update Scene.

Changing the Background Color

1. Choose Set Background from the Render menu.

2. Click the background color and set it to an orange color and click OK.

Animating the Can

1. From the Animate menu, select Animation Controls.

2. In the Animation Controls, enter 30 for the end frame. This will create 30 frames for the animation.

3. Select the can.

4. From the Animate menu, select Fast Forward.

5. With the can still selected, choose Auto Rotate from the Animate menu.

6. Enter 360 degrees for the object rotation. Select object's z Axis as the Axis of Rotation.

7. Select Render Setup from the Animation menu. Check the Render Shadows box and click OK.

8. Save the scene.

Rendering the Animation to a file

 CD ROM   You can use the file Project/CANSCENE.e3d from the disc.

1. Select Render to Disk from the Animation menu.

2. Enter the frame or frames you want to render.

3. Select QuickTime or AVI movie.

4. Click the Render button.

5. Enter a name for the movie you are about to render.

6. A dialog box for AVI or QuickTime movie settings will appear. Enter 10 frames a second and click OK.

Wait. Your computer will churn away, creating your animation frame by frame.

Your first project takes advantage of all FreeHand Graphic Studio has to offer. This project should give you more ideas and lead the way for more complex projects in the future. Have fun and create something wonderful!

Index

Symbols

A

C

F

P

REGISTRATION CARD

FreeHand Graphics Studio Skills

Hayden Books

Name _____ Title _____

Company_____Type of business _____

Address _____

City/State/ZIP _____

Have you used these types of books before? ☐ yes ☐ no

If yes, which ones? _____

_____

How many computer books do you purchase each year? ☐ 1–5 ☐ 6 or more

How did you learn about this book?_____

    ☐ recommended by a friend   ☐ received ad in mail

    ☐ recommended by store personnel   ☐ read book review

    ☐ saw in catalog   ☐ saw on bookshelf

Where did you purchase this book? _____

Which applications do you currently use? _____

Which computer magazines do you subscribe to? _____

What trade shows do you attend? _____

Please number the top three factors which most influenced your decision for this book purchase.

    ☐ cover   ☐ price

    ☐ approach to content   ☐ author's reputation

    ☐ logo   ☐ publisher's reputation

    ☐ layout/design   ☐ other _____

Would you like to be placed on our preferred mailing list? ☐ yes ☐ no e-mail address _____

☐ **I would like to see my name in print!** You may use my name and quote me in future Hayden products and promotions. My daytime phone number is: _____

Comments _____

_____

_____

Hayden Books Attn: Product Marketing ◆ 201 West 103rd Street ◆ Indianapolis, Indiana 46290 USA

Fax to **317-581-3576**   Visit out Web Page **http://WWW.MCP.com/hayden/**

Fold Here

BUSINESS REPLY MAIL

FIRST-CLASS MAIL PERMIT NO. 9918 INDIANAPOLIS IN

POSTAGE WILL BE PAID BY THE ADDRESSEE

HAYDEN BOOKS
Attn: Product Marketing
201 W 103RD ST
INDIANAPOLIS IN 46290-9058

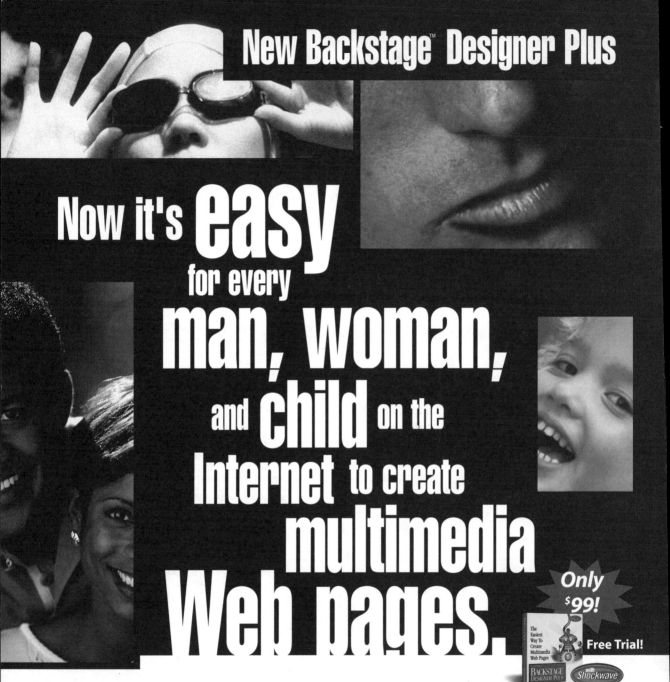

New Backstage™ Designer Plus

Now it's easy for every man, woman, and child on the Internet to create multimedia Web pages.

Only $99!

Free Trial!

Welcome to a place where anyone can **create an amazing Web page**, right out of the box.

It's a place where simple, intuitive page layout takes away the pain of HTML programming. Where tasks like hyperlinking, text formatting, and spell checking are all as easy as point and click. Where Macromedia

PowerApplets™ bring Java™ and Shockwave™ to your web page with the click of a mouse.

The place is Backstage™ Designer Plus for Windows. And it's here today as a demo version to download free. Or for only $99,* complete with Macromedia xRes™ image editing and paint tools, and Macromedia PowerApplets for automatically creating

multimedia banners, bullets, slide shows and more.

You've always been able to imagine a multimedia Web page. Now you have an easy place to create one.

http://www.macromedia.com/
1-800-945-4052

1-800-COMP USA

1-800-THE CITY

EGGHEAD
1-800-EGGHEAD

MACROMEDIA®
Tools To Power Your Ideas™

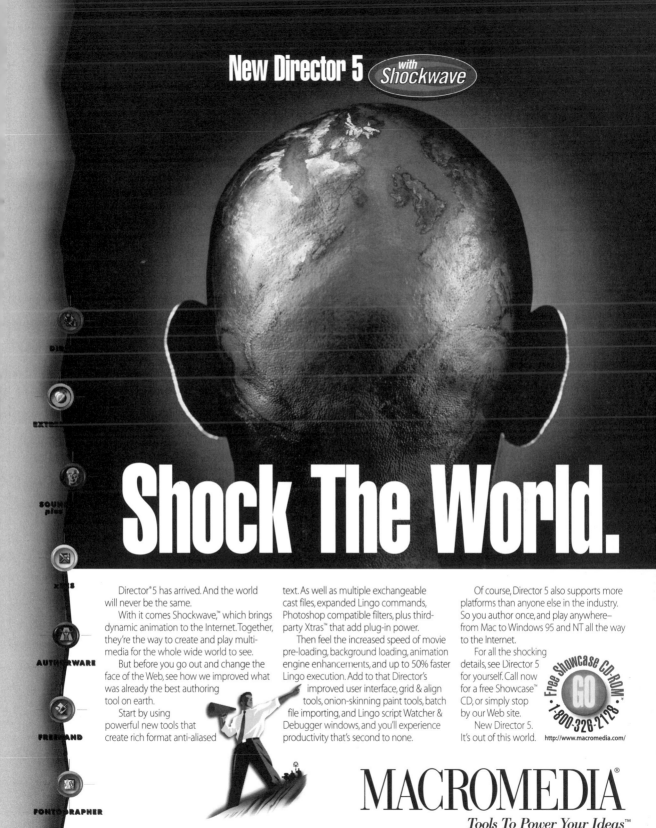

About the CD ROM

The CD-ROM included with this book contains demo versions of the four applications in the FreeHand Graphics Studio, provided by Macromedia. The Macromedia folder or directory contains a read me file and install packages for the latest versions of FreeHand, Fontographer, Extreme 3D and xRes. The folder or directory titled Software also contains the Shockwave for FreeHand Xtras.

The disc also contains exercise files for use in the FreeHand and Fontographer sections of this book, and files that can be used with the project.

To begin, just pop the disc in and go to it! Follow paths given in the text to find project and exercise files; follow installation directions in the read me file in the Macromedia folder or directory to install the demo software.